HARD BARGAINS

HARD BARGAINS

THE COERCIVE POWER OF
DRUG LAWS IN FEDERAL COURT

MONA LYNCH

Russell Sage Foundation · New York

The Russell Sage Foundation

Library of Congress Cataloging-in-Publication Data

Names: Lynch, Mona Pauline, author.
Title: Hard bargains : the coercive power of drug laws in federal court / Mona Lynch.
Description: New York : Russell Sage Foundation, 2016. | Includes bibliographical references and index.
Identifiers: LCCN 2016017917 (print) | LCCN 2016041734 (ebook) | ISBN 9780871545114 (paperback) | ISBN 9781610448611 (ebook)
Subjects: LCSH: Drugs of abuse—Law and legislation—United States—Criminal provisions. | Drug traffic—United States. | Criminal justice, Administration of—United States. | Sentences (Criminal procedure)—United States. | Plea bargaining—United States. | BISAC: SOCIAL SCIENCE / Criminology. | LAW / Criminal Law / Sentencing. | SOCIAL SCIENCE / Sociology / General.
Classification: LCC KF3890 .L96 2016 (print) | LCC KF3890 (ebook) | DDC 345.73/0277—dc23
LC record available at https://lccn.loc.gov/2016017917

Text design by Suzanne Nichols.

RUSSELL SAGE FOUNDATION
112 East 64th Street, New York, New York 10065
10 9 8 7 6 5 4 3 2 1

For my father

Table of Contents

═ List of Illustrations ═

About the Author

Mona Lynch is professor in the Department of Criminology, Law, and Society and, by courtesy, in the School of Law at the University of California, Irvine.

═ Acknowledgments ═

This book would not have been possible without the help and support of so many. First and foremost are the wonderful people who allowed me into their professional worlds to conduct this study. Although I cannot name them individually, I was the beneficiary of so much generosity, especially from those in the federal defenders' offices who gave me time, space, and a wealth of thoughtful insights. They brought this project to life. In particular, I owe a huge debt of gratitude to Amy Baron-Evans, who made that happen and who has been my go-to person for questions. Lou Reedt, at the U.S. Sentencing Commission, has been another go-to person whose help has been invaluable.

I benefitted from considerable financial support for this project. The Department of Criminology, Law, and Society at the University of California, Irvine, awarded me a seed grant to get the field research off the ground. The National Science Foundation's Law and Social Science Program provided the crucial funding for the field research (1251700). The National Institute of Justice's Data Resources Program provided funding for the quantitative data analysis piece of the project (2010-IJ-CX-0010). The Russell Sage Foundation invited me to spend a wonderful, productive year as a residential visiting scholar, where I wrote much of the first draft of this book.

I am also indebted to the excellent, talented research assistants who worked on different stages of the research: Alyse Bertenthal, Marisa Omori, and Anjuli Verma, and especially Kevin Lerman whose critical read strengthened the book in so many ways. As I finalized the writing of this book, I benefitted immensely from the sometimes blunt, always on-target advice of my editor, Suzanne Nichols, as well as from the insightful comments of the anonymous reviewers.

I have been challenged and inspired by exchanges with many friends and colleagues over the course of this project. Among those people are Rachel Barkow, Doug Berman, Devon Carbado, Sharon Dolovich, James Forman, John Gleeson, Marie Gottschalk, Craig Haney, Kelly Hannah-Moffat, Bernard Harcourt, Paul Hofer, Jim Jacobs, Brian Johnson, Sasha Natapoff, Paul Passavant, Keramet Reiter, Carroll Seron, Carol Steiker,

Kate Stith, Marjorie Zatz, and Frank Zimring. The writing process was also immeasurably enriched by the day-to-day engagement with my fellow Russell Sage Foundation scholars, at lunch, in our seminars, in the halls, and out on the town. A special, special thanks goes to friends and colleagues who read chapter drafts and gave me honest feedback: Jesse Katz (whose editorial suggestions were invaluable), Susan Silbey, and Jonathan Simon. They pushed me where I needed to be pushed.

My love and thanks go to my family, who are my foundation. I am especially grateful for my husband, Gregory Coben, who helped make this research and writing project an adventure. Without him, it would not have been nearly as much fun. And as always, I owe so much to my father, Thomas Lynch, who remains my inspiration.

Finally, I thank "Devon," whose story propels this book. I reached out to him as I was writing to ask if I could share with readers his experience in federal court. He agreed and has since become a long-distance friend. For him and others in his situation, my hope is that this book will have some impact in changing laws, policies, and practices that lead to such injustices.

= Introduction =

A System out of Whack

Devon Harrison had a drug problem. Heroin had gotten under his skin early in his adult life. By the time he landed in federal court, he was stuck in an all-too-common cycle of addiction.[1] To maintain his habit, he occasionally sold or traded several rocks of crack cocaine—the prevailing drug market in the mid-sized southern city where he was born and raised—a solution of expedience. He was not getting rich. He was not blazing new territory. In our nation's war on drugs, he was not the public enemy for whom we imagine the most draconian, least forgiving consequences of the federal criminal justice system are reserved.

In that fateful summer of 2004, Devon had reignited a friendship with Charles, a former high school classmate. By this time, Charles was a relatively large-scale local crack dealer, his distribution network many orders of magnitude greater than Devon's sporadic, piecemeal sales. Charles regularly made runs to his supplier, who was located in a town about 150 miles southwest; Charles's girlfriend, Marina, often helped by renting a transport car. Unbeknownst to either Charles or Marina, federal law enforcement had been actively surveilling the couple for months, thanks to a tip from a confidential informant. Agents had documented the near-weekly trips to the same supplier, including Marina's car-rental patterns. In late August, just weeks after the old classmates had reconnected, Charles and Marina invited Devon and his girlfriend along for the ride. It was a bad idea. But as the surveillance operation confirmed, this was the one and only time Devon accompanied his friend on a run. This was also the night that federal agents had decided to take down Charles.

The group headed back to the city well past midnight, after Charles had purchased close to a kilogram of crack from his supplier. Alert to the possibility of being tailed by law enforcement, Charles twice ditched the drugs en route, each time deciding he was not being followed after all. The second time, he enlisted Devon's help in finding the stash. Devon retrieved the small Foot Locker bag of crack from the brush on the roadside, then tucked it under the front passenger seat near his feet. Back on the highway, they were soon pulled over by a state patrol officer, who searched the car with the aid of a trained dog and found the drugs. The official reason for the stop was for speeding, but the trooper was working with the federal agents to initiate the arrest. Those agents, who had been tracking the car all night, swarmed in and arrested its four occupants.

Less than twelve hours later, three of the four suspects—Charles, Marina, and Devon—were making initial appearances in federal court, about to face charges of conspiracy to distribute crack cocaine.[2] Eight months later, the three federal defendants stood convicted and sentenced. Marina received a term of federal probation and home confinement. Charles was sentenced to twenty years in prison (later reduced to about fifteen). And Devon, who had just gone along for the ride, got a sentence that eclipsed them all: life without parole.

How could it be that the person with the least culpability—a fact not disputed by anyone in this case—would end up receiving the gravest sentence? It was not only merely possible, it was in fact the near-inevitable result once Devon was charged in federal court and declined to plead guilty. Indeed, nearly every aspect of Devon's experience exemplifies the most troublesome features of the federal criminal justice system, from how he ended up charged in federal court in the first place to the legal provisions that allow for a life-without-parole sentence for his tangential participation in this crime.

Ultimately, Devon's story illustrates the consequences of the extreme power imbalance between the adversarial parties, which was the result of numerous criminal justice developments since the 1970s. These developments created the conditions under which prosecutors can wield the law to obtain the outcomes they seek, and wield it even more forcefully in the face of defendants' noncompliance. Devon's case thus throws into sharp relief the ideals of fairness that are supposed to underpin our justice system, and the inequities that come from affording an overabundance of power to prosecutors.

Devon, who had done two short stints behind bars for drug-related state convictions in his twenties, ended up with a life-without-parole sentence because the prosecutor had the absolute power to compel it. Even the sentencing judge could not have altered that outcome. Devon's case demonstrates a fundamental perversion of due process that underlies contemporary criminal justice: the costs of asserting one's rights in criminal court are so high few people dare take the risk. Devon properly exercised his constitutional right to a jury trial, and, as we will see, he had good reason for doing so. Yet his unwillingness to knuckle under was the key factor in his ultimately being condemned to the custody of the Bureau of Prisons for the rest of his life.

This book is about the power to punish and its consequences. I use the case of federal criminal law—in particular, the set of formidable drug laws that were enacted in the 1980s—as a window into the contemporary life of penal power. Two distinct components of this expansion of power help explain how and why the criminal law has been wielded so forcefully against defendants such as Devon in recent years. The first has to do with the institutional conditions—the rules of the game, as it were— by which criminal justice actors operate. Those conditions have changed dramatically in the federal justice system.[3] The seeds were planted well before the 1980s, but it took a confluence of structural factors to realize their potential.

The most significant structural factor was sentencing reform. Aiming to completely overhaul how criminal defendants were punished in the federal system, Congress passed the Sentencing Reform Act of 1984, which authorized the development of a mandatory sentencing-guidelines system designed to constrain judicial discretion.[4] Also in the 1980s, Congress directly enacted a bevy of mandatory minimum sentencing statutes, including the Anti–Drug Abuse Act of 1986, which mandated multiyear sentences for a panoply of drug offenses. Most infamously, a provision of the Anti–Drug Abuse Act incorporated a 100-1 powder-crack cocaine disparity in the drug weight triggering mandatory minimums. Under the new law, for example, a distribution offense involving just 5 grams of crack cocaine triggered the same five-year mandatory minimum sentence as an offense involving 500 grams of powder cocaine. This law armed authorities with a hugely powerful weapon for obtaining long prison sentences even in cases with relatively small amounts of drugs.[5]

These new laws set in motion dramatic changes in day-to-day federal criminal justice operations, largely by shifting a massive amount of discretionary power from judges to prosecutors.[6] Under the new regime, the federal prosecutor in effect subsumed most traditional judicial functions to become, in practice, "the adjudicator—making the relevant factual findings, applying the law to the facts, and selecting the sentence or at least the sentencing range."[7] The shift in power catalyzed a rush of activity in districts across the nation, where vastly more defendants were brought into federal court and charged by prosecutors fortified with the new powers.

Overall criminal caseloads grew, and the number of drug cases skyrocketed. Federal prosecutors filed felony drug charges against about eight thousand defendants in 1980, before the sentencing reforms. By 2000, that number had grown to nearly twenty-nine thousand.[8] The explosion in caseload size in turn fueled considerable institutional growth, including increased resource allocations to federal criminal justice. We now have a formidable federal law enforcement machine, with thousands of front-line prosecutors initiating criminal cases in federal courts across the country.

The second critical piece—indeed, the core—of the story told in this book is the human element of power's deployment, including the variety of ways that those given the power to punish put it to use. Legal actors not only use the force of criminal law to obtain desired outcomes but also use their myriad tools to suppress defiance and punish noncompliance. And the more unequal the power relations are between the prosecution and the defense, the worse it gets for those who do not go along with the program. So for defendants like Devon Harrison, who was prosecuted in a place, and at a time, that was especially hostile to the defense, the ultimate punitive tools available to prosecutors have been wielded with relative frequency. The creative, coercive, on-the-ground deployment of drug laws as it occurs in specific contexts and moments in time is detailed and illuminated in chapters 3 to 6.

To tell this story about the coercive use of power, I examine the day-to-day drug case adjudication practices in three federal court districts, which I call Northeastern District, Southeast District, and Southwestern District.[9] I traveled to the three districts between late 2012 and summer 2014, visiting courthouses in each jurisdiction and observing firsthand how cases in all three places were negotiated and sentenced. I conducted in-depth interviews with defense attorneys, current and former federal prosecutors, judges, and others. I also reviewed and analyzed case file materials, including sentencing memoranda, plea agreements, hearing transcripts, and other documents from sentenced drug cases in the districts. And I used the official data specific to the districts from the Executive Office for U.S. Attorneys, the courts, and the U.S. Sentencing Commission (an independent agency in the judicial branch of the government) to put my observations in the larger historical context of drug law deployment in each site.

In each of the case studies, I look behind the scenes to understand the logic of who gets brought to federal court on drug charges in the first place, and how those choices influence the way cases are resolved. I show how, in each locale, federal drug defendants are under immense pressure to waive their Fifth and Sixth Amendment rights, including their rights to appeal any part of the judgment or sentence, and plead guilty to charges that will usually bring long prison sentences. By following cases as they unfold, I reveal how prosecutors, judges, and others deploy those very laws that were supposed to tame discretionary excesses to obtain their desired outcomes.

But each district has its own norms and imperatives, so cases that may look alike on paper have very different trajectories depending upon where they are prosecuted. In some courts, guilty pleas are derived through prosecutors' demands for "cooperation" in exchange for plea deals; the prosecutors simultaneously threaten to increase the defendant's exposure to a longer sentence if he or she declines the deal. In other courts, the pressure is time and expediency; plea offers will be taken off the table if the defendants drag their feet about accepting the plea deal or ask for too much due process. For those who do not succumb to the pressure to plead guilty, like Devon Harrison, the consequences are almost always magnitudes worse for having asserted their rights in federal court.

My goal with this book is to reveal the deep risks to our system of justice when the power to punish is not kept in check. Therefore, I examine on-the-ground legal action because it offers a view into a core challenge of democratic life: how power is authorized, negotiated, used, and abused in modern institutional operations. Indeed, the deployment of criminal law is among the most obvious, explicit, and extreme exercises of institutional power in modern democratic societies, a tool openly wielded to dominate, coerce, and control.

Power, the French philosopher Michel Foucault reminds us, "brings into play relations between individuals (or between groups)," and those relations constitute the crux of sociality: ever-present, in motion, and shifting as a function of time, place, people, and context.[10] Accordingly, dominance, as produced by power relations, can be best understood by examining the social conditions in which it is produced.[11] Through an examination of the dynamics of power—resistance to the force of power as well as the strategic games played in power struggles—we can discover deeper insights about how and why social relations take the shape they do in different contexts.[12]

In the context of criminal case negotiations, the powerful potential of law on the books can be put into action in a variety of ways, depending upon the players involved, the local norms and constraints, and the particular strategies marshaled. Changes in the federal laws that took place in the 1980s amplified the potential for extreme punishment outcomes, especially since mandatory minimums deepened the imbalance in power relations among the key actors.[13] The opportunities for wielding power are vast in contemporary federal criminal law, and the agents of power, especially law enforcement officers and prosecutors, embody roles that are imbued with enormous potential to compel the submission of criminal suspects to the legal system. And no matter how objective and by-the-book it may be portrayed, the exercise of such power is always selective. The question I grapple with here, then, is not whether power is in play, but rather why is it in play in the shape that it takes at any given time and place?

I could have chosen many other sites to examine how the coercive power of criminal law is deployed, but there were compelling reasons for examining the federal system. At first glance the federal system may seem like an odd choice, since it is a relatively small player in American criminal justice. According to the most recent available data, federal courts account for only about 6.5 percent of the nation's felony drug convictions.[14] For a large number of drug cases brought into federal court, state-level courts would seem to be the more logical venue for prosecution. Each of the states has ample criminal law available to prosecute drug posses- sion, manufacturing, and trafficking, and local and state agencies have enforced those laws with considerable zeal. Yet analyzing how drug cases live in the federal system can offer some critically important lessons about the force with which criminal law is wielded in our contemporary justice system.

Because federal prosecutors' drug caseloads are usually very discretion- ary as to case selection, examining these prosecutions provides a clear view of the choices made by legal actors. We can make stronger inferences about the decisionmaking that constructs those caseloads, especially as they vary from district to district. The balance of criminal case types in a given dis- trict, the way charges are filed, and the particular mechanisms used in the adjudication process all expose the policy choices and practical norms of local actors and their organizations. Thus, these comparative case studies offer new insights into the durable features of institutional life to answer the questions of how and why social institutions—such as trial-level courts and the interconnected offices and agencies that constitute them—develop their own particular sets of logics, motivations, and practices.

And the federal "drug war" constitutes an important case of the late twentieth-century "mass imprisonment" phenomenon in its own right.[15] The federal deployment of modern criminal drug laws has been spec- tacular in its scope, its racially disproportionate impact, and the extent of its growth, outdoing the states on many measures of punitiveness. This was most evident in the dramatic rise in the relative share of the federal criminal caseload composed of drug cases. From 1940 through 1960, only 5 percent or fewer of federal criminal cases annually involved drug defen- dants. That share began to edge up over the next two decades: In 1980, 17 percent of federal defendants were convicted on drug charges. By 1990, once the sentencing-guidelines system was up and running, that share had more than doubled: 39 percent of federal defendants were convicted of drug offenses. Drug defendants have since accounted for 30 percent or more of all federal convictions each year, even as the overall number of federally convicted defendants also grew.[16]

Furthermore, under the sentencing guidelines and mandatory mini- mums, almost all who were convicted of drug charges have been sen- tenced to lengthy prison sentences. As a result, the growth in the federal imprisonment rate outpaced that of the states. Between 1980 and 2010, the federal prison population grew ninefold, nearly double the growth rate of state systems. A disproportionate share of that increase in the fed- eral system was made up of sentenced drug defendants (see figure I.1).

Nor has the federal drug war been evenly distributed among the potential population of defendants. The sentencing guidelines and man-

Figure I.1   Federal Prison Growth Attributable to Sentenced Drug
Defendants, 1970 to 2012

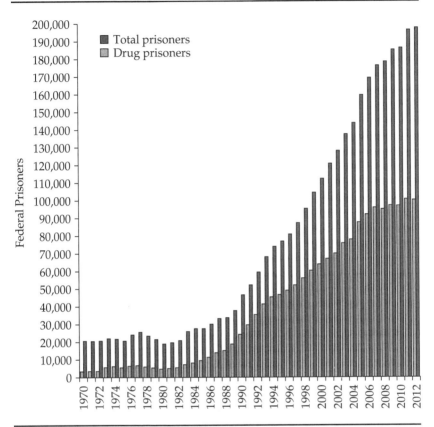

Source: Author's compilation. Data from 1970 to 2004 is based on University at Albany, Sourcebook of Criminal Justice Statistics, table 6.57. Data for 2005 to 2012 is based on Bureau of Justice Statistics, Federal Justice Statistics, table 7.9.
Note: Annual single-day population counts.

datory minimums contributed to a dramatic demographic shift among the federal drug defendant population. In 1986, on the eve of the implementation of sentencing reform, 58 percent of federally sentenced drug defendants were white; by 2013, just 23 percent were white.[17] This demographic skewing is not simply attributable to differences in offending. Rather, it reflects district-level enforcement policies and practices: how law enforcement resources are deployed and where law enforcement looks for illicit drug activity, what kinds of contraband are prioritized, and who is identified as being an appropriate target for the heavy hammer of federal drug prosecution.[18]

Some, but not all, of the demographic shift was due to the extreme racial disparity in federal prosecutors' choices as to whom to charge under the disproportionately punitive crack cocaine laws. For instance, white defendants have consistently constituted a mere 5 to 10 percent of the annual federal sentenced defendant population for crack offenses, even though whites make up the overwhelming majority of crack users in the United States.[19] Conversely, blacks have been vastly overrepresented as crack defendants, making up 80 to 95 percent of the annual sentenced population for federal crack convictions. Defendants in crack cases have also been disproportionately likely to end up with life sentences; more than half of all federal defendants sentenced to life for drug offenses were convicted of crack offenses. Like Devon Harrison, 94 percent of those crack-offense-sentenced lifers have been African American. Latinos have also accounted for an increasing share of all federally sentenced drug defendants in the guidelines era, accounting for nearly half of the overall drug-sentenced population in 2014.[20] One source of this increase has been stepped-up immigration enforcement along the southern border (discussed in detail in chapter 5).

But to fully explain the legal, political, and human impacts of the 1980s sentencing revolution requires more than just documenting its quantifiable results. The guidelines imposed by the U.S. Sentencing Commission represented a major shock to the entire federal system and set many institutional actions in motion, some visible in outcome data, others not. This structural change played a critical role in the subsequent proliferation of criminal cases entering the system, especially drug cases, and it catalyzed punitive legal innovations in how cases were adjudicated, above and beyond its intended effects of both toughening formal sanctions and constraining judicial sentencing discretion.

The guidelines—which aimed to "provide certainty and fairness . . . by avoiding unwarranted disparity among offenders with similar characteristics convicted of similar offenses"—seem on their face to have come up short in at least half that goal.[21] They do provide certainty of punishment, but disparities in sentencing persist, diverging over time and as a function of place.[22] A close examination of adjudication practices reveals why policy "failures" like these are neither wholly unintended nor wholly unpredictable.

This leads to the normative importance of appraising the federal system, and my situating of the study within trial-level courts. The federal government has often followed rather than led in policy trends, but it was right out front on drug prosecutions, especially in regard to the innovation of the crack-powder disparity.[23] The fine-grained distinctions made between drug types in the new federal drug laws institutionalized racism in the system of punishment, which was revolutionary in the post–civil rights era.[24] Thirteen states directly followed suit by building a crack-powder disparity into their drug laws.[25] More treach-erously, crack's highly publicized, elevated seriousness in the federal system gave rise to a new era of aggressive, racially targeted frontline law enforcement.[26]

Furthermore, myriad other legal tools, such as a defendant's criminal history, are used by prosecutors in this system to enhance punishment and foreclose mitigation that also institutionalize racial disparities in sen-tences. By uncovering the mechanics of how these legal strategies have been variously deployed, we can assign responsibility for their effects. Prosecutorial ethics—as a systemic concern—and the power bestowed on the prosecutorial role lie at the heart of the normative questions I raise here. It will be impossible to significantly reform the justice system without first constraining and reorienting the prosecutorial power that has accumulated. Although the federal system may be qualitatively dif-ferent than most state systems in its relative resources and its particular role in crime fighting, the structural shift in power to the prosecutor is emblematic of changes that have occurred in jurisdictions nation-wide.[27] Indeed, empirical studies "consistently identify the same insti-tutional actor as the central engine of [state] prison admission growth: the prosecutor."[28]

Because of the nature of how power works in legal institutions, we need to beware of complacency as the political ethos around the drug war, and the larger war on crime, begins to change. At first glance, a reversal appears under way, with several legal and policy developments signaling a taming of these "wars." For instance, in the 2005 case *United States v. Booker*, the United States Supreme Court rendered the federal sentencing guidelines advisory rather than mandatory, thereby giving judges more leeway to deviate from guidelines-determined sentences in all federal criminal cases, including drug cases.[29] Although mandatory minimums are still in force, judicial sentencing in cases not subject to mandatory minimums has been considerably liberated.[30]

A few years later, after decades of refusing to take action, Congress tempered the harsh crack cocaine mandatory minimum statutes when it passed the Fair Sentencing Act of 2010, which reduced the crack-powder disparity from 100:1 to 18:1. Since then, Congress has demonstrated some willingness to reconsider, across the board, the punitive nature of the fed-eral drug laws. This is driven in part by fiscal concerns and prison over-crowding, and in part by justice considerations. Thus, there remains broad (although not full) bipartisan support for modest sentencing reforms that have been proposed—but not yet passed—in recent years.[31] In light of this changing political tenor, the U.S. Sentencing Commission reformu-lated the guidelines by reducing drug offense levels across the board, a move Congress assented to in 2014. The practical effect of this change was to reduce the advisory guideline minimum sentences by anywhere from six months to more than sixty months, depending on the offense level and the criminal history category of the defendant.

The executive branch has also gotten on board with tempering the punitive reach of federal drug laws. In 2013, then attorney general Eric Holder directed U.S. attorneys across the nation to revise their criminal charging policies so that low-level drug defendants, even if legally eligible, would no longer be charged with offenses that "impose draconian mandatory minimum sentences."[32] Beginning in 2014, the attorney general's office has also partnered with the White House to implement a clemency initiative that offers those convicted of drug offenses who have served at least ten years in prison with no major disciplinary problems an opportunity to petition for release. Although only a small share of those petitioners have successfully earned sentence commutations so far, this effort represents a significant shift in recent presidential clemency policy.[33]

These developments have generated praise and excitement among activists, advocates, members of the press, and the public, yet optimism about the ability of such reform efforts to meaningfully rein in the power of federal drug laws may be misplaced.[34] The legal changes of the 1980s created the capacity and incentive for astounding growth of the federal justice system, in ways that render contraction very difficult. Legal scholars Kate Stith and Jose Cabranes warned us of this about ten years into the guidelines regime: "History teaches that it is always easier to create a bureaucracy than it is to reform or dismantle one."[35] This time around, a number of vested stakeholders, including some federal prosecutors as well as federal, state, and local law enforcement coalitions, have already mobilized to protect and maintain the punitive drug laws, working with members of Congress in these efforts.[36] This is no surprise, given that institutions like the federal justice system are inhabited by people whose livelihoods, professional identities, and in many cases ideological and moral commitments motivate them to maintain, if not enhance, the size and stature of their professional homes.

Moreover, the recent reforms have largely left intact a body of substantive law that subverts legal standards related to proof and evidence, ensuring that prosecutors can easily secure guilty pleas and convictions. The law also equips prosecutors with a stockpile of enhancements and add-ons they can wield to exponentially increase potential sentences, as well as a set of incentives (most notably for "substantial assistance" to the government) that they can dangle to extract guilty pleas. So although the reform movement now gaining momentum has much potential to make a dent in the overproduction and harsh punishment of federally imprisoned drug defendants, a more comprehensive dismantling of the legal machinery responsible for that overproduction is a much more daunting and distant goal.

Ultimately, as I hope to convey in the coming pages, it will take more than tweaking to undo the broader human and institutional damage inflicted by a system whose balance of power is so out of whack. The erosion of core legal ideals, along with the steep human costs exacted by the adjudication practices I document here, threaten the very legitimacy of our system of justice for a large and growing share of our society.[37]

= Chapter 1 =

The First Drug War:
Laying the Groundwork

R onald Reagan famously declared a war on drugs in 1982, during one of his weekly radio addresses.[1] In the popular imagination, this declaration set off the punitive contemporary drug war that took on a life of its own in subsequent decades. While rhetorical politics—in Reagan's era and in future ones—have certainly played a role in raising public and political concern about illicit drugs, this was not the first time in American history that a drug war had been declared. The first "call to arms," many decades earlier, had neither the scope nor the impact of the Reagan-era war, but it laid some of the groundwork for what was to come. That groundwork went beyond modeling and foreshadowing anti-drug political rhetoric of the sort Reagan used. New legal weapons were devised to be used against those charged with and convicted of drug-related crimes.

A half century before President Reagan's election, in 1930, Harry J. Anslinger, an itinerant law enforcement officer dedicated to stemming the international drug trade, was appointed to head up a brand-new domestic narcotics enforcement agency, the Federal Bureau of Narcotics, housed within the Treasury Department.[2] Commissioner Anslinger was an innovator in that role, firmly planting drug law enforcement as a core concern for the nation. Over the course of his thirty-plus-year career with the bureau, Anslinger positioned drug crimes as among the most serious threats facing the nation and successfully advocated for federal laws that provided severe sanctions for drug violations.[3]

When Anslinger became commissioner, there were few laws on the books for him to enforce. The first federal drug law of any substance had come into existence with the passage, in 1914, of the Harrison Narcotics Tax Act.[4] The Harrison Act imposed registration, taxation, and record-keeping requirements on all those authorized to prescribe or administer controlled substances, and it severely limited the amounts of morphine, cocaine, heroin, and opium that could be included in medicinal compounds that were sold directly to consumers.[5] Anslinger built on this base, his stated goal being the expansion of federal power to completely stamp out drug use in America.

In the early years, Anslinger's strategy was twofold. First, he actively encouraged states to adopt more stringent criminal laws prohibiting all forms of illicit drugs, including marijuana. This was a calculated move, since he knew federal judges would balk if low-level drug cases involving ordinary citizens began to flood their dockets.[6] Second, as Anslinger settled into his role, he became a much more vocal advocate for expanding federal law to criminalize drug manufacturing, distribution, and use. Therefore, Anslinger was one of the key architects of the original infrastructure upon which the modern drug war would be built.

Anslinger nabbed an early win when Congress brought marijuana into the fold of regulation by passing the Marihuana Tax Act of 1937.[7] This victory was the culmination of an intense lobbying and public relations effort spearheaded by Anslinger, who portrayed marijuana as a highly dangerous drug that also inspired violence among its users.[8] The Marihuana Tax Act regulated marijuana distribution and use much along the lines of the Harrison Narcotics Tax Act, thereby adding to the Narcotics Bureau's enforcement arsenal.

Anslinger was just getting started. Over the next decade and a half he helped propel drug regulation right into the punitive heart of criminal law. The Harrison Act and the Marihuana Act both regulated drug use indirectly: the primary enforcement targets were medical doctors, dentists, and pharmacists. These early laws aimed to funnel the power to distribute substances to legitimate medical practitioners and medicinal suppliers, whose patterns of distribution could then be monitored. Indeed, the fact that the governing agency responsible for enforcement was the Treasury Bureau signaled the primary devices—improper registration, record-keeping, or tax remission by distributors—through which violations would be identified and punished.

In 1951, Anslinger celebrated the passage of the Boggs Act, which directly and forcefully criminalized users and dealers through a novel set of mandatory minimum sentences for violation of drug laws.[9] The Boggs Act authorized five- and ten-year mandatory minimum prison sentences for drug distribution convictions, and two-, five-, and ten-year mandatories for unlawful possession convictions. The length of mandatory sentences in both instances depended on the prior criminal record of the defendant, so this legislation also introduced rigid criminal history enhancements specific to drug cases. Under this "recidivist" provision, prosecutors were required to determine whether eligible prior convictions existed and then certify those prior convictions in court. Judges then were required to impose the enhanced sentences.

Anslinger had actively lobbied members of Congress for years in this effort. He also published writings in popular and professional outlets that lamented the relative inadequacy of the drug laws available at that time and that touted the importance of mandatory minimums to his organization's law enforcement efforts. The core components of his argument are captured in a brief law review article he published in the midst of congressional consideration of mandatory minimum legislation:

> For some time the Bureau of Narcotics has favored a strengthening of the penalty provisions of the federal narcotics laws by providing minimum and maximum sentences, with mandatory sentences for second and subsequent violators. A bill, H.R. 3490, which has passed the House of Representatives and is pending action in the Senate has these provisions. . . .
>
> If enacted into law it should prove a most important aid to narcotic law enforcement by removing the persistent peddler from his illegal activity for a longer period of time while acting as a strong deterrent to those who would normally seek to be his successor in such traffic.[10]

Although Anslinger certainly was a motivator and catalyst, Congress did not need to be dragged into passing punitive drug laws. The political chorus from the 1920s through the 1950s bellowed about the dangers of narcotics and other substances, and dissenters who urged noncriminal modes of managing the problem of drug use and addiction were altogether ignored in the political arena.[11] At its most extreme, Congress passed the Narcotics Control Act of 1956, which authorized the death penalty for adults who sold heroin to persons under the age of eighteen.[12] Congress also expanded drug law enforcement's arsenal of investigative tools via statutes passed in the 1930s. The Vehicle Seizure Act of 1939 gave law enforcement the power to seize vehicles suspected of being used for transporting illegal drugs.[13] The seized vehicles were to be forfeited to the federal government and could then be used by law enforcement in the "investigation, detection and arrest of other violators."[14] Another early statute authorized the Bureau of Narcotics to pay informants to provide information about suspected drug law violations.[15]

This earlier period can be seen as both a prototype and an opening of possibility for what was to come in the 1980s in the wake of Reagan's new war on drugs. The modes of regulation that emerged in the earlier period all have powerful and important successors in the modern federal drug war, including the establishment and solidification of legitimate drug distribution avenues within the medical realm (which themselves could be abused for illicit purposes); the introduction of mandatory minimum sentencing statutes to constrain judicial sentencing discretion in drug cases, as well as mandatory sentence enhancements for those with prior narcotics convictions; the development of specialized narcotics law enforcement units; and the tactics of asset forfeiture and the cultivation of informants as key drug law enforcement strategies.

The earlier period was characterized by racial demonization of drug users and traffickers, likewise a notable feature of the 1980s war on drugs. Numerous scholars have documented the way that politicians, interest groups, and law enforcement figures, in their narratives of the drug scourge, linked the "menace" of drugs to people of color, who were said to pose multiple threats to whites, especially to white women and youths.[16] The Chinese were tied to the scourge of opium; African Americans, especially in the South, were characterized as cocaine "fiends" who could only be controlled by harsh criminal laws; and marijuana was portrayed as causing Mexicans and African Americans to become violent.[17] These linkages elevated the threat posed by illicit drug use to new heights, which was key to the eventual federal passage of early narcotics laws.

Anslinger was among the most sensational racial demonizers.[18] In support of proposed marijuana laws, he suggested that white women who were high on marijuana were seduced into having sex with black men and that fully half of all crime committed by blacks and Latinos was committed under its influence.[19] This theme that people of color were especially susceptible to drug addiction and that they then corrupted whites also animated Anslinger's arguments for mandatory minimums.

Missing in this period, however, were the scope and scale of implementation that would come three decades later. These earlier laws and policies were put on the books, but the number of federal drug convictions did not increase as the laws were toughened. In other words, although the political will and bureaucratic interest was there (at least in Anslinger's unit) both to build the federal drug enforcement infrastructure and to pass very punitive federal laws, federal actors did not appear to be committed to going out and using these new powers in court to get more convictions. Also, in the earlier period the fiscal investment in federal drug law enforcement never came close to matching the heightened rhetoric that prompted legislative change.

Anslinger was well aware that federal judges actively discouraged federal prosecutions of run-of-the-mill drug cases. The federal laws expanded the prosecutorial capacity of assistant U.S. attorneys, but on-the-ground district court norms served as a check on the actualization of that potential. Indeed, after the punitive drug laws were enthusiastically enacted by Congress in the 1950s, federal drug caseloads actually declined. The year before the Boggs Act was enacted, federal prosecutors initiated 2,400 cases against drug defendants and obtained 2,136 convictions. Those numbers slowly and steadily dropped over the next decade. By 1962, the annual number of federal drug cases initiated in the federal system hit a low of 1,643, with 1,403 convictions.[20] If anything, federal prosecutors seemed to be using their discretionary power more frugally after the first set of drug mandatory minimums came on the books.

This was, in fact, recommended as policy and practice, as suggested by the prosecutors' policy manuals of the time. The *U.S. Attorneys' Manual* is the official internal policy manual that informs U.S. attorneys of their role and responsibilities and provides guidance on how to manage various aspects of their duties. The 1953 and 1967 versions of the manual cautioned federal prosecutors that with narcotic law violations, "The emphasis should be on prosecutions of the sellers or purveyors, particularly those who deal with minors, and not the mere addict possessors. . . . Moreover, prosecutions for minor offenses which are considered to be local in character may well be and often are left to the state or local authorities."[21] Such restraint did not characterize the discussion of most other criminal offenses in the manual. The manual also reminded prosecutors that they "must file" on eligible prior convictions to trigger the doubled sentences under the Boggs Act mandates. The only way prosecutors could mitigate the harshness of the recidivist provisions was to not bring eligible cases at all.

But the key reason that the 1950s law did not lead to a jump in cases and convictions had to do with the larger legal infrastructure in which prosecutors were operating at the time. Before the 1970s, the jurisdiction of federal criminal law was largely limited to crimes that took place on federal property or that crossed state or national borders.[22] Assistant U.S. attorneys were limited in the kinds of criminal cases involving drugs or common criminal offenses that they could pursue for federal prosecution.

Anslinger's crusade did not let up after the antidrug legislative successes of the 1950s. He fought efforts to divert addicts from the criminal justice system domestically, arguing that the new mandatory minimums were already proving successful in reducing addiction. He also pushed for stronger interdiction and suppression efforts abroad.[23] But Anslinger's retirement from the Federal Bureau of Narcotics in 1962 helped usher in a notable shift in political rhetoric about the problem of drugs. Most pointedly, even though the punitive drug laws that Anslinger had heralded saw more life on the books than in practice at the time, the executive branch had considerable interest in rescinding them.

This less punitive "inter-drug-war" period was kicked off by the 1962 White House Conference on Drug Abuse.[24] Following that conference, the Kennedy administration appointed a special President's Advisory Commission on Narcotics and Drug Abuse that was directed to develop new strategies for dealing with the problem of drugs.[25] The report generated by the commission was not released until 1964, three months after President Kennedy's assassination. Its "guiding principles" and finer-grained recommendations pivoted away from a purely law enforcement-punishment mode of regulation while also solidifying drug regulation as a federal concern. It recommended reorganizing narcotics law enforcement by centralizing all efforts in the Department of Justice. This ensured that when political tides changed again, as they would less than two decades later, the jurisdiction and legal structures to relaunch a punitive drug war at the federal level were in place. The report was hardly radical in its recommendations; among other things it called for rehabilitation programs for users, including within-prison rehabilitation for small-time dealer-addicts, while maintaining a law enforcement strategy for traffickers.

The Advisory Commission's report was criticized on all sides. Bureaucrats in both the Federal Bureau of Narcotics, now headed by Henry Giordino, and the Treasury Department attacked the very mission of the Advisory Commission—in their view law enforcement efforts had been successful. Not surprisingly, leaders of both entities also opposed centralizing all law enforcement efforts in the Department of Justice. On the other end of the spectrum, some experts criticized the report's conflation of drug use with drug abuse, especially since, even if desirable, setting a policy goal of no illicit drug use was unachievable as a practical matter.[26]

Nonetheless, the Advisory Commission's report set off a march down a reform road that tempered the purely hard-line, punitive politics that had reached its apex in the 1950s, at least for a time. Part of the reform was structural: a new federal agency, the Bureau of Drug Abuse and Control (BDAC), was authorized by Congress in 1965, housed within the Food and Drug Administration. The BDAC represented a direct attack on Anslinger's legacy and the power of the Federal Bureau of Narcotics. Three years later, the Federal Bureau of Narcotics and the Bureau of Drug Abuse and Control were consolidated into a single Justice-housed agency, the Bureau of Narcotics and Dangerous Drugs (BNDD).

The kind of compromise vision expressed by the Advisory Commission's report largely guided federal drug law and policy developments over the subsequent sixteen years. Incarceration remained a central component of the intervention strategy, although it would be rehabilitative in nature and—most radically—a "civil commitment," whereby addicts would be diverted from criminal prosecution and institutionalized for treatment.[27] The Narcotic Addict Rehabilitation Act (NARA),[28] signed into law by President Johnson in 1966, epitomized the duality inherent in federal drug policy of the time. Title I of NARA provided federally charged drug "addicts" with a diversion program that imposed up to thirty-six months of treatment under the care of the surgeon general; criminal charges were dropped against those deemed cured of their addiction after the thirty-six-month period.[29] Title II provided specialized within-prison treatment for eligible defendants who were deemed addicts and who had been convicted of a subset of non-violent offenses.[30] This program's popularity was short-lived; by 1978, all of the stand-alone NARA units within the federal prison system had been dismantled.[31]

The key target of the reform efforts of this period were the mandatory minimums under the Boggs Act. There was considerable political will to repeal these laws—but not because the nation's drug problem was deemed solved. Indeed, in 1967 the President's Commission on Law Enforcement and Administration of Justice published the *Task Force Report: Drug Abuse and Narcotics* on the "growing and critical" problem of narcotics trafficking and drug abuse in America.[32] Despite this characterization, the Advisory Commission recommended eliminating the federal mandatory minimum drug penalties that had been in force since 1951. Finding the evidence inconclusive as to whether these laws were effective in reducing drug crime, the Advisory Commission viewed judicial discretion to assess the individualized circumstances of defendants as essential to effective criminal justice policy:

> Within any classification of offenses, differences exist in both the circumstances and nature of the illegal conduct and in the offenders. Mandatory provisions deprive judges and correctional authorities of the ability to base their judgments on the seriousness of the violations and the particular characteristics and potential for rehabilitation of the offender.[33]

Within three years of this report, Congress passed the Comprehensive Drug Abuse Prevention and Control Act of 1970,[34] repealing the drug mandatory minimums, decreasing maximum possible drug sentences, creating a drug scheduling system, and expanding treatment and education programs as a means to combat the drug problem.[35] Thus, where NARA had primarily addressed the quality of sanction that was best imposed for certain drug-related crimes, favoring rehabilitation over punishment, the Comprehensive Drug Abuse Prevention and Control Act of 1970 directly addressed the scope of sanctions.

Elements of this legislation were several years in the making, spanning the Johnson and Nixon administrations. Although Nixon held this law up as a centerpiece to his law-and-order campaign, it was actually a contradictory accumulation of provisions that scaled back punishment for drug defendants and dramatically increased funding for treatment and research, while also further solidifying drugs as a core federal law enforcement concern.[36] To that end, the act consolidated most drug-enforcement-related activities within the Department of Justice, while delegating border-related drug law enforcement to the U.S. Customs Service. It also set the stage for the drug-related federalization explosion, in that Congress dramatically expanded federal jurisdiction to cover more intrastate drug-related crimes.[37] This legislative move was easily translated into action as a result of the concurrent jurisdictional expansion of federal criminal law. Specifically, the opportunity for a tighter coupling of legislative changes and expansive drug enforcement practices opened up after a United States Supreme Court ruling that upheld the federal government's right to prosecute intrastate crime.[38]

The scope of federal law enforcement power was further extended through the establishment of the drug dangerousness "scheduling" scheme that was authorized in the act. This responsibility was and continues to be held by the Drug Enforcement Administration (DEA), which succeeded the Bureau of Narcotics and Dangerous Drugs in 1973. Much to the dismay of medical and other experts, law enforcement was given the power to designate the degree of medical efficacy of and health risk posed by regulated substances, which in turn helps determine the severity of punishment.[39]

Nonetheless, the 1970 act largely accomplished the goal that had been previously set by the Johnson administration: to eliminate mandatory minimum prison sentences for most federal drug offenses. Although it still authorized increased punishment for recidivists, it made the imposition of longer sentences in such cases discretionary. Like the Boggs Act recidivist provision, prosecutors needed to file an information, a form of charging document initiated by a prosecutor, to certify eligible prior offenses. However, unlike under the Boggs Act, the choice to file was at the U.S. attorney's discretion rather than mandated by statute.[40]

The net effect of these changes was to shift discretionary sentencing power back to federal judges, who had been so maligned by Anslinger and others as being "too soft" on drug defendants.[41] Through its part in shaping this act and other drug-related legislation, the first Nixon administration talked tough about drugs and crime and consolidated institutional resources, including considerable law enforcement resources, around the problems of both drug abuse and trafficking. Yet it also expressed confidence in the legal system to determine appropriate sentences on a case-by-case basis, provide meaningful sanctions that would do more than just punish those convicted, and even determine who could be best served by interventions outside the formal criminal justice system. To that end, it provided significant institutional and fiscal support to drug abuse research and treatment, to be housed in and directed by the Health, Education and Welfare Department.

The 1970 Act also headed down a path of divvying up the "drug problem," by both substance and persons, into categories that needed either social and medical intervention or forceful law enforcement action. Marijuana was increasingly exempted from the law enforcement category, as were the "misguided youth" who became involved in using and selling marijuana. Ruth Peterson's analysis of the congressional debates over the act demonstrates the race- and class-based nature of these divisions. She argues that by devising a law that distinguished between "'saving' users and punishing pushers," lawmakers could present the policy as race- and class-neutral even though it was explicitly underpinned with concern about how the lives of privileged youths who got involved with drugs would be ruined if they were brought into the criminal justice system.[42]

Members of Congress cautioned against using the hard hammer of the federal criminal justice system against "the sons and daughters of some Members of Congress as well as other leading members of the business, industrial, and political community of these United States" or against "college students . . . on the road to professional careers" who were caught violating the law.[43] Consequently, the distinction between type of drug offense and the special leniency toward marijuana that was incorporated in the act institutionalized bias in a more fine-grained manner than had prior punitive drug laws, by carving out categories of culpability that correlate with race and class. This was in some sense a cautionary tale about what could happen should the punishment winds shift direction.

The act also codified the notion of an especially culpable drug defendant by defining a "dangerous special drug offender" who, to ensure public safety, needed to receive a longer sentence than would otherwise be allowed by law.[44] Under this provision, a prosecutor could seek a sentence above the statutory maximum sentence for convicted drug defendants who were determined to be habitual offenders, professional drug dealers, or part of an organized criminal network.

By the second Nixon administration, the bifurcation between the addict and the trafficker and the differential concern with specific illicit substances depending on the using populations had become hardened. This had implications for subsequent federal policy and practice. The suppression of drug trafficking became both a political and administrative mission, and the innovation of the multi-agency, cross-jurisdictional task force emerged.[45] And even though the mandatory minimum sentences for drug offenses had been repealed, the concept was now firmly established as a possibility.

In fact, President Nixon called for restoring mandatory minimums for heroin traffickers in his 1973 State of the Union address, explicitly voicing discontent with federal courts that provide "little more than an escape hatch for those who are responsible for the menace of drugs."[46] While Nixon was soon diverted to his own political and legal troubles, the dual infrastructure born of the 1970 Act impelled growth and competition in the national fight against illicit drugs. One key mechanism for growth was an infusion of federal funding in selected communities to support both the law enforcement and treatment sides of the policy mission.[47]

Absent the Watergate fiasco, the threat of Nixon's impeachment, and his resignation, the second federal drug war may have taken off in earnest in the early 1970s, just a decade after initial retreat. But Nixon's successor, Gerald Ford, was not committed to sustaining this effort. The short-lived Ford administration worked hard to deemphasize the problem of drugs, both to avoid acknowledging their widespread use and to scale back the enormous amount of funding that had been dedicated to both sides of the federal drug policy during Nixon's administration.[48]

The grandstanding style of Nixon, who spoke publicly of a war against drugs, and the fiscal commitment that underpinned the rhetoric were replaced by a much more tentative stance by President Ford. Research and treatment took a huge hit, as Ford dismantled several cabinet entities dedicated to drug abuse. On the enforcement end, the Ford administration continued the practice of categorizing priorities by perceived dangerousness of substance and abuser. Cocaine and marijuana were deemed low priorities for enforcement, whereas opiates such as heroin remained a top priority. Moreover, the Ford administration floated the politically radical idea that drug use could be distinguished from drug abuse as a policy matter, with only the latter being the appropriate focus for governmental intervention.

The most notable articulation of the Ford administration's policy was made in a report, published in 1975, *The White Paper on Drug Abuse: A Report to the President from the Domestic Drug Abuse Task Force.* The report recommended that the federal government concentrate its efforts on international trafficking organizations and the major dealers within the nation and leave the other concerns to entities outside the federal government. Members of Congress and other stakeholders were quite critical of its recommendations. Ford responded by retreating from the sensible vision presented in the report, at least rhetorically, especially as the 1976 presidential election campaign heated up. Echoing his predecessor, he began to call for lengthy mandatory minimums for major traffickers, and increased support for the DEA's enforcement efforts. After his loss to Jimmy Carter, during the final lame-duck months of his presidency, Ford reverted to the position outlined in the report: to be prudent, the federal government must prioritize the most serious drug threats to the nation and learn to live with the more recreational uses that were now prevalent, especially of marijuana.

President Carter's drug policy closely tracked the recommendations of the task force's report. Carter inherited a budget crisis and so worked to continue cutting back on spending, including on drug abuse research, treatment, and enforcement. Consequently, he was reluctant to invest in a cabinet-level infrastructure devoted to drug policy even though Congress pushed for it. Concerning marijuana, Carter took a step further than Ford, coming out in favor of decriminalization in 1977, a reform also urged by several Democratic lawmakers at the time. Like his predecessors, Carter maintained federal enforcement focus on heroin while deemphasizing marijuana and cocaine. His administration also favored a strategy to suppress the international supply of drugs, so DEA and other federal agencies were deployed in programs to eradicate poppy harvests in countries around the globe.

The outlook of both Ford's and Carter's administrations seemed to trickle down to U.S. attorneys' offices. Drug prosecutions and convictions steadily declined from their post–Boggs Act high-water mark in 1974. By 1980, the last year of Carter's presidency, the annual number of federal drug convictions was just 58 percent of what they had been five years earlier. Nonetheless, toward the end of Carter's term in office, the executive branch began to waver on its more libertarian approach to federal drug policy. As more and more cocaine came into the United States, the substance's status as a benign, even glamorous, recreational drug began to change.[49] In a 1979 report on drug strategy, cocaine was elevated to the rank of "serious" drug worthy of federal attention, right behind heroin and barbiturates.[50] Policy staff recommended a supply-suppression strategy similar to that used against poppy growers, whereby the federal government would put resources into discouraging coca leaf cultivation in South America.

The Carter administration also began to show renewed interest in the problem of addiction. This was driven in part by a counter-movement of suburban parents decrying the laissez-faire federal approach to drugs and propelled by a shake-up within the White House drug policy advisory team.[51] The Parents Movement put considerable pressure on the White House to change its approach, and the administration responded with rhetoric and even some resources directed at preventing drug abuse among youth and countering the glamorization of drugs in American culture.[52]

By the time Carter left the White House, federal drug policy was at a crossroads. The Carter administration was unable to articulate a clear vision of the federal government's goals or mission vis-à-vis illicit drugs. Nor did it project confidence in the effectiveness of any specific policy path, whether it be harm reduction, liberalization of drug laws, and the treatment and rehabilitation of users and addicts, or hard-line prohibition. The future was wide open for the Reagan administration and the broader New Right coalition that consolidated its power in the 1980s.[53]

= Chapter 2 =

The Great War: Creating an Infrastructure of Legal Power

E ven more critical to the incipient drug war than the floundering executive branch policy was a concurrent criminal justice reform revolution quietly brewing in Congress. Paradoxically, this initiative, spearheaded by the liberal Massachusetts Senator Ted Kennedy, aimed to further tame federal criminal law and make it more equitable by completely overhauling the entire existing sentencing structure. The effort was ultimately realized in the passage of the Sentencing Reform Act of 1984 (SRA). The SRA was not particular to drug convictions, but it would have huge implications for drug cases. This large-scale restructuring, along with myriad smaller changes to federal criminal law, created a much more complex legal landscape in which federal criminal cases, including drug cases, have since been prosecuted and adjudicated.

The idea that the federal sentencing system needed reform was rooted in a broader political and legal struggle over the predominant sentencing structure used in most jurisdictions at the time. Since the early twentieth century, indeterminate sentencing had been the prevailing practice. Under indeterminate sentencing schemes, judges, at sentencing, and parole boards, at the back end, exercised broad discretion in individual cases to determine the appropriate sentence in light of both offense and defendant characteristics. In its idealized version, indeterminate sentencing was necessary to achieve rehabilitation, so each defendant could be treated individually to address his or her therapeutic needs. And each would be released from prison when experts determined rehabilitation had been achieved. In practice, however, there was a growing sense that the system did not rehabilitate very effectively nor did judges and parole boards treat the convicted very fairly.[1]

Initially, the calls for reform to indeterminate sentencing were sympathetic to the plight of criminal defendants and prisoners, since sentences could vary wildly from judge to judge and between similarly convicted defendants. A central critique propelling this movement was that racial discrimination ran rampant under such indeterminate conditions. Critics supported reforms that constrained judicial sentencing discretion on the theory that they would temper inequality in outcomes. The liberal elite was motivated to make these reforms happen, which they did in jurisdictions across the country.[2]

In the federal system, Judge Marvin Frankel, of the Southern District of New York, was among the most vocal critics of indeterminate sentences, publishing his indictment of them, *Criminal Sentencing: Law Without Order,* in 1973. Frankel's book inspired Senator Kennedy to tackle reform in the federal system.[3] Drawing on Judge Frankel's recommendations as well as those from a group of scholars at Yale Law School, Senator Kennedy made the establishment of a sentencing commission that would be authorized to develop binding sentencing guidelines a centerpiece of his reform plan. Between 1975 and 1984, Kennedy sponsored or cosponsored a number of pieces of sentencing reform legislation, including two compromise bills that would revise criminal law statutes as well as reform sentencing procedure.[4]

Early versions of the bills included provisions to lower maximum prison terms and explicitly encouraged the development and use of alternative sanctions to prison, pegging current prison capacity as a limit on how punitive sentences could become under the new system.[5] But the legislative process involved considerable political compromise on every attempt to achieve passage of the bills, and all of these provisions disappeared by the final version of the SRA. As Kate Stith and Steven Koh have documented, the SRA's very passage was made possible by being packaged within the larger, explicitly punitive Comprehensive Crime Control Act of 1984, which toughened up the criminal code in several areas.[6]

By the time the Sentencing Reform Act was enacted in 1984, the nature of political and popular concern about crime had changed dramatically. Consequently, the bill passed by Congress and signed into law by President Reagan was in many ways the antithesis of its original vision. The enacted law did mandate the establishment of a sentencing commission, which was tasked with drafting guidelines and monitoring sentences to ensure consistency in outcomes and reduce sentencing disparity.[7] However, the underlying ethos of the final product had more to do with crime control than with due process. Put simply, sentencing reform had moved from an antidiscrimination and relatively antipunitive effort to a critical building block of the national tough-on-crime movement.[8] Although the executive branch's targeted war on drugs and the concurrent legislative activity on the Sentencing Reform Act were distinct political phenomena, they became deeply conjoined as the SRA was transformed into nuts-and-bolts policy. Indeed, the new system was structured in a way that would allow sentences to be dramatically ratcheted up from the prevailing norms, which is exactly what happened in the case of drug offenses.

The U.S. Sentencing Commission (USSC), as established by the SRA, was administratively housed in the judicial branch. By law, the USSC was appointed by the president and comprised seven voting members, of which at least three were federal judges and no more than four could be from the same political party.[9] A designee from the attorney general's office and the chair of the U.S. Parole Commission were also authorized as ex officio nonvoting members. The USSC was given "broad authority to review and rationalize the federal sentencing system."[10] Among its specific mandates was to devise a system that would "provide certainty and fairness in meeting the purposes of sentencing, avoiding unwarranted sentencing disparities among defendants with similar records who have been found guilty of similar conduct."[11] The uniformity and fairness goal was to be achieved solely through constraining judicial decisionmaking in the sentence determination, via the Sentencing Guidelines promulgated by the USSC. The commission had no say over who was dragged into the front door to be prosecuted.

The SRA did not specify a single purpose of criminal punishment. Instead, Congress delineated four distinct and somewhat contradictory purposes that judges must consider in making sentencing determinations. According to the statute, federal sentences should be retributive and should "promote respect for the law"; serve as a deterrent; provide for public safety; and provide rehabilitative opportunities for those convicted.[12]

Despite the nod to rehabilitation, the law made clear that those who committed drug-related crimes were to be treated harshly. The USSC was directed to set the guidelines for certain drug and violent offenders, whom it came to dub "career offenders," to the statutory maximum sentences allowed by law.[13] The SRA eliminated discretionary parole and authorized a maximum of fifty-four days per year served (roughly 15 percent) of good-time credit that inmates could earn.[14] This good-time credit ratio was considerably more austere than was common in most determinate state sentencing systems at the time, which was most typically either "day-for-day" (one day off for one day served, or 50 percent) or one day off for two days served (about 33 percent).[15] In place of parole supervision, the SRA authorized determinate periods of supervised release to be imposed after the prison term was completed.[16] Finally, the SRA included an enforcement mechanism to discipline judges into following the guidelines. For the first time, judges' pronounced sentences would be subject to appellate review when they departed from the guidelines.[17]

While the USSC went to work on devising a system that could meet the directives of the SRA, Congress added to the mix by passing a series of new mandatory minimum and mandatory sentencing enhancement statutes that were then incorporated into the emerging scheme. These new statutes dictated that lengthy minimum prison sentences be imposed for certain kinds of offenses and defendants. Several of these statutes had huge implications for drug sentencing under the new system.[18]

First, the Anti-Drug Abuse Act of 1986 included a set of new mandatory minimum penalties for drug trafficking crimes.[19] The "Narcotics Penalties and Enforcement" subsection of this act distinguished among various forms of controlled substances by setting different trigger weights for mandatory sentences of five or ten years. In the original scheme, crack cocaine became the punitive anchor.[20] Even heroin, which had consistently been the demon drug throughout most of the twentieth century, was supplanted by crack. It took twenty times the amount of heroin to trigger an equivalent sentence for crack under the new mandatory minimum scheme. Congress then intensified its disparate treatment of crack with the passage of the Anti-Drug Abuse Act of 1988. A provision in this new law specified that mere possession of crack cocaine triggered a mandatory prison sentence of five years whereas no other possession offense required a prison sentence at all, and otherwise a *maximum* one-year sentence was specified.[21]

In addition to introducing the rash of harsh drug mandatories, the 1986 Anti-Drug Abuse Act included a provision that allows prosecutors to seek a doubling of both the five- and ten-year mandatory minimums if the defendant has a single prior drug felony conviction.[22] Two years later, the ultimate enhancement was passed into law: in cases ordinarily subject to a ten-year mandatory minimum, prosecutors could seek a mandatory minimum of life without parole when defendants had two or more prior convictions on drug charges.[23] The device to obtain these enhanced drug sentences was already in the criminal code—21 U.S.C. § 851—which had been enacted in 1970 to give prosecutors the discretion to *not* seek mandatory enhanced punishments against repeat drug defendants.[24] So assistant U.S. attorneys seeking to enhance drug sentences under the new statute file a prior-felony information with the court, documenting the specific prior conviction(s). These enhancements have come to be known colloquially as "851s" or "851 enhancements." Notably, they apply only to drug defendants in federal court. And unlike convictions that count against defendants for criminal history points and for the career offender guideline, prior drug convictions have no expiration date for qualifying for the "851" enhancement, so decades-old priors can be leveraged against drug defendants.

To achieve a unified sentencing system, the USSC incorporated the new mandatory minimums into the Sentencing Guidelines, which came to serve as key sentencing benchmarks around which all other drug sentence ranges within the guideline scheme were built.[25] In some sense, then, the mandatory minimums answered the question for the USSC of what drug sentencing should look like under the guidelines: it was to be very punitive, rather than rehabilitative, and individual culpability was devalued, since sentences were largely driven by drug type and quantity.[26]

The USSC spent its first few years of existence crafting an intricate set of guidelines that tried to incorporate all of these congressional mandates. The basic structure put forth by the USSC for sentencing determinations was a Sentencing Table: prescribed sentence ranges were a function of forty-three offense characteristics, quantified as "Offense Level" on the y-axis, and prior criminal record of the sentenced defendant, quantified as six "Criminal History Categor[ies]" on the x-axis (see figure 2.1). Sentence ranges overlap vertically and horizontally,[27] but the guideline minimums nonetheless escalate quite rapidly as the offense level or criminal history category increases. This structure remains in place as of 2016, although the prescribed sentence ranges are now advisory rather than mandatory, as they were until 2005.[28]

Although the Sentencing Table seems on its face to be relatively straight-forward, the calculation to determine the case-specific applicable levels on the two axes is not. The USSC's *Guidelines Manual,* which is used to determine both offense level and criminal history category, ran to 326 pages in its first iteration in 1987; the most recent version, published in 2015, is now close to 600 pages, not including the additional 1,600 pages of appendices.[29] Within those pages lie complex rules about valuing and quantifying offense and offender characteristics. And these rules and valuations provide ample opportunities for frontline actors to negotiate around those values, as we shall see in the coming chapters.

Chapter 2 of the *Guidelines Manual* explains the offense level calculation, which sets the base offense level according to the offenses of conviction and all "relevant conduct" surrounding those convictions. Chapter 3 provides for a number of offense level adjustments, mostly to increase the level, depending on certain specific offense characteristics.[30] Relevant conduct is an especially important innovation of the USSC's.[31] It allows a judge to consider criminal conduct that was never formally charged, that was charged but dismissed, or even that was charged, tried, and acquitted to be used to increase sentences so long as a judge finds by a preponderance of the evidence that the purported "relevant conduct" occurred. In the context of drug cases, relevant conduct often includes uncorroborated reports by informers who allege and detail past drug transactions with the defendant.

In the case of certain offenses, including drug violations, the single most important driver of offense level is quantity—the illicit substance's weight or the number of pills or dosages. An individual's relative culpability can be altered a bit through the adjustments outlined in chapter 3. But the quantity measure, including "relevant conduct" quantities above and beyond the amount for which the defendant was convicted, is the overwhelming determinant of the y-axis portion of the calculus. The

Figure 2.1   Sentencing Table (Months of Imprisonment by Offense Level and Criminal History Category)

Zone	Offense Level	Criminal History Category (Criminal History Points)					
		I (0 or 1)	II (2 or 3)	III (4, 5, 6)	IV (7, 8, 9)	V (10, 11, 12)	VI (13 or more)
	1	0–6	0–6	0–6	0–6	0–6	0–6
	2	0–6	0–6	0–6	0–6	0–6	1–7
	3	0–6	0–6	0–6	0–6	2–8	3–9
Zone A	4	0–6	0–6	0–6	2–8	4–10	6–12
	5	0–6	0–6	1–7	4–10	6–12	9–15
	6	0–6	1–7	2–8	6–12	9–15	12–18
	7	0–6	2–8	4–10	8–14	12–18	15–21
	8	0–6	4–10	6–12	10–16	15–21	18–24
	9	4–10	6–12	8–14	12–18	18–24	21–27
Zone B	10	6–12	8–14	10–16	15–21	21–27	24–30
	11	8–14	10–16	12–18	18–24	24–30	27–33
Zone C	12	10–16	12–18	15–21	21–27	27–33	30–37
	13	12–18	15–21	18–24	24–30	30–37	33–41
	14	15–21	18–24	21–27	27–33	33–41	37–46
	15	18–24	21–27	24–30	30–37	37–46	41–51
	16	21–27	24–30	27–33	33–41	41–51	46–57
	17	24–30	27–33	30–37	37–46	46–57	51–63
	18	27–33	30–37	33–41	41–51	51–63	57–71
	19	30–37	33–41	37–46	46–57	57–71	63–78
	20	33–41	37–46	41–51	51–63	63–78	70–87
	21	37–46	41–51	46–57	57–71	70–87	77–96
	22	41–51	46–57	51–63	63–78	77–96	84–105
	23	46–57	51–63	57–71	70–87	84–105	92–115
	24	51–63	57–71	63–78	77–96	92–115	100–125
	25	57–71	63–78	70–87	84–105	100–125	110–137
	26	63–78	70–87	78–97	92–115	110–137	120–150
	27	70–87	78–97	87–108	100–125	120–150	130–162
Zone D	28	78–97	87–108	97–121	110–137	130–162	140–175
	29	87–108	97–121	108–135	121–151	140–175	151–188
	30	97–121	108–135	121–151	135–168	151–188	168–210
	31	108–135	121–151	135–168	151–188	168–210	188–235
	32	121–151	135–168	151–188	168–210	188–235	210–262
	33	135–168	151–188	168–210	188–235	210–262	235–293
	34	151–188	168–210	188–235	210–262	235–293	262–327
	35	168–210	188–235	210–262	235–293	262–327	292–365
	36	188–235	210–262	235–293	262–327	292–365	324–405
	37	210–262	235–293	262–327	292–365	324–405	360–life
	38	235–293	262–327	292–365	324–405	360–life	360–life
	39	262–327	292–365	324–405	360–life	360–life	360–life
	40	292–365	324–405	360–life	360–life	360–life	360–life
	41	324–405	360–life	360–life	360–life	360–life	360–life
	42	360–life	360–life	360–life	360–life	360–life	360–life
	43	life	life	life	life	life	life

Source: U.S. Sentencing Commission 2015.

quantity driver of sentence lengths thus exposes many very low-level couriers, who often transport large quantities of drugs for relatively small sums of money, to lengthy prison sentences.[32] In addition, individual defendants even at the lowest rungs of a drug selling operation, including street dealers, can be held responsible via the conspiracy statute for the total amount of illicit drugs involved in that larger operation.[33] A conspirator does not need to have any direct involvement or even knowledge about the larger operation; involvement in any part implicates culpability for the entire network. As we will see, this aspect of the law provides a huge hammer that can be wielded by prosecutors to induce cooperation and compel guilty pleas.

As noted previously, quantity means different things when it comes to different illicit substances. To clarify those differences, the Sentencing Guidelines provide a drug quantity table, which lists how much of each substance of a given quantity is translated into an offense level. For defendants charged with offenses involving multiple substances, chapter 2 of the guidelines includes a drug equivalency table to convert all illicit substances into a standardized "marihuana" weight for ease in combining relative quantities and determining the appropriate offense level.[34]

"Criminal History Category," which has values from I to VI on the x-axis of the Sentencing Table, is calculated following the rules set out in chapter 4 of the guidelines. The fact that criminal history took on such an outsize role in this sentencing structure reflects political choices made by the original USSC.[35] The SRA directed the USSC to consider a broad range of defendant-related factors to be incorporated into the guidelines' formula, including traditional sentencing factors such as age, family ties and responsibilities, mental and emotional condition, and employment history.[36] Criminal history was only one item among eleven factors delineated for consideration. But by the time the guidelines were devised the traditional mitigating defendant characteristics were excluded as standard sentencing criteria, while criminal history had been elevated to be the sole occupier of the x-axis. This ensured that defendants' prior record would play a determinative role in all sentences under the guidelines.[37]

Criminal history was also incorporated into the guidelines through a provision for those dubbed "career offenders" that was devised by the original USSC and that remains in substantially the same form today. This provision has special significance for drug defendants. Specifically, it defined a career offender as an adult defendant whose "instant offense is a crime of violence or trafficking in a controlled substance, and . . . the defendant has at least two prior felony convictions of either a crime of violence or a controlled substance offense."[38] In directing the USSC to treat "career offenders" more punitively, Congress lumped drug priors in with violent priors as the predicate offenses that would trigger the career offender guideline. And it lumped drug defendants in with those accused of violent offenses as deserving of extraordinary punishment, so even those convicted of low-level street dealing and who have no criminal history other than drug convictions are subject to this enhancement. Seen in a broader context, then, the 1970 statutory invention of the "special dangerous drug offender" who needed extra punishment had morphed into the more generic "career offender" in the new scheme.[39]

For defendants who fall under the guidelines' career offender provision, the sentence ranges shoot up exponentially. Qualifying defendants are automatically placed in the highest criminal history category, category VI, and their offense levels are significantly increased. For example, under the original guidelines for a drug defendant with two prior drug convictions as the total criminal history and who is found responsible for distributing 100 grams of heroin, the base offense level would move from 26 to 34 and the criminal history category would move from III to VI. This more than triples the resulting sentence range, from between 78 and 97 months to between 262 and 327 months—just as a function of the career offender guideline provision.

Congress also authorized an avenue for escaping mandatory minimums, by directing the USSC to have the guidelines "reflect the general appropriateness of imposing a lower sentence than would otherwise be imposed, including a sentence that is lower than that established by statute as a minimum sentence, to take into account a defendant's substantial assistance in the investigation or prosecution of another person who has committed an offense."[40] The USSC fulfilled this directive by devising a prosecutor-initiated sentencing departure, "5K1.1 Substantial Assistance to Authorities," which has become a key tool used by prosecutors to induce both cooperation (informing on others) and guilty pleas in federal drug cases.

The other way out from under the harsh drug mandatory minimums is the "safety valve," which can be granted to defendants who have no real criminal history, among other requirements.[41] Specifically, to obtain safety valve relief, a defendant must satisfy a five-prong test:

1. The defendant had no more than one criminal history point (so generally no more than a petty misdemeanor).
2. The defendant did not use violence or possess a gun during the offense.
3. No serious bodily injury or death resulted from the offense.
4. The defendant was not a leader, manager, supervisor, or organizer in the offense.
5. The defendant must truthfully provide all information and evidence about the offense to the government.

Those who are awarded the safety valve are released from the mandatory minimum, and their guidelines' offense levels are decreased by two.

Congress authorized this escape valve in 1994, under pressure from advocacy groups such as Families Against Mandatory Minimums (FAMM) after it became evident how punitive and inflexible the drug laws had become under the new sentencing regime.[42] In practice, however, this provision is less straightforward than it appears on paper. In particular, the fifth prong can become a sticking point, as some U.S. attorneys expect defendants to inform on their coconspirators in order to earn the safety valve. Therefore, they may not sign off on that requirement without receiving detailed information that in some cases amounts to substantial assistance without the protections afforded when a defendant agrees to cooperate for a sentencing departure. Notwithstanding the safety valve concession, the bulk of sentencing reforms through the mid-2000s served to ensure lengthy sentences, especially in drug cases, and to close any loopholes that judges could use to impose sentences that were below the guidelines' ranges.

All of this political and legal action has since translated into a much larger, meaner, and more proactive drug law enforcement regime at the federal level. The dramatic uptick in the annual number of drug convictions began not long after President Reagan declared his renewed war on drugs in 1982 (see figure 2.2). Describing drugs as "an especially vicious virus of crime," he identified south Florida as the first "battlefield" in his drug war, where federal law enforcement resources had been beefed up, and drug arrests and prosecutions had increased by 40 percent.[43] Reagan promised to "duplicate the south Florida experience for the entire United States" and expressed optimism that he had devised a coordinated strategy to "win the war on drugs."[44]

Following that declaration, Reagan began to rebuild the executive branch infrastructure devoted to drug policy, and he pushed for and obtained significant fiscal investment in federal drug law enforcement. The administration's efforts were then fortified by the structural legal innovations that came with the new laws passed by Congress. Beginning in the 1980s, funding for federal drug law enforcement was significantly increased, and a vast network of federal-local law enforcement collaborations emerged, which translated into many more drug arrests that had the potential to be charged in federal court.[45]

The ranks of federal prosecutors also began to dramatically expand. In 1980, 1,636 assistant U.S. attorneys (AUSAs) were employed as prosecutors; by 1990 that number had nearly doubled, to 3,107.[46] By 2000, 4,938 AUSAs were employed nationally, and a decade later, that number had risen to 6,075.[47] Since it takes prosecutorial action to initiate a criminal case, this strong and steady growth in personnel propelled case growth;

Figure 2.2   Annual Number of Federally Convicted Drug Defendants, 1945 to 2013

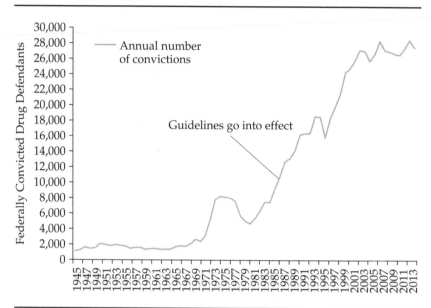

Source: Author's compilation based on University at Albany, Sourcebook of Criminal Justice Statistics; Bureau of Justice Statistics, Federal Justice Statistics, 2011 and 2012 statistical tables.

as a consequence, exponentially more defendants came to be criminally charged under federal statutes.[48]

The caseload growth was not simply a matter of more drug arrests landing on the desks of AUSAs, but was part of a proactive strategy at the federal level to get into the business of drug prosecutions. Indeed, the expanded federal jurisdiction that came in the 1970s did not in any way eliminate state and local power to prosecute intrastate drug crime. To the contrary, over the same period most states were toughening up their own drug laws and prosecuting larger numbers of people charged with drug crimes.[49] Thus, the new trend was heightened drug law enforcement and prosecution at both the state and federal levels.[50] For federal prosecutors that meant bucking the longstanding practice over the twentieth century of pursuing only those drug cases that seemed serious enough to be federally charged.[51]

This new ethos was made explicit in the 1984 revision of the *U.S. Attorneys' Manual.* An entire section in title 9 of the *Manual* discusses when drug cases should be left to state or local authorities.[52] In that section, prosecutors are discouraged from declining cases just because the amount of drugs is small. Rather, federal prosecution of drug cases is generally encouraged for reasons both ideological and strategic, where there is sufficient evidence to convict. The *Manual* advises that "it should be recognized that the federal government has grave responsibilities in the vital area of controlled substance law enforcement. Thus, care should be taken by federal prosecutors in deciding which is the most appropriate judicial forum in which to prosecute a controlled substance offense."[53]

Prosecutors were also reminded of the strategic benefits of bringing federal charges against drug defendants. Thus, they were encouraged to consider (among other things), "whether the offender would, if federally prosecuted, cooperate and furnish evidence of narcotic violations committed by his/her confederates or by others."[54] And they were given a mandate to use their federal powers in jurisdictions where the "professional competence" of local prosecutors was in question or where those convicted of drug offenses face "unduly light sentences."[55]

The aggressive adoption of cases was aided by the relative ease with which drug conspiracies could be proved in the federal system. Under the drug conspiracy statute, defendants do not have to actually complete illegal acts, so simple agreements to engage in or aid in drug deals could be prosecuted.[56] This, then, eliminated the need to have actual drugs as evidence. Since the drug conspiracy statute provides for sentences equal to the underlying offense for all involved in the conspiracy, seeking conspiracy convictions was often easier and more expeditious than pursuing actual trafficking. As the sentences grew more punitive for drug crimes, prosecutors began to prioritize conspiracies as a primary enforcement strategy. By the 1984 *U.S. Attorneys' Manual,* the chapter on narcotics offenses included a new section on how offices should set up "controlled substance units" in conjunction with the Drug Enforcement Administration (DEA), which would "primarily [initiate] narcotic conspiracy prosecutions."[57]

A short article in the *FBI Bulletin* written in 1994 by an active DEA agent, Gregory Lee, pointedly illustrates this new logic. Extolling the virtues of drug conspiracy laws to convince jurisdictions beyond the federal system to adopt the practice, Lee listed ten "advantages of drug conspiracy cases." The first three were cost efficiency benefits, in that conspiracy cases "eliminate the need to purchase drug evidence, serve as sources of asset forfeiture funds, [and] reduce undercover and surveillance expenses."[58]

Even more telling were the advantages Lee put forth for lowering the evidentiary bar while maximizing the legal culpability of all who could be charged in a given conspiracy. Agent Lee let his readers know that drug conspiracy cases "provide an exception to the hearsay rule of evidence; permit evidence against one defendant to be used against all defendants;

[and] enable prosecution and conviction without drug evidence."[59] As to maximizing the government's ability to aggressively prosecute everyone involved, Lee listed the advantage of "allow[ing] for indictment of conspirators for crimes committed by co-conspirators throughout the life of the conspiracy" and courts' ability to "apply the same penalties for conspiracy and the actual crime."[60]

The Office of the Attorney General in Washington, D.C., also became much more hands-on in directing prosecutors' plea negotiations, once the guidelines came online.[61] In 1989, Attorney General Richard Thornburgh issued a directive urging prosecutors to "charge the most serious, readily provable offense or offenses consistent with the defendant's conduct."[62] The memo strongly discouraged any concessions in plea bargaining that would detract from "honesty in sentencing . . . [whereby] the totality and seriousness of the defendant's conduct" is punished.[63] The acceptable items for negotiation were sentence recommendations within the prescribed guidelines range, "acceptance of responsibility" adjustments, and "the most important departure," substantial assistance.[64] Attorney General Janet Reno softened this language just slightly, to allow for more individualized assessment by prosecutors. That ended, though, under Attorney General John Ashcroft, who explicitly directed prosecutors to seek convictions on the most serious charges. Moreover, he "strongly encouraged" using 851s and other statutory enhancements, including as an "incentive" by threatening to file them if the defendant does not plead guilty.[65]

The bottom line was that, beginning in the 1980s, the federal criminal justice system got seriously into the business of prosecuting drug crimes and punishing drug defendants. This was facilitated by the expanded capacity made possible by increased resource allocation to law enforcement personnel and was further fueled by the punitive sentencing reforms. So not only were vastly more drug defendants being charged in federal court, but once convicted, their average prison sentences were much longer under the new regime. The average federal drug felony sentence in 1980 was just under four years; by 1991 it had more than doubled, to eight years. Since then, federal drug sentences have been six to seven years, on average.[66]

Moreover, under the new regime, nearly all of those who have been federally convicted for drug crimes have been sent to prison, as Congress had hoped. In 2014, 95 percent of all sentenced drug defendants, including those convicted of simple possession, received prison terms, up from 72 percent in 1984, at the cusp of the sentencing changes. Consequently, the exploding imprisonment rates at the federal level are disproportionately accounted for by drug defendants, who now constitute about half of all federal prisoners (see figure I.1 in the introduction). This characteristic of the federal system sets it apart from state courts, where both the likelihood of going to prison and the length of sentences imposed for drug offenses are consistently much lower.[67] Most critical to the realization of the new drug war was the redistribution of discretionary legal power within the system. The changes to the formal law created the capacity for a punitive explosion, but the shift in the balance of power from judges to prosecutors that came with the sentencing reforms ensured its actualization. Under the new rules of the game, prosecutors became, in essence, "first-look sentencers" who could largely dictate punishment outcomes by their charging decisions and plea offers.[68] Because the guidelines were mandatory, judges had to sentence within the calculated guideline range, with very limited exceptions.[69] The mandatory minimum and enhancement statutes were (and continue to be) afforded even less judicial discretion. Judges can sentence below them only at the prosecution's request, usually for cases in which the defendant provided "substantial assistance" to the government by serving as an informant. In addition, mandatory minimums became particularly potent in drug cases: there are over 170 mandatory minimum statutes on the federal books, but the most frequent to be actually applied involve drug offenses. In fiscal year 2010, 77 percent of the federal mandatory minimums imposed were for drug convictions.[70]

The shift in power, and the resulting drug law enforcement bonanza, was drastic—yet its effects were not uniform across U.S. districts. There was considerable jurisdictional variation in prosecuting drug crimes and in the degree of punitiveness meted out to drug defendants. At the low end of the spectrum, in several western U.S. district courts, the drug caseload has remained a small share of the overall criminal caseload, with drug defendants constituting only about 20 percent of sentenced defendants over the period from 1992 to 2012.[71] At the high end of the spectrum, in several West Virginia and Illinois districts, those rates over the same period were three times that, about 60 percent.

Average sentence lengths for drug trafficking have also varied considerably by district and region over the same twenty-year period. At the low end, average drug trafficking sentences in several southwestern border districts have been less than three years; at the high end is the U.S. District Court for the Northern District of Florida, where the average was more than twelve years. And the meting out of life-without-parole sentences for drug trafficking—the most draconian punishment in the federal drug war—has also varied by locale. Some districts simply do not impose life sentences as a general practice. At the high end, in the same twenty-year period, 6.5 percent of all convicted drug traffickers in the Northern District of Florida have been sentenced to life.[72]

Such variation in case composition and outcomes also characterizes the three districts I studied. In the following chapters I show why and how

Figure 2.3   Drug Trafficking Caseload as Percentage of Total Criminal Cases Sentenced in Three Case Study Districts, 1992 to 2014

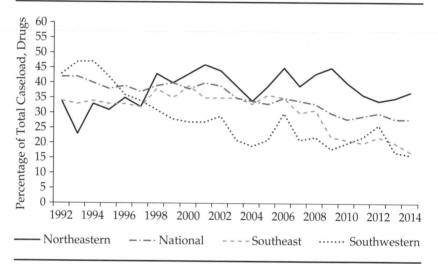

——— Northeastern   —·— National   - - - - Southeast   ······· Southwestern

Source: Author's consolidated dataset of U.S. Sentencing Commission sentencing data.

districts can differ so much from each other despite the overarching goal of uniformity that was the original aim of sentencing reform. Formal laws can live very divergent lives depending upon local norms, legal actors' motivations, and the on-the-ground power dynamics in which drug cases are charged, negotiated, and sentenced. Before I dive in, though, let me provide some general context and background about each district (the three districts are described in detail in appendix B).

I begin in Northeastern District, where, since the late 1990s, a higher percentage of criminal defendants have been convicted of drug charges than the national average (see figure 2.3). Prosecutors in Northeastern District have been very proactive in bringing what look like small, state cases to federal court. As I detail in the next chapter, AUSAs there often partner with local law enforcement to target certain kinds of suspected drug dealers by using several potent legal tools at their disposal. The gap between drug sentences meted out in state court and federal court is stark in this district, so the consequences are severe for those targeted for federal prosecution. In some sense, then, prosecutors in this district seem to have taken to heart the advice to use the federal law as a corrective on the perceived "unduly light sentences" imposed in the state court.[73]

The decision in *United States v. Booker* has considerably liberated sentencing in Northeastern District, as has been the case in most of the districts in the northeast region of the United States. Only 32 percent of drug sentences imposed here have been within the guidelines advisory

Figure 2.4   **Mean Length of Drug Sentences in Three Case Study Districts, 1992 to 2014**

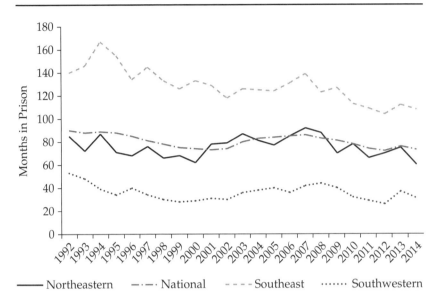

—— Northeastern   —·— National   - - - - Southeast   ······· Southwestern

Source: Author's consolidated dataset of U.S. Sentencing Commission sentencing data.
Note: These means were calculated using a dataset assembled from "Defendants Sentenced Under the Sentencing Reform Act" data, and include only defendants who received prison sentences. Drug trafficking cases were identified using the Sentencing Guidelines offense, according to the U.S. Sentencing Commission method of coding.

range since 2007. Sentences for drug trafficking were, on average, about two years below the bottom of the guidelines range in 2012. This is not simply the product of judges' newfound discretionary power. The rates of government-sponsored departures for reasons other than substantial assistance have also increased significantly.[74] Put simply, there appears to be a collective post-*Booker* commitment to mitigating the harsh drug sentences, which seems paradoxical given the investment in bringing small cases here in the first place. Moreover, mean sentence lengths for drug trafficking in this district come closest to the annual national average of the three districts in this study (see figure 2.4). So although, on the books, Northeastern District looks as though it deviates considerably from the dictates of the guidelines, its actual outcomes conform to national sentencing norms.

Southeast District, the subject of chapter 4, has some things in common with Northeastern District—but a norm of below-guidelines sentences is not one of them. Averaging 98 percent of the guidelines minimum from 1992 to 2012, Southeast District hewed the closest to the guidelines of my three cases.[75] Consequently, Southeast District's drug trafficking sentences have, on average, been well above national means, amounting to years more meted out in this district for drug convictions (see figure 2.4).

Indeed, it was not until 2010 that the average drug trafficking sentence here dropped much below ten years. This is due in part to the high rate of drug mandatory minimum cases, especially crack cases, that are prosecuted here. From 1993 to 2012, more than 75 percent of sentenced trafficking defendants in this district were subject to mandatory minimums, above the national rate of 64 percent.[76] And about half as many defendants who face a drug mandatory minimum in this district, compared to the national average, have been granted the safety valve escape from the mandatory minimum: 35 percent of those facing a drug trafficking mandatory across the nation were granted safety valve relief, whereas only 18 percent in Southeast District received that relief.

Yet it is not as if the drug defendants prosecuted in federal court in Southeast District are all kingpins who deal large amounts of drugs. As in Northeastern District, a substantial portion of the drug caseload in Southeast is made up of cases that look like run-of-the-mill state court cases involving street dealers. Many cases, in fact, started in state court and ended up going federal as a way to compel cooperation, among other motivations.

Southwestern District, the subject of chapter 5, looks like neither of the other two districts. It is among the highest-volume district courts in the country, and that status extends to its drug caseload. In 2011, 82 percent of those sentenced here for non-petty criminal convictions had been convicted of either immigration or drug offenses.[77] There has been astounding growth in the volume of both immigration and drug convictions in this district, especially since 2008 (see figure 2.5). This is largely the product of much more aggressive enforcement by the Border Patrol and the stepped-up use of criminal charges against people snared by those enforcement efforts.

Unlike in Northeastern and Southeast Districts, federal prosecutors in Southwestern District engage in little to no proactive targeting of "state" drug cases. AUSAs do not need to go looking for more cases to prosecute, given that their drug caseloads are also among the highest in the nation. In 2014, Southwestern District sentenced about ten times as many defendants on drug charges as were sentenced in Southeast District that year, and eighteen times as many as Northeastern District. The trafficking cases here often involve relatively large quantities of drugs that have been transported across the border by couriers who typically have little or no criminal history and who are on the bottom rung of the larger drug operation. As a consequence, many of the drug trafficking defendants here are eligible for and receive safety valve relief.

There is also a "fast track" program available to drug defendants in the largest court in this district, in which prosecutors agree to a four-level

Figure 2.5   Drug and Immigration Convictions in Southwestern District, 1992 to 2014

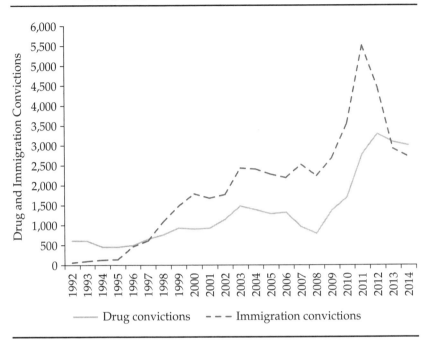

Source: Author's consolidated dataset of U.S. Sentencing Commission sentencing data.

reduction in the guideline offense level for defendants who plead guilty very early in the criminal process and who waive a number of basic procedural rights. This program is an import from the immigration world and speaks to both the high volume of cases here and the blurred boundaries between drug and immigration cases at the border.[78] The institutionalized incentives have resulted in an exceptionally high rate of guilty pleas. The distance between what is being offered and the potential sentencing exposure for those who go to trial is so large that few defendants take the risk of turning down the offer. Although Southwestern District looks by quantifiable measures to be among the most lenient U.S. district court districts in the nation, there are deep costs and consequences for defendants in this district that raise troublesome implications of their own.

═ Chapter 3 ═

Paternalism and Power:
The Deployment of Drug Law
in the Liberal Northeast

In April 2014, Aaron Crenshaw appeared in Courtroom 6 of the main division of Northeastern District, where he would formally change his plea from not guilty to guilty on two counts of distributing heroin and cocaine. Unlike the majority of drug defendants in federal court, who appear in orange or maroon jumpsuits with institutional names plastered on their backs, Aaron was dressed in street clothes: black slacks, dark shirt. This meant he was out of custody pending resolution of his case, at least until today.

The gallery of the stately courtroom, featuring three rows of beautiful tiger oak benches, held more than the usual number of spectators. Among them was Aaron's mother, who wept both before and during the proceeding, at times so loudly that the others in the room could not help but notice. She was periodically comforted by other members of the family, who were all there to support Aaron. Aaron himself was visibly distressed as well. As he waited for the judge to emerge from chambers and take the bench, his foot shook nervously, he tapped on the table, and he too cried, more noticeably when he heard his mother's wails. Neither Aaron nor his family knew exactly what his fate would be once he formally pleaded guilty and returned for sentencing, but they had been forewarned by his lawyer that it would be prison, and potentially for many years. It was an uncomfortable proceeding to witness, the penultimate hearing in a long legal process.

Two and a half years earlier, when he was twenty-three, Aaron and his then girlfriend had sold 1.3 grams of crack cocaine and 0.25 grams of heroin to an undercover agent, a $200 deal. Aaron and his girlfriend were arrested and charged in the local municipal court, which processes misdemeanor and low-level felony cases in the state. Six months into that case, the U.S. attorney's office in Northeastern District decided to indict

Aaron in federal court, which meant he faced an exponentially longer sentence than he would if his case had remained where it started. His girlfriend stayed in state court, where the charges were eventually dismissed in exchange for her staying out of trouble for a year.

Aaron's case seems an unlikely candidate for federal prosecution. His girlfriend had been the original target of the undercover sting; she had set up several drug deals with the undercover agent and Aaron just helped deliver the drugs. He certainly seemed to be the less culpable of the pair. The total amount of drugs he had sold was minuscule, no guns were involved, and he was not being charged for any larger-scale or more serious offenses.

Aaron's case also seemed at odds with the changing political winds on harsh drug sentencing. Aaron was pleading guilty just weeks before the Obama administration unveiled its major clemency initiative, which explicitly aimed to address the past overuse of long federal prison sentences for low-level, nonviolent drug defendants. It was also happening months after Attorney General Holder had issued a memorandum directing U.S. attorneys not to pursue long sentences for low-level drug defendants. And it was happening in one of the nation's most liberal federal districts, where one might expect cases like Aaron's to disappear from the dockets in light of the shifting political environment.

Yet although his case seems at first glance to be anomalous, it perfectly represents one of the most common types of federal drug cases prosecuted in Northeastern District: a small-time street dealer, almost always a young African American man, who has been set up by a confidential informant or an undercover law enforcement agent to make a hand-to-hand sale of small amounts of drugs, usually crack. The particular young men so targeted for federal prosecution are often those who have the requisite criminal history to qualify them for the career offender guideline or other very severe sentence enhancements.

Aaron fit that profile. Aaron's two qualifying prior convictions for the career offender guideline happened in the state's lower criminal court when he was just eighteen. The first was for felony possession with the intent to distribute crack cocaine, which qualified as a prior controlled substance offense. The second was for resisting arrest, stemming from his protest of a friend's arrest at a shopping mall. No one was hurt in the incident, but it still counted as a crime-of-violence prior. Aaron had served a total of six months in the local jail for these priors, which constituted the only sentence of incarceration that he had ever served until this point.

This history transformed the guidelines calculus for Aaron, dramatically increasing his sentencing exposure and giving the prosecutor enormous power in negotiating a plea and sentence. Qualifying to be sentenced under the career offender guideline meant that Aaron's advisory sentencing range catapulted from 2 to 8 months to 151 to 188 months, after getting a reduction for acceptance of responsibility.[1] Had either of Aaron's prior sentences been for property offenses, his guideline would not have budged from 2 to 8 months, and he likely would not have been brought up to federal court in the first place.

As noted in chapter 2, under the career offender guideline, a total of two prior convictions for a "violent offense" or a "controlled substance offense" that have a potential maximum sentence of more than a year qualify certain defendants for dramatically longer sentences upon conviction.[2] Drug defendants like Aaron have borne the brunt of the career offender guideline. In the year Aaron was sentenced, three-quarters of those who qualified for career offender sentences had been convicted of drug offenses.[3]

The frequency and persistence of the low-level cases like Aaron's becomes even more understandable when they are placed in the local historical context of prosecutions in this district. In Northeastern District, the aggressive prosecution of drug cases is partially rooted in a local-federal task force initiative that aimed to reduce the number of youth homicides. In 1996, the federal government sponsored a multi-jurisdictional program to reduce youth violence in the urban hub of the district. The program encouraged prosecutors to use federal gun laws, and the corresponding long sentences, against those identified by local police and other stakeholders as incorrigible, gun-toting gang members.

That program was subsequently hailed as a model for violence reduction, in part through its use of the formidable federal criminal law hammer as both threat and promise. Federal prosecutors in Northeastern District expanded their focus beyond interstate gun crimes to pursue intrastate gun trafficking and possession when the suspect was identified as a major problem for the community. The geographic areas they targeted for intervention were all minority neighborhoods within the larger city. Those who found themselves in federal prosecutors' sights, therefore, were young men of color, like Aaron, who lived in those neighborhoods.

This model spun out to include drugs, despite the original program designers' commitment to decouple gun violence from drug crime. The expansion to drug crimes happened in two notable ways. The first was through the practice of incorporating intrastate cases into the federal caseload, which extended from guns to drugs, where targeted suspects were often set up by undercover agents in low-level transactions. In essence, the lines between guns and drugs as serious criminal matters became blurred, as did the lines between state and federal cases. The second way this program expanded to include drug crimes was through the reliance on local law enforcement, and the partnerships between local and federal agents, as a way to identify the "bad actors" for eventual federal prosecution.

From there, the prosecutorial norm of federal adoption of state drug cases became routinized, well after the original program had come and gone and the rates of youth homicide had plummeted. Relationships had become cemented between federal prosecutors and local law enforcement assigned to the neighborhoods where the original program was concentrated, and from which cases like Aaron's continued to be plucked. Moreover, defendants like Aaron are categorized within a triad of risk—guns, gangs, and drugs—that, in the view of law enforcement and prosecutors, sometimes needs the heavy hammer of federal criminal law to manage and contain.

Consequently, the long-established, localized prosecutorial norms in Northeastern District helped gloss over the seeming incongruity of the persistence of federal low-level drug prosecutions in one of the least likely places to defy the new kinder, gentler prosecutorial ethos. Indeed, the historical continuity from the original homicide intervention to targeting low-level street dealers two decades later is evident in both the population and neighborhood demographics of the small-time dealers who continue to be prosecuted in federal court. And it is evident in the structural makeup of the local U.S. attorney's criminal division. These cases are primarily prosecuted out of a specialized guns, violence, and drugs unit that continues to partner, both formally and informally, with local law enforcement and county prosecutors. As a result of this structural arrangement, guns, gangs, and drugs are linked together as a federal interest when they are thought to be present, in particular within several targeted neighborhoods that constitute just a small portion of the jurisdiction.

Perhaps the best way to understand why Aaron and so many others like him make up a substantial share of Northeastern District's drug caseload is by examining both the structure of the region's state law and the particular logic of these prosecutions in this district. First, the law: Northeastern District, it turns out, has one of the highest rates of career offender sentences in the nation. This is not because the defendants charged here are more hardened than in other places; it is because the mechanics of the federal career offender guideline are such that even some misdemeanor convictions imposed in state court here can count as predicate offenses. The state law has the unusual feature of authorizing maximum sentences of more than one year for certain misdemeanor convictions, so if they qualify as violent or are related to drug trafficking they can be used as "career offender" priors. As a result, some state misdemeanor convictions, such as for the misdemeanor crime of resisting arrest, have regularly qualified federal defendants for sentencing under the career offender guideline in Northeastern District.

This legal anomaly is what helped elevate Aaron's sentencing exposure, and it's what made his case a target for adoption by federal prosecutors.[4] Although his resisting arrest prior was a misdemeanor conviction, it counted as a qualifying prior since a judge could have conceivably sentenced him to more than a year in jail for it. In this district, Aaron's case is more typical than atypical.

The gap between what we might imagine as a career offender and the reality of Aaron Crenshaw was evident in so many ways. It also typifies how the career offender guideline functions in Northeastern District. In this instance, Aaron had been allowed to stay out of custody for nearly two years pending resolution, which is not an option for the majority of drug offenders, especially those with serious records. During this time, he lived with his parents, held down two jobs in which he excelled, learned new skills in auto repair, and entered into a stable romantic relationship. His own fear and apprehension exhibited at the plea proceeding, as he came to terms with the possibility of going to prison for the first time in his life, also does not comport with the image of a hardened career offender. And, of course, his record itself reveals the gap between the government's goal to severely punish the most serious repeat offenders and what happens in practice. In trying to account for the many different ways that states define criminal acts, the USSC had constructed a formula that was over-inclusive, especially in certain jurisdictions, of which Northeastern District was one.

To be sure, there are qualifying defendants with significant records in this district, but there have been hundreds of Aarons prosecuted here as well. And their numbers have grown over the years, despite an ostensible softening of the drug war. In the early and mid-1990s, before the initial anti-violence initiative was implemented, just a small handful of drug defendants here were sentenced under the career offender guideline, generally constituting less than 7 percent of the annual drug trafficking defendant population. The numbers and share of drug defendants sentenced as career offenders multiplied after that, peaking in 2010 when more than a quarter of all drug traffickers were sentenced in Northeastern District under the career offender guideline.[5] In Northeastern District, most defendants sentenced as career offenders were convicted of drug crimes rather than crimes of violence. Over the two-decade period from 1992 to 2012, nearly three-quarters of the defendants subject to the career offender guideline in Northeastern District were sentenced for drug trafficking.

And, like Aaron, these criminal suspects do not generally just land on the desk of federal prosecutors, who then may feel some obligation to file charges if the evidence is sufficient. Rather, they are sought out specifically because they are so vulnerable to long prison sentences.[6] As a result, once defendants like Aaron are brought to federal court, prosecutors are in the driver's seat, steering plea negotiations and sentencing. As Aaron's lawyer explained to me, "There's not a lot of wiggle room in terms of litigating" these cases because they are usually airtight transactions, often with video and audio recordings of the sales to seal the defendant's fate.[7]

But just because prosecutors can federally charge low-level defendants like Aaron does not fully explain why they actually do it. In Northeastern District, the logic underlying this initiative reflects a paternalistic ethos where federal intervention is deemed a necessity for the defendants' and their communities' own good. That is, the career offender hammer functions as just another tool in the prosecutor's legal toolkit to save "at-risk" defendants from themselves while protecting their communities. Under this logic, the targeted defendant is rhetorically constructed as a hybrid being—a troublemaker who is the cause of ruin in the neighborhoods targeted for enforcement but someone also vulnerable because of his lifetime exposure to the impoverished, degraded conditions in those same places. And the deployment of federal criminal law is viewed as a solution to both problems.

In this district there are several prosecutors assigned to the specialized task force who bring the majority of these cases. Each has close, well-established relationships with officers on the local beat, and each relies on those local law enforcement sources to help supply defendants to prosecute. These sources assure the prosecutors that the targeted defendants are the "bad guys" or "troublemakers" whose removal from the community will alleviate problems in the neighborhood.[8] The prosecutors then bring that logic to court when justifying the decision to file charges and the content of those charges, making their plea offers, and crafting their recommended sentences.

One of the primary assistant U.S. attorneys (AUSAs) in this unit, Thomas Hendley, is a career prosecutor whom defense attorneys characterized as a "true believer" in his quest to save the poor black community in the urban center of this district from itself.[9] Hendley himself described his approach as an "Al Capone" strategy, in which he uses drug prosecutions to combat gangs and violence. Thus, he explained, he targets those identified by local police as active in other kinds of crime with two goals in mind: to "send a message to gang compatriots" that they too may be charged federally if they don't cease illegal behavior, and to interrupt the pattern of gang-related crime by giving those prosecuted a "time-out." For Mr. Hendley, these tactics are for the benefit of the young men and occasional women who get prosecuted, convicted, and sent to prison, while also benefitting the larger community.

Notably, the more serious criminal activity alleged by police is merely suspected but not easily proved; otherwise, those charges would themselves likely be filed. So the drug prosecutions skirt the formal requirements of conviction by using proxy charges that are themselves the product of proactive (often undercover) law enforcement tactics. Because it is relatively easy to obtain federal drug convictions that trigger significant punishment, law enforcement and prosecutors can together determine who they think needs to be locked up, for any number of reasons, then deploy the federal drug laws as the means to make that happen.[10]

The tools used by Mr. Hendley and his colleagues are not limited to the career offender guideline. So although career offender eligibility enhances the likelihood of federal prosecution, it is not a prerequisite for Mr. Hendley or others in his unit to pursue a case. One favored strategy, deployed even against those with minimal records, is to set up those they have identified as "trouble" in very small drug sales, usually of less than a gram of crack, to occur within 1,000 feet of a protected zone such as a school, playground, or public housing facility. These drug sales in a protected zone trigger a one-year mandatory minimum for those with no drug priors, and longer mandatories for those with prior convictions. They also mandate a doubling of the supervised release period following incarceration, which typically means six years of community control.[11]

Mr. Hendley's sentencing memoranda reflect the underlying ethos of these small-time street-dealing drug prosecutions. His memoranda are well-known in this district for their length and narrative structure. They often open with a very detailed retelling of the defendant's crime of conviction, framed to highlight his culpability and his general disregard for the law. This is followed by a detailed recitation of the defendant's prior criminal justice contact, not limited just to prior convictions. It may include every police call made where the defendant's name appeared, even if there was no actual contact (much less arrest), and even in cases where the defendant was a victim. This section typically offers a narrative of a person for whom soft intervention has not been effective given his continued failures, such as repeatedly being where there is "trouble." All of this is then underscored by his current legal predicament. These two sections, although lengthier and more floridly detailed than most, do not necessarily diverge from the predominant prosecutorial sentencing narrative. But they are just the prelude for the real story Mr. Hendley tells about the defendant and his interventional needs.

With the criminal defendant's past and present story spelled out for the reader—mainly the assigned judge and the defense attorney—the narrative often takes one of two tacks. The first, for the more serious and less vulnerable defendants who typically sell drugs for commerce and are not themselves users, begins with a discussion of how drugs wreak havoc upon poor minority neighborhoods. This narrative is both local and global. Mr. Hendley provides numerous citations and summaries of criminological research, published legal and policy documents, and other kinds of expert accounts of how harmful drugs, particularly crack, are for communities. He connects these sources to the particulars of the defendant's case to highlight their relevance to the sentencing at hand. The citations and summaries of the empirical and expert record are often repeated verbatim from memo to memo, and they set the stage for local-izing the problem posed by the defendant.

That global argument is then bolstered by citations that hit closer to home. The memos sometimes excerpt the same quote from a local black minister, made after a particularly violent period in the city, that includes this snippet: *"The Black Church must take the hard line that, if you do the crime, kid, you should go to jail. The Black Churches have to challenge the judges to stop coddling criminals and then putting them back on the streets to wreak havoc in the Black Community"* (emphasis in original).[12] The memorandum also sometimes attaches an actual CD recording of this minister's full speech as an exhibit. Of course, using this minister's words to make such a racial-ized exhortation has the effect of distancing Mr. Hendley, a white man, from accusations of racial paternalism or subordination. The minister's words also provide the bridge back to the individual defendant who has, in the view of law enforcement, been part of that havoc wreaking in the very communities the minister serves. This moves the memo to the spe-cific set of recommendations the prosecution advocates: to "interrupt" problem behavior, provide a "time-out" in the form of a prison sentence, and reset the life course of the defendant.

In more sympathetic cases, the narrative skips over the gloom and doom caused by drugs and goes right to the particular recommendations for sentence and release. In both typologies, Mr. Hendley relies on selected published research, especially related to the causes of recidivism and methods for reducing it, to support each of his recommended interven-tions. In this more sympathetic version, he often narrates the defendant's life as one that is broken, littered with a string of interventional failures. Hendley's recommendations are then framed as a last resort of sorts.

Hendley is especially well known for including a laundry list of spe-cial conditions for supervised release, justified with citations from the criminological literature on the positive effect of the recommended inter-ventions and supported with a range of documentation. Along with seek-ing a particular prison term that will serve as the "time-out," he and his colleagues typically request that the judge impose both geographic and associational restrictions on the targeted defendants upon their release from prison. The proposed geographic restrictions are mapped for the judge, and may declare as off-limits places where family, potential work and living opportunities, and support resources are located. The geo-graphic restrictions are generally accompanied by proposed associational restrictions, which contain a list of people with whom the defendant may not associate while under supervision. These lists contain anywhere from just a handful of names to dozens.

Both sets of restrictions are represented as working on both sides of the interventional formula: benefitting the defendant and protecting the community. The geographic restrictions head off "trouble" by removing the defendant as troublemaker from places that are under siege from him and his ilk (or, as one fairly typical sentencing memo puts it, "the defendant grew up in a troubled area, choosing to add to the misery that crack cocaine and other drugs wreak on these neighborhoods and their residents"). They also purport to protect the defendant himself from the contamination of those places, thereby enhancing his chances of reform. The associational restrictions similarly do double duty. Henley seemingly proposes them as a way reduce the risk of bad human alchemy and its negative impact on the neighborhoods in question, by keeping separate those people who, when together, make trouble. He promotes them on the logic that the restrictions will encourage the defendant to develop positive new relationships as part of his life turnaround.

Ronald Cherry, a small-time drug defendant prosecuted by Hendley, was one of the more sympathetic cases. Mr. Cherry, a twenty-five-year-old African American, pleaded guilty in 2014 to selling 0.8 grams of crack cocaine. The local police had arranged for an undercover officer to purchase the drugs from him in a protected zone, in this case within the vicinity of a school, park, *and* public housing. Mr. Cherry appeared to be eligible for the career offender enhancement, so Hendley would have considerable leverage in plea negotiations and at sentencing. But Mr. Cherry's lawyer was able to vacate a prior drug conviction due to lab improprieties, thereby avoiding the career offender guideline.

Despite the fact that Mr. Cherry was no longer subject to the enhancement, Mr. Hendley did not want his sentence to fall within the regular Sentencing Guidelines range of fifteen to twenty-one months. So he threatened to seek a significant upward departure (an increased sentence that departs from the Sentencing Guidelines) on the theory that the prior crime actually happened even if it was legally vacated.[13] After a "protracted negotiation," the two sides hammered out a binding plea agreement of thirty-six months in prison and four years of supervised release. If the judge accepted the agreement terms, this would be Mr. Cherry's sentence.

Mr. Cherry was an especially sympathetic defendant. His attorney documented in his sentencing memorandum that Cherry had experienced severe and sustained deprivation growing up, continued to have a chaotic, unstable life, and was very vulnerable to others' influence. In the sentencing memorandum setting out the prosecution's position on the appropriate sentence, Mr. Hendley acknowledged Mr. Cherry's mitigating circumstances and then framed the punishment he sought as remediating the effects of that painful childhood: "These are among the most difficult issues to deal with at Sentencing. On the one hand, the conditions under which the defendant grew up make him less culpable for the crimes he has committed as a teenager and a young adult. On the other hand, those very same conditions also increase the risk of recidivism."

After detailing Mr. Cherry's past and present criminal justice involvement, Mr. Hendley began his "Proposed Judicial Recommendations" section with an imperative for legal intervention to save the defendant: "Any plan designed to give the defendant the maximum chance at fundamental life change must of course begin with the terms and conditions of his incarceration." He recommended that the judge order both drug treatment and vocational training for Mr. Cherry during his incarceration. He reserved most of his recommendations for the four-year supervised release period though.

This section of the memo began by asking that the defendant be placed in a halfway house for the first six months, unless his sister was willing to take him in. If the government's recommendations were granted, Mr. Cherry would be barred from drinking alcohol (and of course taking any drugs), would be subject to regular drug testing, and would be required to attend drug counseling and mental health counseling. Mr. Hendley also wanted to require Moral Reconation Therapy (MRT)—a program purchased and used by federal probation in Northeastern District, among many others—for Mr. Cherry. This is a proprietary cognitive-behavioral therapy based on the premise that the solution to criminality is to deal with the purported underdeveloped or failed moral reasoning of the individual defendant.[14]

Then came the slew of geographic and associational restrictions. Mr. Hendley asked for a 7 p.m. curfew for the first nine months of release, and wanted to bar Mr. Cherry from entering the very large neighborhood where he had been arrested for the entire four years of supervised release.[15] Finally, Mr. Hendley appended a list of twenty-seven names of men and women with whom Mr. Cherry could not associate for the four-year supervised release period, if the judge agreed. He argued that all on the list "have figured in his prior arrests or other interactions with the police." The judge accepted every one of Mr. Hendley's recommended special conditions.

The paternalistic ethos whereby the use of punitive law is justified by its supposed ability to save defendants from themselves and to rescue the black community from its troublesome members extends even to those much older than the typical young men busted by the task force stings. I observed the sentencing of a black man in his early fifties, Alvin Carson, who had a long history of criminal justice involvement, mostly related to his own drug addiction. He seemed to be another unlikely target for federal prosecution. Mr. Carson was sitting on a bench in a protected zone—a playground outside a public housing development—when two men approached him and asked him for help obtaining "three-twenties," meaning three bags of crack each containing 0.2 grams of the drug. Mr. Carson retrieved the drugs from his partner, Elizabeth Elders, a small-time dealer, and asked for a modest commission—a rock of crack—for connecting them. Of course the two men were working for police, and Mr. Carson and Ms. Elders were subsequently arrested and charged in federal court.

The court allowed Ms. Elders to enter a drug rehabilitation program on pretrial supervision while her case proceeded; she ultimately received credit for time served (mainly in the drug rehabilitation program) and was sentenced to three years of supervised release, which included a geographic restriction. Mr. Carson was held in custody at the local jail during the ten-month period that his case was adjudicated. Carson's negotiated sentence was a year and a day, with a six-year period of supervised release.[16] The issues up for debate at sentencing were the supervision conditions.

In his sentencing memorandum, Assistant U.S. Attorney Hendley narrated a version of Mr. Carson's life that characterized his prosecutorial intervention as a life-saving endeavor. He argued for his usual panoply of "special conditions," including geographic restrictions that banned Mr. Carson from three to four square miles of the city, as well as from all city-owned housing developments. He also produced a list of eighteen people, including Ms. Elders, with whom Mr. Carson could not associate for the six-year period, and asked for a curfew to be imposed for the first period of release. Then he called for a series of therapeutic interventions, including anger management counseling, drug treatment, vocational training, and the MRT program.

In justifying his position, Mr. Hendley described his use of legal power as a hybrid weapon-prod in the state's coercive yet therapeutic mission. Specifically, in Mr. Carson's case, the prosecutor asserted that the specter of a very long career offender sentence in the future had a place in the reformation process:

> With the right type of supervision and services, the defendant can move the rest of his life in a different direction and become a productive member of our community. But there is another reason why the government thinks that a year-and-a day is the right sentence in this case. As a result of this conviction and his 2009 conviction for [assault and battery], [the defendant] will now be a career offender. Should he return to drug dealing, or commit any crime of violence that can be prosecuted here [in federal court], he will be looking at a Guideline sentence of 12–15 years. It is hoped that, at this point in his life, the reality of such a sentence, along with the assistance of our Probation Department, can help ensure that this court appearance will be his last.[17]

At Mr. Carson's sentencing hearing, this dual-edged theme continued. The defense strenuously objected to the scope of the associational restrictions, especially the bar on Mr. Carson's future contact with Ms. Elders. When the judge expressed reservations about imposing the geographic and associational restrictions, Mr. Hendley argued that it not only was good for public safety but also would help Mr. Carson refrain from recidivating. He then went on to discuss the defendant couple as a joint project of his. Even though Ms. Elders was not being sentenced that day, and was not even in court, Mr. Hendley told the judge, "I prosecuted her not to put her in jail, but to save her life." And restricting Mr. Carson from seeing her was out of that concern. He said he "didn't do it lightly," but thought it necessary to help them withstand the "rough road ahead of them." He concluded by assuring the judge that all his recommendations were for the long-term benefit of both defendants, citing criminological research to bolster his arguments. In the end, the judge granted Hendley everything he asked for.

There is plenty of evidence from the public health field that addicts such as Mr. Carson would be better off if routed out of the criminal justice system rather than steered into it.[18] The kind of drug sales that he and others like him engage in are primarily to ensure access to what they need for their own habit. Yet once their acts are charged as crimes, especially in federal court, the interventional tools center on the coercive and punitive powers inherent in the criminal statutes and sentencing guidelines. Consequently, the lens for understanding causes of, and solutions to, the criminal behavior is necessarily constrained by the very place in which they are being processed: federal criminal court.[19]

In Northeastern District, there is considerable engagement with other expert fields, especially psychotherapeutic ones, as exemplified in how these small drug cases are adjudicated. But even those therapeutic interventions are delivered through criminal law and with the force of that law behind them. Defendants are not encouraged to take advantage of such resources like drug treatment or MRT; they are ordered to do so. Failures to comply result in time back in prison and other punishments. Moreover, purely punitive sanctions—like prison terms, geographic banishments, and bars on associating with friends and loved ones—get offered up as therapeutic even though they pack the same punch to the lived experience of defendants as if they were imposed under a purely retributive logic.

This conundrum is no more evident than for defendants such as Ronald Cherry and Alvin Carson, once on supervised release in Northeastern District. They not only need to keep their noses clean; they generally have multiple obligations, all meant to deal with their purported psychological and moral shortcomings, that complicate the landscape. Minefields abound—ending up in the wrong part of town, talking to the wrong people, missing a meeting or therapy session, failing to juggle all the supervised release obligations while also trying to work and establish life stability. And because there is an explicit strategy among those in the taskforce unit to obtain extra-long periods of postincarceration supervision, the risk of failures is heightened even more.

That is the story of Ray Wilkins, who was originally arrested by local police for his part in a single hand-to-hand sale of crack in 2007, when he was twenty-two years old. Mr. Wilkins had driven his friend to deliver a half gram of crack (unknowingly) to an undercover officer. Mr. Wilkins remained in the car while his friend completed the sale, which had been arranged by the buyer-agent to occur within 1,000 feet of a school. Mr. Wilkins was not the original target of this sting—his friend was—but both eventually ended up charged in federal court. After about a year in jail custody while proceeding in state court, Mr. Wilkins and his friend were indicted in federal court. Mr. Wilkins's case was likely adopted because of his prior conviction for a nonfatal shooting when he was seventeen years old, marking him as a risk in need of federal prosecution.

In the crack sale case, Mr. Wilkins negotiated an eighteen-month sentence with Assistant U.S. Attorney Hendley, who also insisted upon a six-year period of supervised release as part of the plea agreement. Although Mr. Wilkins was able to shave one year off the supervision period by successfully completing an intensive court-based reentry program that included MRT, he remained stuck after that.

After two years on supervision with no violations and with some strong markers of success, Mr. Wilkins petitioned for termination of supervised release. By this point he had obtained a full-time job, was volunteering with an inner-city youth group, and had successfully completed some community college courses. His request was opposed by probation as well as by Mr. Hendley, who nonetheless "applaud[ed] the defendant's efforts to date."[20] The judge denied Wilkins's petition and told him, "Keep up the good work and reapply in a year."[21] A year later he reapplied, citing a continued record of success and absence of violations. The judge denied it once again but suggested to the probation department that Mr. Wilkins "should be considered for low-intensity caseload," which would lighten the supervision obligations he was under.[22]

A year after that, he was once again back in court—only this time on a serious supervised release violation. He had been arrested and charged in state court for selling crack, which also constituted a violation of his federal supervised release. I attended the final disposition hearing on the supervision violation; the agreed-on sentence, negotiated between probation, Mr. Hendley, and Mr. Wilkins's lawyer, was eight months of incarceration, concurrent to whatever sentence he received in state court, followed by another year on supervised release. Before the judge came out to the bench, Hendley spoke to the probation officer, making it clear that he would have preferred a longer incarceration term than eight months but would go along with the deal. He then spoke directly to Mr. Wilkins when his lawyer briefly left the courtroom. "I know you don't want to be here. I don't want you to be here. But we're doing our jobs. You have a lot of smarts and potential."

This theme continued in the formal hearing. In his argument to the judge, Mr. Hendley asked for even more extensive geographic and associational restrictions. He spoke of Mr. Wilkins's potential, which he characterized as the greatest of all the young men he had "worked with" from the neighborhood in the past six years.[23] Mr. Wilkins, who opted to speak at the hearing, played on this logic. He first expressed his sorrow for letting down Mr. Hendley, probation, and his family, then acknowledged his bad choices. This led to his request, which was, after completing his prison sentence, that he would please be allowed to move out of the country to where his father had relocated, to have a fresh start, far away from his hometown where his troubles have been.

The judge then formally pronounced the disposition. She turned down Hendley's request for geographic and associational restrictions: "I see too many technical violations [come from these]. That's home, family, friends." And she granted Mr. Wilkins's request to suspend supervised release and move out of the country upon release from prison, expressing hope that the move would allow him to get his life on track.

In some sense, both Mr. Wilkins's request and the judge's order in the case highlighted a fundamental flaw in using coercive legal strategies as therapeutic intervention. By calling out Mr. Hendley on his repeated requests for associational and geographic restrictions, the judge acknowledged that many situations are, in her words, "complicated." Indeed, she seemed to suggest, because of the binds these restrictions can put people in, the practice *itself* produces unnecessary violations even if it prevents others. She ended the proceeding by telling Hendley that there was a "longer conversation" about geographic and associational restrictions she'd like to have with him.

To some extent Mr. Wilkins's request may be read as confirmation of Mr. Hendley's working theory of the powerful negative influence of place. By requesting to leave everything he'd known his whole life, he seemed to acknowledge that this was a necessary precondition for embarking on a crime-free life. But at the same time, this move freed him from the powerful constraints of the law, via the long and demanding supervision period, which itself may have barred Mr. Wilkins from getting a fresh start.

Although these small kinds of cases constituted the most common typology in Northeastern District's drug caseload during my period of study, more traditional federal drug cases were also prosecuted here. These are typically multidefendant conspiracies involving transportation of larger amounts of drugs, often across state and federal borders, and where federal law enforcement agents have utilized wiretaps, GPS, webs of informants, and other forms of surveillance to bring down distribution rings. As such, they often include defendants who sit at different rungs of the operation, from the lowliest couriers to high-level managers and organizers. Although they ranged in size and scale, these conspiracies handled in federal courts were much heftier, at least in drug weight, than the "Hendley cases."[24]

One might expect that the conspiracy cases flowed naturally from the Hendley cases—that those busted in the hand-to-hand street sales would be used to go up the chain to suppliers and wholesale distributors. This is not the typical pattern in Northeastern District, however. The drug conspiracies here only occasionally intersected with the Hendley cases in terms of the players involved or places where they occurred. Instead, the prototypical defendant in the conspiracy type of case was Dominican by birth or heritage, especially in cases that involved heroin and cocaine, which predominated. A growing number of conspiracy defendants were also immigrants from Mexico and Central America. Overall, there was considerably more racial and ethnic diversity in the conspiracy defendant pool than in the Hendley cases, even within individual cases. Cases involving designer drugs such as MDMA (known as ecstasy), marijuana, and prescription drugs such as OxyContin often involved some white defendants, and a number of the larger cases included defendants from a variety of backgrounds within them.

Even though these cases look more like what we think of as federal cases, in that they involve interstate transport and larger networks of participants, they still pose several challenges for justice. Indeed, they illustrate some of the core features of contemporary federal drug cases, especially the integral role of cooperation, or "snitching," both for making the cases and for adjudicating them. The reliance on informants opens up a powerful prosecutorial weapon in federal drug cases: "historical weight." Informants provide information that is used to estimate drug weight for alleged past trafficking acts—they tell the case law enforcement agents how much was sold, how often, and for how long.[25] This information constitutes historical weight—no drugs have to be found or tested or put on the scale for it to be the basis of conspiracy convictions and subsequent "relevant conduct" at sentencing. And it can dramatically increase sentencing exposure against those informed upon.

In conspiracy cases, codefendants are often among the informants, which sometimes creates perverse outcomes. Those with the most information are typically higher up in the conspiracy, so they may get the largest breaks by informing on those on the lower rungs.[26] Since drug weight is the primary factor in determining the guideline offense level and the drug mandatory minimum thresholds, sentences within a single conspiracy can vary considerably depending upon what one defendant offers up as "historical weight" to be used against the others. It is not hard to see the risks that come with these adjudication dynamics, especially when the informants have the opportunity to lower their own risk on sentencing exposure. The last to plead often gets the worst of it, with no one left to inform upon and often no information to give.

The result is that the conspiracy cases—such as that of Rodrigo Ortega, whose sentencing I attended—usually live a longer and more contested life in federal court than the Hendley cases. Mr. Ortega was one of nine defendants, all from the Dominican Republic, indicted after a long investigation for drug conspiracy in 2012. Mr. Ortega, who was in his early forties, was the first defendant named in the indictment, which indicated that he had been identified by prosecutors as a "leader," and thus, the most culpable.

Each defendant was charged with conspiring to distribute a kilogram or more of heroin and five kilograms or more of cocaine.[27] Tracking this case was complicated by the fact that several of the defendants had aliases under which they were originally charged. It took months for the court to sort out the true names of the defendants, so at times it appeared that some defendants came and went as if ghosts.[28]

The original complaint (the basis for arrest warrants) named eight suspects, but only six ended up getting arrested. Two of the named suspects became fugitives from the outset of the case and remain so as of this writing. Nonetheless, they were formally indicted by the grand jury, and the cases against them remain open in federal court. Their names appeared on the docket all the way through the process. The ninth defendant was quietly added to the case about two weeks after the original arrest warrants were issued. No criminal complaint or warrant was issued in his name; the first indication that he was a defendant in this case was that an appointed attorney appeared on the court record the day before formal indictment. This may indicate that this defendant had started cooperating before the other defendants were arrested.[29]

The defendants appeared to be united in strategy for about nine months. Their attorneys, a mix of privately retained and court-appointed counsel, collectively requested additional discovery from the prosecution and filed joint motions on several issues, including their disagreements with the prosecution about the evidence to which they were entitled. Then, nine months in, the first group of three defendants agreed to plead guilty, having "engaged in productive discussions [with prosecutors] regarding resolution short of trial."[30]

Among the first to plead was the last defendant brought into this case. He had a written plea agreement that potentially got him under the ten-year mandatory minimum he faced, via the safety valve. In this district, the prosecutors' demands for disclosure under the safety valve's fifth prong (requiring truthful disclosure of the facts of the crime) was quite expansive. Defendants were expected to provide information that was functionally equivalent to what would be required to obtain a "substantial assistance" departure. Therefore, many defense lawyers would rather have their clients do a 5K1.1 substantial assistance proffer than a safety valve "disclosure" because it actually offers more protection to the defendant if the prosecution is not satisfied.[31]

In this case, it appears that this safety valve proffer included some informing. The defendant made a motion, which was granted, to seal his and the government's sentencing memoranda—a tip-off that the sealed documents show that the defendant provided some information to the government. His sentence ended up at seventy-two months. The other two early pleaders were likely lower-level operatives. One was able to get under the mandatory minimum via the safety valve and received fifty-six months. The other was granted both the safety valve and a substantial assistance departure. He ended up with the lowest sentence of all in the conspiracy: forty-five months.

The three remaining nonfugitive defendants, other than Ortega, agreed to plead guilty two months later, but one of them backed out before the change-of-plea proceeding. One of the defendants who pleaded guilty in this second round was a lower-level member of the conspiracy; he had merely delivered drugs and was involved for a shorter period in the conspiracy. He received sixty-three months after being granted the safety valve and a departure for providing substantial assistance. The other also received sixty-three months. His plea agreement was sealed, but according to the recorded judgment he got under the ten-year mandatory minimum solely by providing information to the government (a 5K1.1 reduction).

With all the other defendants rolling over and assisting the government, Mr. Ortega—the top man in the conspiracy—jumped on board. He was the second-to-last to plead guilty. His sentencing hearing, which I attended, took place about twenty-one months after the case was initially filed. The first order of business had to do with Mr. Ortega's receiving a break for providing substantial assistance to the government. Both sides asked the judge to seal the sentencing memo in the court files. The judge agreed to that request.

As with all sentencing hearings, the proceeding moved on to confirm, on the record, that the sentencing guidelines were correctly calculated.[32] The probation officer, who was in court, had calculated considerable drug weight as "relevant conduct" for setting the guideline offense level. This opened up an interesting tussle between the probation officer and the lawyers who had crafted an agreement based on a lower drug weight total. Thus, both the prosecutor and the defense attorney objected to probation's weight calculation.

After a host of objections to the guideline calculations by both sides, the judge made the determination that Mr. Ortega would be responsible for eight kilograms of heroin, higher than what the lawyers wanted, which garnered a base offense level of thirty-four. Four more levels were added, since Mr. Ortega was a "leader" in the conspiracy; then three levels were taken off for "acceptance of responsibility." Mr. Ortega's criminal history category was I, so his advisory guidelines range was 168 to 210 months. Both sides asked the judge to reduce the offense level two more levels in anticipation of a future amendment to the Sentencing Guidelines, which he granted. That brought the advisory guideline range to 135 to 168 months. With that calculation settled—a sort of anchoring point of departure—the actual sentence determination process began.

Both sides had previously agreed to recommend an eighty-seven-month sentence for Mr. Ortega, but that did not preclude either side from recounting the offense and the defendant's criminal history. The prosecutor opened by stating the government's recommendation of eighty-seven months followed by three years of supervision. He then described the defendant as "an energetic leader of an entrenched, high-volume heroin and cocaine operation." The drugs involved in this case, he said, totaled seventeen kilograms of heroin and an additional two kilograms of cocaine, as well as hundreds of thousands of dollars in drug proceeds. This invocation of such a hefty drug weight seemed incongruous with the litigation that had just preceded it. Nonetheless, nobody remarked on the irony of this being the same prosecutor who had just tried to keep weight amounts out of the guideline calculations.

The AUSA went on to acknowledge that not all the drugs could be directly attributed to Mr. Ortega, especially after he had returned to the Dominican Republic for a period of time. Nonetheless, he argued, the sentence was necessary to serve as a deterrent, to both Mr. Ortega and others like him. He pointed out that heroin "is a particularly dangerous and noxious drug," which had resulted in many overdoses within the district in recent months. He concluded by pointing out that Mr. Ortega, although not formally educated, is intelligent and could have applied his intelligence to different, legal pursuits.

The two lawyers then requested to talk to the judge at the bench. The public nature of the proceeding was put on hold, and a loud static noise began to emanate from the courtroom's audio system. The two attorneys approached the judge's bench from the right side, and the judge came over to confer. The three spoke for several minutes, presumably about the nature of the substantial assistance provided, so as to justify the 35 percent reduction from the bottom of the guidelines that was being jointly recommended. This judge is a guidelines judge—he typically sentences within the guidelines unless there is a motion or request from the prosecutor to go below, as in this case, so the recommended sentence may have taken some convincing.

At the end of the sidebar conference, the static noise ceased and Mr. Ortega's attorney began his sentencing argument. He opened by concurring with the prosecutor on the eighty-seven-month recommendation. He appealed to the circumstances of Mr. Ortega's life—that he had only a third-grade education, that he spoke no English, and that he had no idea how serious his crime was. The lawyer also pointed out to the judge that Mr. Ortega would undoubtedly be deported postincarceration, implying that even after the lengthy sentence there was little worry about him recidivating in this country. Mr. Ortega himself then issued an apology to the court, in Spanish, which was translated by a court interpreter.

The judge pronounced sentence. "Stand, Mr. Ortega. You are about to be sentenced for your role as a leader in this operation." Mr. Ortega stood up. "You enter this country illegally for the sole purpose of selling illegal drugs. How many drug addicts have you succeeded to create? I will grant your departure [for substantial assistance], but this does not reduce the enormity of your crime. I must sentence you to deter you and others in the Dominican Republic from coming here to spread poison in our midst." He then sentenced Mr. Ortega to the agreed-on eighty-seven months, followed by a five-year supervised release period.

With Mr. Ortega pleading guilty, the remaining defendant (besides the fugitives) was the last man standing without a deal in hand. His earlier missteps may have come back to haunt him. This defendant, Ernesto Vélez-López, was not the ringleader but a supplier who was peripheral to Mr. Ortega's operation. In this case, Mr. Vélez-López was convicted for a multikilogram sale of heroin to Mr. Ortega, for which he received close to $400,000 cash as payment. He was arrested right after being paid, so the money was seized and eventually forfeited to the government. He worked out a plea deal with the prosecutor, which he officially signed off on about three months after Mr. Ortega had pleaded guilty. As with all the other defendants in the case, his agreement allowed him to get out from under the ten-year mandatory minimum by fulfilling the criteria of the safety valve. If granted the safety valve, the recommended sentence would be seventy to eighty-four months.

But something happened between the plea agreement and the actual sentencing. Mr. Vélez-López met the first four criteria for the safety valve, regarding his criminal history and his role in the crime, but did not fulfill the fifth prong, requiring disclosure. At sentencing, both sides reported to the judge that he "did not engage in a proffer with the government" so was ineligible for the safety valve. As a consequence, the floor on his sentence became the ten-year mandatory minimum. And that's what he received.

The federal drug laws in these kinds of cases operate under a distinctly different logic than the Hendley-type cases. The law is not justified as a tool to save defendants and their communities. Rather, there is a bit of an insular quality to these cases that makes the stakes internal to the world of drug conspiracies. The most valuable commodity defendants have here is information to give—it is essential to escaping the mandatory minimums, either through the safety valve or through 5K1.1 substantial assistance departures. Within any given conspiracy there is often pressure to make the first deal by giving up information on the others. As one defender explained, "There's this rush . . . to get on the bus because even if you're one of the major players, if you can get in there and start talking and they like you, the world is your oyster, and you can end up doing very, very well."[33]

In the Ortega case, the defendants held tight for a while as a group, but once a few decided to plead and talk, the prospects got worse and worse for the remaining defendants. There was an ascending nature to the negotiated sentences. With the exception of the one anomalous defendant who came to the case late and settled first, the sentences grew longer the longer the defendants held out. As for the final defendant, the record does not make clear what went wrong on the safety valve proffer, but the fact that he got hit hardest as the last to plead fits with the more general pattern of these cases.

The web of informing that is created through these kinds of cases also expands the net for prosecutors. This case intersected with at least two other conspiracies that were prosecuted within months of the Ortega case. The evidence in this case included recorded calls and observations that linked alleged conspirators from one with those from the other two. One linkage was to an even larger conspiracy, involving ten defendants, all also of Dominican heritage. There was even a linkage, by the evidence of conspirators in the Ortega case, to a three-defendant case that originated in Mexico and involved two Mexican nationals and a U.S. citizen from a district a thousand miles away. Once arrested, defendants can and do offer up information or other assistance beyond their own cases, thereby fortifying the prosecutors' cases in other ongoing conspiracies and further entangling the network of drug conspiracies. Given Mr. Ortega's place in his own conspiracy—as the leader and as one of the last to plead—it is likely that information about others outside of his immediate case was the kind of assistance he could fruitfully supply.

In the Ortega case, there was some semblance of proportionality relative to individual culpability of codefendants within the group. Although there were relatively large and potentially troubling differences in sentence lengths among the nonleaders, Mr. Ortega as the identified leader did get a more substantial sentence than most of the others. But this may not be the norm: the USSC's analysis has indicated that managers in conspiracies are the most likely by far to receive sentencing breaks for cooperation, followed by organizers. Street-level dealers get the worst of all worlds and are least likely to qualify for any sentencing break when facing a mandatory minimum.[34]

And when we widen the scope and compare the kinds of outcomes in these cases to what happens in the Hendley cases, the picture of how sentence length comports with justice and relative culpability is even more troubling. This is partly an artifact of the guidelines themselves. All of the defendants in this conspiracy had negligible criminal history—all fell into criminal history category I—which is likely in part due to the fact that only U.S. convictions formally count in the criminal history calculation, and most of the defendants had spent only limited time in the United States.[35]

Consequently, even though federal agents gathered evidence for more than a year and chronicled thousands upon thousands of grams being distributed, the lack of applicable criminal history provided an escape hatch through the safety valve from the drug weight side of the sentencing hammer. Mandatory minimums could be avoided and some below-guidelines sentences were imposed. Even with one of the toughest sentencing judges in the district, the sentences for at least some of the defendants looked remarkably close to those meted out to the small-timers in the Hendley cases, especially where the career offender guideline was in play.[36] This is not to say that the drugs should "count" more and that the Ortega conspirators should have been punished more harshly. I raise it to question the very calculus that undergirds all federal sentencing in drug cases: that drug weight times criminal record equals the appropriate sentence. Rather, as I have illustrated, this formulation masks the qualitatively diverse cases that get prosecuted in federal court and can itself produce injustices and inequalities.

Ultimately, the Hendley-type cases seem to be the most troubling of drug cases prosecuted in Northeastern District. No matter how noble the goals of this prosecutorial mission, many stakeholders in this district have pointedly asked why these cases are in federal court in the first place. For instance, in early 2004, one of the judges in the district, himself a former federal prosecutor here, publicly called out the U.S. Attorney's Office for charging small cases that originally had been developed by state and local agencies. He suggested that such cases were not appropriate for the federal docket because they wasted federal resources. In his view they were being brought in lieu of "important" federal cases that needed significant resources to be developed and pursued. The relative share of drug cases subsequently dropped, temporarily, but headed back up in 2006.

The low-level defendants prosecuted in federal court by Mr. Hendley and his colleagues were characterized by several defense attorneys as "low-hanging fruit," ripe to be picked off and sent away.[37] They viewed the practice of setting up and federally prosecuting small-time street dealers as a cynical way both law enforcement and prosecutors ensure easy-to-obtain, frequent convictions that help keep their case numbers up.[38] As one federal defender put it, "I'm *confounded* by some of the choices because I just don't see why particular people are plucked out, brought in, and . . . in effect launched into sentences that are outrageous."[39]

Although all the defense attorneys I spoke to thought Mr. Hendley, in particular, was committed to using his power to improve troubled communities, it was not lost on them that these cases also functioned as fodder for a criminal justice system that requires numbers to be sustained. Nor was it lost on them that this segment of the drug caseload was primarily African American. The prioritization of small state cases plucked from targeted minority neighborhoods appeared to contribute to the racializing of the federal drug caseload in Northeastern District. In the early to mid-1990s, between 50 and 55 percent of the sentenced drug defendants in this district were white. From 2008 to 2012, the annual percentage of white drug defendants hovered between 13 percent and 23 percent, even though the general population in the state is 75 percent white.

Numerous attorneys pointed to the selection process of who comes into Northeastern District's federal court on drug charges as the source of stark racial disparities:

Those cases that they handpick . . . I mean, it's all poor black people from the projects. It's all [city] police telling the prosecutor's office, "This guy needs to be off the street. He's a menace [to his neighborhood.] Or he's the menace at wherever."[40]

Take Tom Hendley's cases, right? I mean he's busting up gangs in [two urban neighborhoods], you know, African American communities. And those clients are black. That accounts for the race, you know, the neighborhoods that they're targeting.[41]

Yet these cases keep getting filed here.[42] This brings us back to Aaron Crenshaw, whose case was ultimately resolved more than three years after he was first arrested, at a time when the national conversation was more critical of the racialized war on drugs than ever.

The judge assigned to Aaron's case came out to the bench to take the plea. He found a distraught young man before him. The judge had expected to hear a motion to suppress evidence filed by Aaron's lawyer. For months, Aaron had gone back and forth on whether to fight his case or take a plea offer. The night before this proceeding, after a long, emotional meeting with his lawyer and his family, Aaron relented to the strong pressures to plead guilty: the slim likelihood of winning the motion and the even slimmer likelihood of an acquittal at trial. With the career offender guideline and a potential 851 enhancement hanging over him, the risk outweighed the potential reward in this calculus. Defendants are typically hammered at sentencing when they go to trial and lose: all deals disappear, acceptance of responsibility deductions are moot, and some judges add a "price" at sentencing for the time and resources expended in going to trial on a losing case.[43]

After Aaron's lawyer clarified for the judge that a plea agreement had been reached and that today's proceeding would be the formal change of plea, the ceremony began. It opened with a close reading of the terms of the agreement. It was a nonbinding agreement, which meant that the judge did not have to follow either party's recommendation. The agreement specified that the prosecutor would recommend a sentence of sixty months, considerably below the career offender guidelines, along with a three-year period of supervised release. Aaron was then asked the laundry list of questions to establish that he was competent to enter a plea, and that the plea was voluntary and knowing.

Aaron provided the correct answers to proceed, through tears and with considerable distress. The judge did not like what he saw: "I understand you are feeling emotional about this. Is this truly your own decision?" Aaron said yes, but the judge was not convinced and asked again. Aaron reiterated that it was his decision. With that, the judge asked the prosecutor to recite the facts of the crime that would be proved if the case had proceeded to trial. Then the wrap-up: Aaron was asked how he pleads to the charges, to which he responded, "Guilty." Was he pleading guilty because he did in fact commit the crimes as outlined by the prosecutor? Aaron confirmed.

Because Aaron was now officially guilty and facing a prison sentence, the whole calculus of pretrial release changed. The probation officer, who was seated in the jury box during the proceeding, reported to the judge that she did not want Aaron to remain out of custody. She was worried about his safety, she said, given the display of anxiety and despair that we had all just witnessed. The prosecutor piped up in agreement, that taking Aaron into custody right then was the best course of action for his own safety. Aaron's lawyer argued against it and pleaded for at least forty-eight hours so that Aaron could wrap up his affairs and say goodbye to his family. "His parents are a rock," the lawyer said, and would be in the best position to care for him in this time of distress. That plea did not work. The judge ordered Aaron into custody, and he was taken out of the courtroom to the marshals' holding pen, his family's wails joined by his own.

Aaron remained in local custody for the next six months while awaiting the final judgment—his day of sentencing. Both sides submitted written sentencing memos in support of their recommendations to the judge. Aaron's attorney opened his by pointing out that Aaron "is anything but the career offender the United States Sentencing Guidelines say he is, and, the government agrees." He followed with his sentencing request— twenty-four months—which he pointed out was still three times higher than the low-end of the guidelines would be, absent the career offender guideline. The next section offered a detailed biography of Aaron's life, moving on to a retelling of the crime of conviction to highlight how minor it was in the scope of federal drug crimes. He then made a robust legal argument based on proportionality, especially in light of the anomalous misdemeanor career offender predicates that count in this district (and in this case). Attached to the memo were letters from loved ones, former employers, and clergy.

The prosecutor opened his memo by casting himself as a victim of his own generosity. "No good deed goes unpunished. The government lowered its sentencing recommendation to the Court dramatically—a full ninety-one months below the low-end of the [career offender] guideline sentencing range set by the U.S. Probation Office. Yet, the defendant uses the government's reduced sentencing recommendation to justify a sentence that is even lower still." He then went on to justify why this case was in federal court, stating that local police had alleged that Aaron had been involved in a street gang known for guns and violence. He did not explain why, then, Aaron's girlfriend had been the original target of the undercover buys instead of Aaron himself, or why Aaron's actual record did not reflect that more dangerous portrayal. His recitation of the crime itself also did not support the contention that Aaron was somehow dangerous and that the drug bust was necessary to contain the risk he posed.

The judge split the baby, with two-thirds of the difference going to the prosecution: forty-eight months in federal prison plus three years of supervised release, for $200 worth of drug sales.

═ Chapter 4 ═

Hammers and Nails
in Southeast District

About nine months after his client had been sentenced by Judge
Jeremiah Jenkins, a.k.a. "the punisher," defense attorney Dennis
Younger summed up the experience for me: "When the only tool
you have is a hammer, everything looks like a nail."[1] In Southeast District,
there are lots of big hammers pounding on an endless supply of nails.

Mr. Younger had been appointed to represent Franklin Samuels in
one of the few federal cases he had taken as a criminal defense attorney.
He generally declines federal cases and sticks with those charged in state
court, because he feels there is little that can be done for clients once they
are charged in federal court. As soon as drug defendants are federally
indicted here, said Younger, "The die is cast." If the defense tries to litigate anything, the prosecutors will just up the ante. And as he came to
discover in Mr. Samuels's case, the ante can be upped even when defendants go along with the prosecutor's wishes.

Mr. Samuels, an African American man approaching his sixtieth birthday, had a history in this federal court. He had first been indicted here
in a five-defendant drug conspiracy case fourteen years earlier. In that
case, he pleaded guilty to distributing crack cocaine and was sentenced
to eighty-four months in prison, followed by five years of supervised
release. Soon after he was released, he violated his conditions of supervision when he was caught using cocaine and heroin. Mr. Samuels was
taken into custody and appeared back before his original sentencing
judge, who sustained the violation allegation and returned him to prison
for two more years.

After he got out again, Mr. Samuels stayed clean for more than three
years and got off supervision.[2] His health was failing, and he was occupied with addressing his serious cardiac and pulmonary problems to
stay alive. Given his history of drug abuse, coupled with the aging effects
of prison, he was at this point in his life physically much older than his
chronological age. But Mr. Samuels was momentarily sucked back into

the drug trade in a manner that epitomizes how drug cases develop and proliferate in Southeast District. That is, through the seemingly limitless network of "cooperators" who have no way to escape harsh drug sentences themselves except to name names and set up others for arrest. For Mr. Samuels, this began and ended with a conversation with his son.

Federal agents had decided to target Mr. Samuels's adult son in a controlled buy of heroin after his name had come up in another case. At their direction "a person secretly working for the police" whom they labeled Cooperator phoned Mr. Samuels's son and said he needed to buy a small amount of heroin. The son did not have anything so asked his father for connections to help out. Mr. Samuels was "out of the game," but relented and pointed his son to another potential source. The son obtained the drugs from that source and sold a single gram of heroin to the cooperator, meeting for the deal at his father's house. The cooperator went on to set up Mr. Samuels's son in another sale, of three grams of heroin, a transaction in which Mr. Samuels had no involvement whatsoever.

Both Mr. Samuels and his son were arrested and indicted in federal court for conspiring to distribute 100 grams or more of heroin over a five-month period. This indictment gives some insight into how cooperation and its byproduct, "historical weight," work in Southeast District. The actual heroin sales directly tied to Mr. Samuels and his son were of 1 gram and 4 grams, respectively; the rest was arrived at on the mere say-so of confidential informants. According to Rebecca Frist, the assistant U.S. attorney (AUSA) prosecuting this case, both Mr. Samuels's and his son's names had been bandied about in another conspiracy that her office had recently prosecuted. She described for me how she came to charge the Samuelses' case. "The information that we had, once we brought that case down and we flipped the suppliers, was that [Mr. Samuels] and his son, who was his codefendant, basically were hang-arounds of the main guy [the leader of the previously prosecuted conspiracy].[3] The main guy had been through the federal system. He was friends with . . . the son, and had known the father, [Mr. Samuels], since he was a little kid."[4] In other words, because Mr. Samuels and his son were in the same social networks and may have hung around, they were identified as members of the conspiracy.

She told me that she could have established enough historical weight, through those she had "flipped," to get Mr. Samuels to at least a ten-year mandatory minimum sentence, if not more. So on top of the 100 grams of heroin alleged in the conspiracy charge, she indicated she could also have tagged Samuels and his son with 5 kilograms of cocaine. Not much needs to be established to link someone to weight in a conspiracy. If she could get her highly motivated cooperator to indicate even minimal action on Mr. Samuels's part that was "in furtherance of the conspiracy," he'd be linked, potentially even to deals that he knew nothing about.[5]

And of course, there are few if any checks on veracity and reliability when weight is established only through the words of a cooperator. A federal defender in this division described this as one of the most challenging aspects of handling drug cases in federal court here. She said that in the state system, where she previously worked, drugs had to actually be possessed to charge with intent to sell, "but here we have this historical weight, and you know, trying to explain to a client how the law allows another individual to throw out numbers—'I've known this person for a year. They've been my source of supply for a year. I would purchase this substance in these quantities. And I did that for six months.' . . . It blew my mind when I came to the federal system. What do you mean, drugs that they weren't caught with, and based upon all of these snitches' statements?"[6]

In the end, Ms. Frist decided to let go of the historical weight in exchange for a guilty plea from Mr. Samuels. "I made a very gracious offer to say, 'Look, just take responsibility for what you did.'" So if Mr. Samuels pleaded guilty to aiding and abetting the one-gram drug sale, she would dismiss the conspiracy charge. He took the deal. Based on his applicable criminal record and the offense level for this small offense, Mr. Samuels's guideline sentencing range would be eight to fourteen months in prison. But it was about to get worse than that.

Ten days before the scheduled sentencing proceeding, the defense received a copy of Ms. Frist's motion seeking a sentence above the guidelines, because, in her view, Mr. Samuels's criminal history score substantially underrepresented his "true" criminal history. In the motion, she recounted his entire criminal record dating back to when he came of age in the early 1970s. He did have two decades-old felony convictions from his late teens and early twenties, but other than the previous federal drug conviction (which had been counted), his record was primarily very old misdemeanor convictions. Nonetheless, Ms. Frist argued, his criminal history category should be V instead of II, based on all the older, "uncounted" criminal history. In other words, while the Sentencing Guidelines do not factor in most convictions after they've become stale, Ms. Frist asked the court to make an exception. The practical effect of this, if the judge agreed, would be that Mr. Samuels's sentencing guidelines would increase to twenty-one to twenty-seven months. And that's the range she requested in her sentencing memo.

Mr. Samuels got more bad news four days before his sentencing hearing. The judge issued a notice that he was contemplating an "upward variance" in this case, which was "based on the apparent inadequacy of previous periods of confinement to promote respect for the law and deter criminal conduct."[7] Given these two notices, the defense had no realistic expectations for a sentence in the advisory sentencing range. But they tried.

I attended Mr. Samuels's sentencing hearing in Judge Jenkins's court-room. Before the judge came out to the bench, Mr. Samuels chatted with a few of his family members who were there to support him. He told them that he was fairly certain, given the facts, that the cooperator was his very own nephew, who was working with the police to get time off of his own impending sentence. That nephew had been caught up in another case and ended up getting just four months, a minuscule sentence for any drug defendant in this jurisdiction. Ms. Frist also bantered with Mr. Samuels, who seemed unaware about how much worse things were about to get for him.

The proceeding began with the judge's standard confirmation that the Sentencing Guidelines had been correctly calculated by the probation officer. Mr. Younger then raised a concern about the way his client's health problems were understated in the presentencing report, but to no avail. After that, the critical part of the sentencing proceeding began in earnest, with Ms. Frist arguing her motion for an upward variance. She hammered the themes that Judge Jenkins often echoes: the need for deterrence and to promote respect for law. Her telling of Mr. Samuels's life was—in its entirety—his criminal past and his continued failures to be deterred and to show respect for the law.

Then it was Mr. Younger's turn. In his sentencing memorandum he had asked the judge to sentence his client within the calculated guidelines, as a fair and just outcome for an ailing man "in his twilight years." In court, he could not get through his argument without encountering pushback. First, he made the point that the worst of the offenses not "counted" in the criminal history score happened nearly forty years ago when Mr. Samuels was a young man. He tried an empathetic strategy, saying he himself had also made mistakes when he was young. Judge Jenkins interrupted. "But you learned from your mistakes; he has not." Mr. Younger then pivoted to the health issue, and the litany of problems his client had dealt with, including while in custody this time around. The judge interrupted a second time—"Let's cut to the chase here"—then he listed each sentence Mr. Samuels had served, concluding, "None has deterred him." Younger changed strategy once again, to criticize how Mr. Samuels had basically been reeled into this case. "The Cooperator was out there trawling [on behalf of law enforcement] and the minnow they got was Mr. Samuels."

That did it. Mr. Younger was cut off, and the floor belonged to Judge Jenkins. Referring to himself in the third person, he announced that "the court gave notice of a contemplated upward variance. The guidelines in this case are inadequate." He once again listed each sentence that had not deterred Mr. Samuels in the past, and stated that his goal in sentencing was to promote respect for the law and achieve deterrence. He then declared that rather than move Mr. Samuels's criminal history to a category V, as requested by Ms. Frist, he would move the criminal history to the highest category available, Category VI.

Moreover, even though no one suggested that the calculated offense level—for helping his son sell a single gram of heroin—was too low, Judge Jenkins decided to tinker with that as well. Based on some internal calculation that was never elucidated, he announced that the offense level should really be a fifteen instead of a ten. The consequence of his adjustments was that Mr. Samuels's new guidelines were forty-one to sixty months in prison. Judge Jenkins settled on forty-eight months—six times longer than the low end of Mr. Samuels's calculated guidelines—plus three years of supervised release as the appropriate sentence. Before adjourning, he told Mr. Samuels:

> As a fellow human being, I am sensitive to your health care needs and will recommend you go to a facility to get care. You may get better care than if you were out. . . . I hope you profit from this experience and you do not need to spend the rest of your life in prison.

Exactly a week after I had watched Judge Jenkins sentence Mr. Samuels so far above the guidelines, I was back in his courtroom for a sentencing hearing in a white-collar case. The defendant was a middle-aged woman who had emigrated from India decades earlier. She and her husband had violated bank deposit reporting laws in their efforts to avoid being detected for about $10 million of illegal tobacco sales to out-of-state buyers over a fourteen-month period. She had also involved her daughter in the scheme. Her guideline calculation called for a sentence of fifty-seven to sixty months, but she had cooperated with the prosecutor, so he recommended a "5K1.1" substantial assistance departure to forty-one months.

Before turning the hearing over to the attorneys, Judge Jenkins proclaimed the defendant "fundamentally a good person who used bad judgment and did bad things." The defense attorney asked for home confinement in his argument, and the prosecutor argued for the forty-one months. Judge Jenkins then pronounced sentence. He decided that instead of being an offense level 25, which was her calculated guideline, or even level 22, which she got to with the substantial assistance break recommended by the AUSA, she really should be at level 17. He repeated, directly to the defendant, his moral assessment of her. "You are basically a good person who got involved in illegal activity." His pronounced sentence was twenty-four months in prison, and even then he let her stay out of custody for a month so she could surrender on her own to the Bureau of Prisons. This, he said, "because of your good behavior, will allow you to get to be classified at a lower security level [in prison]."[8]

Unlike Mr. Samuels, this defendant was not defined by her criminal behavior; those acts were aberrations. Her illegal activity was sustained over some fourteen months, and she had even brought her own child into the business, but in this courtroom she was spared being defined only by her criminal acts, as Mr. Samuels had been defined just a week earlier. In Southeast District, drug defendants such as Mr. Samuels got the punch of the iron fist; white-collar defendants had a chance to merely have a brush with a kid glove.

Mr. Samuels's experience also illustrates how different the lives of drug cases are in Southeast District compared to Northeastern District. For instance, the terms of Mr. Samuels's sentence were identical to Aaron Crenshaw's up north.[9] But the underlying logic that brought these two men to federal court and that justified their respective sentences couldn't be more different. In Southeast District, punishment is explicitly identified as such; it is not wielded therapeutically, as is purported in Northeastern District. Drug defendants here are deserving of punishment for punishment's sake, because they do not demonstrate appropriate compliance with and respect for the law. That logic is used to justify the very coercive tactics used against defendants to compel both guilty pleas and cooperation with the government.

Indeed, in Southeast District, drug cases and cooperation go hand in hand, as exemplified by Mr. Samuels's experience.[10] Cooperation was so central to, and pervasive within, the drug prosecutions here that it almost seemed that the prize for the government was the cooperation, not the conviction itself. It was as if some mythical ideal defendant—the ultimate "big fish"—was being sought but never materialized. There is a bit of a domino effect at work here. Those who face federal prosecution are likely to have come to the attention of law enforcement in the first place because their names were given up in a previous arrest or prosecution. And once facing charges, they are under heavy pressure to "work" as cooperators themselves. This may mean flipping on codefendants within their own cases. It may also mean naming others, beyond their own cases, as a way to get credit toward an eventual sentencing break. Or it may mean actually setting up cases by actively seeking drug transactions with others, as directed by their law enforcement handlers. As a consequence, it seems, more and more friends, acquaintances, and family members get sucked into the vortex.

Like Mr. Samuels's prosecution, cases are initiated here through both weak and strong ties within familial and acquaintance networks. Much like the fishing analogy offered by Mr. Samuels's attorney, the more names named and arrests made, the further cooperators need to go to net others. This works in two ways: first is the "minnow" effect. Once information is sufficiently developed about a potential suspect, the government is not interested in offering sentencing breaks for more information on that person—it has what it needs. That means coming up with new targets, who are naturally more plentiful at the bottom of any drug conspiracy than at the higher levels. The "minnows" are also, as a rule, less risky to name, as they do not have the same resources and incentives to retaliate against cooperators that higher-ups typically have. "Flipping" downward rather than upward is both easier and safer, so the cooperation net gets wider, instead of deeper.

Second, from a social psychological perspective, it is much easier to name names of more distant associates than close friends and family. So tangential relationships can result in people getting pulled into the net of those named. If those names are not fruitful for law enforcement, the pressure is on to identify people closer to the cooperator. At times this dynamic is manipulated by the government, as defendants are threatened with blanket arrests of family members—spouses, parents, children—if they do not come clean on a particular target. For defense attorneys, part of the negotiated plea might revolve directly around this problem. A federal defender described how her clients are generally reluctant to tell on a family member. "Sometimes, I can get the agents to sort of back off on that. Certainly with a direct family member, I can usually do that. Cousins are a little harder."[11] Another federal defender mentioned that when clients do give information on family members, she tries to negotiate a larger discount on sentencing since it is more wrenching and damaging, and because it may pose particular danger to clients themselves since they are easier to identify as the informant.

One obvious and foreseeable consequence of making drug cases with an expanding net of cooperation is that original targets largely determine who gets named and busted. The snowballing of suspects will be concentrated in the same neighborhoods and among the same social groups. In Southeast District, that meant that the majority of drug defendants were African Americans, generally from the same poorer neighborhoods and communities.[12] Therefore, the production of racial inequality here was more a recursive, dynamic byproduct of the cooperation imperative. Unlike the Hendley-type cases up north, the Southeast District model needs less proactive police work to maintain. Cooperating defendants themselves help fuel the pattern of racial inequality, albeit under considerable pressure from the government.

Despite the dramatic difference in adjudication and sentencing norms, Southeast District took a familiar path to becoming hyperfocused on drug prosecutions, at least in one of the urban centers of the district. That is, like Northeastern District, the aggressive pursuit of drug cases, especially crack cases, had its roots in an antiviolence effort during the late 1990s. Almost simultaneous to the formation of a multi-jurisdictional task force in Northeastern District, federal law enforcement agencies and the U.S. attorney's office in Southeast District partnered with local agencies to pursue gun-related crimes in the African American–majority city in the middle of this district.

In this case, the program directly targeted persons suspected of drug-related crimes or domestic violence and who possessed guns. Felons in possession of firearms were also targeted. Upon arrest, their cases were prosecuted in either state or federal court, depending on which would yield a stiffer sentence. In the majority of cases, that meant federal prosecution. Thus, from the gun initiative's inception, suspected drug dealers were sought out for arrest and prosecution. Over time the initiative's gun requirement loosened, and drug suspects, armed or not, came to be aggressively prosecuted here.[13] A federal defender who started practicing a few years into this initiative explained that both local and federal actors collectively pushed the small local drug cases to federal court "primarily because the penalties are much more severe with the mandatory minimums in the federal system."[14] As a former prosecutor involved in the regional task force characterized it, the AUSAs in this district "came in with a steamroller . . . and took every possible case," so its application was indiscriminate, capturing "everybody, anybody."[15] The overwhelming majority of those prosecuted were African American.[16]

The overrepresentation of African Americans from poor neighborhoods and communities seemed also to shape the prevailing adjudicatory narrative in this district that justified harsh penalties as deterrence on steroids. Most notorious was one of the old-timer judges, Judge Walter Fridell, who subjected each drug defendant, and sometimes even others who he thought might be involved in drugs, to a lengthy monologue at sentencing about the demise of civilization wrought by drugs. At its conclusion, he brings it home to the defendant and drops his hammer.

"The lecture," as Judge Fridell calls it, opens in 1776, not in the new America but in China, which at that moment in time "had the highest standard of living on Earth." That was also the year in which the East India Trading Company began importing opium into China. According to Judge Fridell's tale, this is the beginning of the end of high civilization for China. Once on opium, users became happy and lazy and completely unproductive. The narrative traverses time and across the globe, through wars, treaties, and empires, highlighting key events in 1800, 1837, 1853, 1876, and 1937 that exemplify China's demise, where, by the time the Communists seize power, addicts are selling their children for nine cents to feed their opium habits. Severe punishment was Communist China's solution:

> Communist China eliminated the problem. If you were caught with opium you went to jail. And nobody ever *sold* opium twice in Communist China and got caught. You know what they did? The first time you sold it the communists shot you. . . . I'm merely telling you what happened in China. It will happen here if we don't stop the utilization of drugs.

This history lesson leads Judge Fridell directly to his contemporary narrative of the demise of society as played out in the poor, primarily African American housing projects in several small towns where many defendants who face him reside. He tells his audience that the people he is sentencing "seem to think there's nothing wrong with drugs" but that soon enough, the addicts in those communities will be selling off their own children to support their habits, just like in pre-Communist China.

Judge Fridell's resulting drug sentences are notoriously long, often measured in decades rather than years, as he generally finds the full extent of relevant conduct to be applicable. This, in his telling, is nothing compared to the summary executions that the Chinese so effectively employed.

"The lecture" excerpted above was given at the conclusion of a lengthy hearing in front of Judge Fridell, where Kelvin Sommers was attempting to withdraw his guilty plea for conspiracy to distribute crack. In his case, the relevant conduct generated from a confidential informant brought 8 grams of crack, the quantity found in Mr. Sommers's possession, up to nearly 1,500 grams. Mr. Sommers told Judge Fridell that he had pleaded guilty due to threats made by the government that his wife would be indicted if he did not accept the plea offer. Judge Fridell said it was "commendable" that Sommers wanted to protect his wife but concluded that he was a perjurious drug dealer. The guilty plea stood.

The hearing had begun in midmorning, and Judge Fridell had allowed only brief breaks for folks to run out and feed the meter and other such essentials. By the time he ruled on the motion, it was after regular business hours of the court. But before Judge Fridell would adjourn, he insisted on giving the lecture.

Judge Fridell: Have a seat [to the defense attorney]. . . . I'm going to tell Mr. Sommers and his wife and brother and friends what drugs are all about.

Defense Attorney: Yes, sir.

Judge Fridell: I'm going to tell them why drugs are such a scourge on mankind. In 1776 the Declaration of Independence was written in the United States. At that time we had no roads. We had little or nothing. At that time the fastest means of transportation was a horse. At that time the fastest means of communication were smoke signals. At that time the most advanced nation on earth was China. We don't learn about China in our history. . . .

And on it went. A month later, Mr. Sommers was back in front of Judge Fridell, who would formally impose sentence. Judge Fridell tried to repeat "the lecture," but the defense attorney reminded him that he had given it to a full audience of the defendant's family at the previous hearing. With nothing left to say, Judge Fridell took into account the full informant-produced "historical weight," and pronounced sentence: 292 months—nearly a quarter-century—in prison.

Beyond producing kilos upon kilos of phantom drug weight in Southeast District, the cooperation imperative has pernicious consequences for defendants' fundamental human and constitutional rights. Defendants are put into impossible binds in which they do not actually have legal choices, largely because of the demand and reward for cooperation. Providing information to the government can be both very dangerous and personally repugnant to those under pressure to provide it, so prosecutors use a panoply of tools at their disposal to overcome reluctance, and they make sure those who do not cooperate pay for declining the opportunity.

I was in court when Tyson Mitchell, charged in an eight-defendant, 280-plus-gram crack conspiracy case, also tried to withdraw from his guilty plea agreement, which in his case had originally included an attempt at cooperation. He initiated his attempt to withdraw by first asking for new counsel, since in his view, his lawyer was part of the effort to coerce him to cooperate and plead. He wrote a long letter to the presiding judge that recounted, from his perspective, the pressures he faced to plead guilty and become an informant from the start of his case.

According to Mr. Mitchell's account, when he was arrested and the agents attempted to interrogate him, he asked for an attorney. The agents told him that if he agreed to cooperate right then, they would put him at the front of the line for a break with the prosecutor. This is a standard tactic, according to several defense attorneys I interviewed, where the time imperative is played up and the divide-and-conquer strategy encourages paranoia, in the target's mind, about codefendants rushing to cooperate ahead of him. Mr. Mitchell did not succumb and insisted on getting a lawyer. He was appointed a panel attorney by the court at his initial appearance.

According Mr. Mitchell, his lawyer's first conversation with him was about cooperating; the lawyer relayed an offer of five years if he agreed to plead and talk. Mr. Mitchell said he wanted to see the evidence against him before making the decision. By the time he was able to even see the criminal complaint, his lawyer told him all the other codefendants had already cooperated. At this point, seeing the writing on the wall, Mr. Mitchell told his lawyer that he just wanted to settle with the best possible outcome without cooperation.

His lawyer came back to let Mr. Mitchell know he was now facing a ten-year mandatory minimum but that the prosecutor still really wanted him to talk. In the course of the AUSA's request to Mr. Mitchell's attorney for his cooperation, the AUSA mentioned possibly charging Mr. Mitchell's fiancée. Mr. Mitchell implored his lawyer to tell the prosecutor and agents that his fiancée was not involved in anything. His attorney also relayed the message that the prosecutor would file an 851 enhancement to double the mandatory minimum to twenty years if he chose to go to trial. Under those circumstances, Mr. Mitchell agreed to identify his supplier. In the meeting, though, the prosecutor and agents turned down that "cooperation" and tried to persuade him to talk about his fellow gang members, which he refused to do. They brought up his fiancée once again. He decided to push forward on testing the evidence in the case and asked his lawyer to obtain full discovery.

After much back and forth with his attorney about the ease with which the prosecutor would be able to prove his part in the larger conspiracy, largely on the word of other cooperators, Mr. Mitchell agreed to plead guilty and signed a plea agreement. He then went through the change-of-plea hearing, consummating the deal. He had a change of heart within days of that hearing, which prompted him to write to the judge. The first hearing on this matter, which I also attended, dealt with the basis for his motion to withdraw his plea—his concern about being adequately represented and his request for new counsel. The judge granted his request, relieving his attorney from the case and assigning him a new attorney.

Mr. Mitchell was not so fortunate a few weeks later when his motion to withdraw his guilty plea was heard. His new lawyer primarily argued that his client's plea was not voluntary, largely because of the joint pressure that had come from both the government and his original attorney to be the first to enter a plea and cooperate. The AUSA argued strenuously against allowing Mr. Mitchell to withdraw his plea, even while acknowledging that doing so would not hurt the government's ability to prosecute the case. He insisted, though, that the courts need to impose a standard of "finality" and to send a message that once a defendant pleads, it is binding.

The judge went through the entire colloquy of the original guilty plea proceeding to demonstrate how each requirement of a legal guilty plea was met. The motion was denied, and a new sentencing date was set. About four months later, Mr. Mitchell was back in this courtroom where he was sentenced to twelve and a half years in prison, exactly what the prosecutor sought in his sentencing position, four years more than what his attorney sought, and seven-and-a-half years more than the original plea offer.

As Mr. Mitchell's case illustrates, the centrality of cooperation to drug cases makes it costly at the individual level to resist the pressure to inform on others. Several defense attorneys shared stories of hardball tactics used against their clients by prosecutors in plea negotiations to obtain that cooperation. The biggest threat to gain cooperation was the 851 enhancement, which functioned not only to force pleas in this district but to force cooperation. In some such cases, the prosecutor will file the 851 even after a plea agreement has been made, and then will let the defense know that the only way out from under that now-doubled mandatory minimum is through cooperation.

This practice can put defendants in a horrible dilemma, since providing assistance can be a deadly endeavor. A federal defender told me about one of her cases, where the very reason the defendant was charged in federal court was because of information that federal prosecutors thought he could supply about some other suspects. The prosecutor's first move was to charge the crime—which had the potential for a ten-year mandatory minimum—as a five-year mandatory minimum case, with the threat of the 851 enhancement if he did not cooperate. The problem for the defender's client was that he was from a neighborhood "where if he cooperates, he's dead . . . or, even worse, his family's dead. And that's what he's concerned about, so he's refusing to cooperate."[17] The attorney went on to describe the prosecutor's persistence even after the client declined:

> [The prosecutor] just called me yesterday and was like, "Look, we really need his help on this guy because he will just make the case for us." And, I was like, "Not gonna do it." And they were like, "Well, just ask him because then we're really gonna file the 851." So even after he's pled guilty, because it's between plea and sentencing now . . . they're trying to get him to cooperate, and that is not going to happen. So, he's probably going to be looking at ten years.

Some prosecutors here made providing assistance a standard requirement in drug case plea agreements. They use the tools and incentives deployed by prosecutors in other districts to compel guilty pleas to also require cooperation as part of the package. To be sure, cooperation is sought and rewarded throughout the system. Here, though, that pursuit has crossed the line to compulsion, especially in the southernmost court in the district. It was not the select defendant threatened with enhancements to obtain cooperation; it was standard operating procedure. As one federal defender told me:

> I've had clients enhanced to mandatory life, mandatory 20, even if they were cooperating. Like part of the deal was, "I'm going to enhance him and then, therefore, he will cooperate, and so he will be able to avoid having this terrible mandatory minimum." . . . [One prosecutor] is just very matter-of-fact with me. She'll give me the discovery at the detention hearing and she says, "By the way, your guy's 851 eligible, I'm enhancing him." I'm like, "Isn't there anything we can talk about?" "Yes. Whether or not he wants to cooperate. That's his choice. Period. But, he's getting it whether he pleads or goes to trial. The plea's not going to save him from getting this enhancement."[18]

Here, anything less than the full force of prosecutors' hammers is characterized as a concession, which justifies the demand for cooperation.

The guidelines-authorized reduction for acceptance of responsibility is not even fodder for negotiation in most places, since it is a given with a guilty plea. Not so here, at least in the southernmost court of this district. Adam Delacroix, a prosecutor from the guns and drugs unit, told me, "If we give something up, you know, an enhancement, a recommendation for a sentence at the low end of the guidelines, [credit for] acceptance of responsibility, we want something in return. And, what defendants ordinarily have to provide us is cooperation."[19] Indeed, informing was so deeply entwined in the whole drug prosecution enterprise in his division that this prosecutor fully conflated cooperators with witnesses in the context of drug cases. Thus, Delacroix described for me how most of his "witnesses" in drug cases had previously been charged in federal court and were working as informants as part of their plea agreement.

I asked Delacroix whether they ever do reach the point where they have finally reeled in the "big fish" and can just prosecute without that cooperation imperative. He responded, "I don't think, here, in [Southeast District] . . . you ever get to the top of the chain, because the drugs all come from someplace else, and even someone who is, by our standards, a major drug trafficker, is probably small potatoes in other districts. A major drug trafficker here can oftentimes provide a lot of valuable information about suppliers in other parts of the country."[20]

The integral role of cooperators in this district ultimately also means that many, many more pounds of drugs are prosecuted than are actually seized. "Historical weight" can come in through the actual charges made in indictments, as in Mr. Samuels's and his son's original indictments. Even more historical weight comes in as relevant conduct when probation calculates the guidelines for sentencing.

It is hard to know how much of that historical weight was fabricated and how much really was dealt in the past. In Mr. Samuels's indictment, only 1 gram of heroin was "actual" weight; the other 99-plus alleged grams were historical. Both of the men who tried to undo their guilty pleas were facing years of added time on historical weight that came in as relevant conduct. In Mr. Sommers's case, the gulf between the actual weight found and the historical weight calculated at sentencing could be measured in decades. He was found with 8 grams of crack but his sentence was based on 1,500 grams. In Mr. Mitchell's case, the disparity was not so great, but it was there. The government could actually tag him with 170 grams of crack, which he sold to an undercover agent, but he was charged with conspiring to sell enough to get over the ten-year mandatory minimum: 280 or more grams of crack cocaine.

In some sense, then, the cases here are sort of a hybrid of the two typologies in Northeastern District. Some may be small cases with small players in terms of actual drugs seized, but the amounts alleged and often pleaded to can be much higher via conspiracy charges. More dramatically yet, even in the small cases like Mr. Sommers's, a huge amount of "historical" weight comes in as relevant conduct as calculated by probation and accepted by the judge. Other cases, like Mr. Mitchell's, look more like the conspiracies in Northeastern, but much more of the weight is soft, established by cooperators, which helps drive up sentences to be dramatically higher than those up north.

Compared to other districts, then, Southeast District is particularly zealous in its use of historical weight in drug cases, especially as relevant conduct at sentencing. A federal defender who had previously practiced in another district in the southwestern United States described her dismay when she began practicing in Southeast District: "I was just astounded by their use of cooperators to drive up drug weight. I just couldn't really believe it when I first [came here]—you have people who get caught with a twenty-dollar rock and all of a sudden you're going to sentencing and it's three hundred grams or something and you're like . . . what in the world!?!"[21] In her previous practice, the only drug weights charged and counted at sentencing were of those seized.

Defendants themselves are sometimes their own worst enemies, serving as the source of the historical weight that is used against them at sentencing. As in Northeastern District, many drug defendants in Southeast District begin in state court, where their cases may remain for one or several months. One common tactic used by federal agents in one of Southeast District's divisions is to pick up the defendant after his case is dismissed in state court, and during a long, leisurely transport to the U.S. marshals for booking (which is in actuality just minutes away) to get the defendant to talk. This is a moment of legal limbo that is exploited to gain information and ensure continued cooperation. The to-be-charged defendants, at least those who are indigent, have not yet been appointed attorneys in federal court, since they have not made their initial appearance. And they are no longer represented in state court, since their cases have been dismissed. A federal defender described this tactic to me:

The DEA [Drug Enforcement Administration] agent or FBI . . . being just these nice guys, maybe they'll run through McDonald's if the [defendant is] cooperative, so when we get appointed to a case, I turn to the government and I say, "All right. Any statements?" And they're like, "Oh, yeah. They talked. . . ." You can get a client who had sold half an ounce, fourteen grams, to somebody, but they confessed to the DEA of selling a half an ounce a week for [however long]. So, all of a sudden, the prosecution's bringing a conspiracy with an unknown person of over five hundred grams, you know, or whatever the math is. So . . . they end up talking their way into a serious conspiracy. Whereas if they would just shut their yap, and let me do something, . . . because if I'm there, I get them immunity, I get stuff done. But, when they tell it all ahead of time, we're sort of hamstrung.[22]

The federal agents lure defendants into waiving their Fifth Amendment rights with promises that telling all will bring leniency, but the reality is that the information is not protected from being used against the would-be cooperator. I got estimates that anywhere from 60 to 85 percent of drug defendants cooperate with law enforcement in this district. If that cooperation is negotiated by defense counsel, she will ensure that all the information given to the government in the proffer (or "free talk") cannot be used against her client unless the client breaks the terms of the agreement.[23] If the government does not find the information useful, then it in essence disappears. Prosecutors will not argue for any of that information to count against the defendant as relevant conduct, and it cannot be used to lodge new charges against the client. If the client talked outside of such an agreement, such as when he is at the McDonald's drive-through on the way to federal booking, everything said can be used against him if the government chooses to do so. The only way to climb out of that hole is to come up with even more to tell in the context of a cooperation agreement.

I asked defense attorneys in this district about whether pleading their clients straight up would be an option, both to escape the pressure to cooperate and to preserve appellate rights. In many districts, including Northeastern District, taking a chance with the sentencing judge has become more and more common since *United States v. Booker* rendered the guidelines advisory in 2005. It allows for a more robust adjudication process at all steps along the way, and the sentencing exposure risks to the defendant are often minimal. That is not the case in Southeast District. Attorneys reported that it would be a rare drug case that would be resolved outside of a plea agreement. "The problem with drug cases is they can always charge more."[24] That typically means more historical weight that can be generated by cooperators. And because the judges here remain faithful to the guidelines, at least in drug cases, pleas for mitigated sentences usually fall on deaf ears.

Moreover, even plea agreements are no guarantee that historical weight can be fully contained in this district. One overriding goal in plea negotiations, across districts, is to lock in weight amounts in the "statement of facts" to control probation's calculation of offense level.[25] But in many instances in Southeast District, the pretrial probation officers conduct their own "independent" investigations to dig up relevant conduct beyond what is specified in the prosecutor's version of the statement of facts. Sometimes this is done with the assistance of the case prosecutor, who turns over the statement of facts but also opens the entire file to the probation officer to mine for additional relevant conduct. It may also happen through phone calls to the law enforcement agents involved in the case, during which the probation officer seeks information that can increase the relevant conduct weight. The consensus among defense attorneys was that although there were some fair-minded probation officers doing presentencing reports, the management in some of the offices enforced a practice that slammed defendants for as much relevant conduct as could be established. These offices required supervisorial approval of presentence reports, which ensured compliance with the practice of counting everything possible against the defendant.

Defendants generally have few allies in the system, other than their lawyers, and in Southeast they face an especially hostile crowd. Probation is a minefield, where guideline calculations are all too often higher than what was expected on the basis of the parameters of the statement of facts. Judges are by and large wedded to those guideline calculations in drug cases. And codefendants, and other associates charged in federal court, are potential cooperators who may well be sources of damaging information. Consequently, defendants are beholden to prosecutors if they want any chance of relief from the very long sentences they face, which mainly comes at the cost of cooperation. This is precisely how prosecutors steer the entire adjudication process and is why "the die is cast" as soon as drug defendants are federally charged here. To put it bluntly, this district looks, on paper, like one of the most compliant districts in the country in its adherence to the guidelines. But the machinations that create cases and produce those outcomes represent an assault on core justice ideals, including those of due process and of equal protection.

Defendants were punished for utilizing basic procedural necessities to be able to even assess the contours of the case against them and to test the evidence in order to make judgments on how to proceed. Defenders related a number of stories about how deals went away and new charges were added if defendants filed motions challenging the constitutionality of searches or other potential procedural violations. As a defender described it to me:

> We have found, and this is one of the true, horrible things about practicing in this jurisdiction, that sometimes when you raise Fourth Amendment issues or Fifth Amendment issues, the stakes get higher for the client. And, that's not just going to trial, that's the pretrial motion stage where you're fighting to get more discovery, you're fighting to suppress the evidence, you're fighting for material that might be favorable to your client, to obtain that. But, unless you get on board with the government in the early stages, to cooperate, you often find that your client is in a much worse position if you are simply trying to exercise the client's constitutional rights. And, to me, that's just a tragedy here. So, you may have a good Fourth Amendment issue on a suppression motion, and the government will say, "Well, if you file this motion or if you go forward with this motion, then I'm gonna move the weight up based on historical confirmation that we have." That's one of the really sad parts of practicing in this district.[26]

He characterized this as "a disgusting way to practice law" that puts defense attorneys in a horrible emotional and moral bind. The defendants are the ones in real jeopardy, since they, not the attorneys, will suffer the consequences of pursuing viable defenses in their cases. Another attorney in the same office offered a specific example, where her client was punished with a 924(c) gun charge, which triggers a mandatory minimum sentence that runs consecutive to the primary sentence, for filing a suppression motion. Her client had a prior drug and gun conviction, and was pulled over while driving. The trooper searched his car and found a gun and a small amount of crack. The client insisted that the search of his car was illegal and urged her to file a suppression motion. The AUSA in the case had offered to cap the sentencing exposure to fifteen years if the client pleaded guilty. When the defender filed the motion, the AUSA pulled the plea offer and filed the 924(c) charge, which upped the mandatory minimum in the case to forty years.[27]

As the defense attorney described it, "It was ugly . . . you know, the guy is just exercising his constitutional right. It's not like [the AUSA is] really putting out a lot more resources. It wasn't like it was the morning of trial and you have all your trial prep done. I mean, this is happening months before a trial date. What's the big deal?"[28] The suppression motion was denied by the judge, so the gamble did not pay off. With the additional charge filed, the defendant had nothing to lose by going to trial since there was no way out from under that forty-year minimum. The client lost at trial, and was indeed sentenced to forty years.

The option of going to trial was viewed as the most risky of all, unless there really was "nothing to lose" because so much time was looming in a given case. As a federal defender characterized it, trials were generally "client-driven," often against counsel's advice: "Clients just say, 'No way, you know, I'm going to trial.'"[29] Once the trial was on the horizon, all the options to worsen the client's situation were typically put into play by prosecutors. For defendants who had made statements to law enforcement, new criminal charges that could be derived from those conversations might surface. The scope of drug weight attributable to the defendant would also be presented to reflect the worst-case scenario. And testifying in one's own defense was particularly fraught, as prior statements could come in directly to impeach and impugn the defendant. In Southeast District, testifying also meant a near-automatic enhancement for obstruction of justice upon conviction. Judges routinely punish convicted defendants who testify, on the theory that they must have been lying if the jury convicted them.

Most brutal of all, prosecutors almost always make good on their threats to file the 851 or 924(c) enhancements against eligible defendants as trial dates approach. This ensures that the so-called trial penalties in Southeast District can run to decades rather than months or years.[30] Making good on such threats also sends a chill throughout the defense bar that ethically compels them to advise clients against taking the risk of asserting their trial rights. Consequently, pressures from all sides propel the high rate of guilty pleas in Southeast District.

Devon Harrison, whose story opened this book, found out just how high the price of going to trial could get. The life course of his case exemplifies how he became a sacrificial lamb in an adversarial system where so much power rests with one side. Devon had been convicted at trial in Southeast District eight years before I first visited there. Devon's indictment included two counts: conspiracy to distribute fifty grams or more of crack cocaine and possession with intent to distribute fifty grams or more of crack. There was little dispute that Devon knew about the drug business his friend Charles was in, or even that he helped retrieve the drugs when Charles had tossed them. Nonetheless, his part in any "conspiracy" was tenuous at best. And his "possession" of the drugs was both fleeting and not at all linked to an actual sale.

Yet for the hubris of taking his case to trial, Devon was pummeled with the largest hammer of them all—the double 851 that transforms a ten-year mandatory minimum into a mandatory sentence of life without the possibility of parole. The road to that sentence reveals the confluence of the vast legal tools at his prosecutor's disposal. It began with the decision about who should be charged, and with what. The prosecutor, Linda Gemelli, who as of 2016 is still an AUSA in this district and who is well known for being especially aggressive in her drugs and guns cases, made a decision out of the gate to include Devon in the federal case but to let his girlfriend, who was also in the car, escape prosecution. Devon may have been more culpable than his girlfriend, and hers may have been an extreme case of being in the wrong place at the wrong time, but as a couple, both seemed to be in a different world of culpability compared to Marina and Charles.

Charles was the name named by the original cooperator to get federal agents interested in watching him, and he had already been set up in a controlled buy as part of this case. Ultimately, he was the primary target of the takedown in August 2004. Marina was also on the radar as an ongoing coconspirator. Federal agents had thoroughly documented her recurrent role in renting the drug-run cars, running "dry heats" to ensure that they were not under surveillance and sometimes accompanying Charles on the weekly pickups. None of the agents had ever caught sight of Devon or his girlfriend over the course of their surveillance until the day of the bust.

But within hours of their arrest on the highway, Devon stood with Charles and Marina in front of a federal judge, and Devon's girlfriend had been let go. From there, things just got worse for Devon. Given his distance from Charles's business, he had little to offer in terms of information. He probably knew a lot less than what law enforcement knew, given their months-long surveillance. Yet, once charged in a case that had a ten-year mandatory minimum, and where the weight of the drugs seized alone would drive up the guidelines well beyond that, he had little hope of relative leniency. The Southeast District has been on the high end, nationally, of life sentence rates for drug convictions, and his prior felony drug possession conviction and prior drug trafficking conviction made him eligible for that. Both of his codefendants also had qualifying 851 priors, so at this time and place, the pressure was immense on all of them to plead out.

The three seemed to be holding tight for the first two months following their arrest, as they went through the discovery process. Then Marina and Charles, almost simultaneously, formally agreed to plead guilty. It turns out that both had been working with the government on fleshing out their own cooperation agreements almost from the start. Once represented by counsel, each had a turn proffering whatever they could to federal agents and the prosecutor as cooperators. In both cases, the plea agreements required that they testify against Devon. And that they did.

Marina got a deal of a lifetime, considering her criminal background and the pending charges against her. Not only did she have a felony drug distribution prior, but on the very morning she was first brought into federal court on this case, she was supposed to be in state court to be placed on electronic monitoring in that prior drug case. The first public indication that Marina was going to be the beneficiary of particularly generous treatment came about three weeks into the case, when she was let out on pretrial release without bond to the custodial care of her mother. The other two defendants remained in custody. Then, five weeks later, Ms. Gemelli dismissed the conspiracy and distribution charges in the indictment against Marina. Marina pleaded guilty instead to "illegal use of a communications facility," which essentially charged that she used the telephone to further an illegal activity. She remained out of custody while pending sentencing, which happened six months later—on the same day, in the same courtroom, as Devon's sentencing. At sentencing, she received a sentence of five years' probation, with the first six months to a year in home confinement. Three years later, she was discharged from probation, well before her maximum term was complete.

Charles's plea deal was not so great, but better than the alternative, especially given his exposure on historical weight and his prior criminal history. He agreed to plead guilty to the conspiracy count with a twenty-year sentence, reducible in the future for cooperating with federal agents, which he continued to do even after he was sent to federal prison.[31] And at sentencing, that's what Charles received—240 months in prison.

Devon had been offered a dozen years in exchange for a guilty plea, but he tried his luck at trial. This seemed a defensible position given that he was not part of any sales or conspiracies involving the hundreds of grams of crack. He was not by any stretch of the imagination a drug trafficker the way Charles and Marina were; he had only ever been a small-time dealer who sold enough to keep himself supplied with the heroin needed to maintain his habit. But that did not stop Ms. Gemelli from going all in on Devon's prosecution once he declined her offer. As soon as Devon's trial date was set and pretrial motions began, she filed the 851 enhancement information, which was the notice that she would seek a mandatory life sentence if Devon was convicted. The notice included evidence of his two qualifying prior state court convictions. Eleven years earlier, just shy of his twenty-first birthday, he had been convicted and sentenced to a short stint in state prison as a low-level street dealer. Three years later, Devon ended up back in state court facing felony drug possession charges; he pleaded guilty and was given twelve months in jail. These two priors ensured that the judge would have to sentence him to life without parole if he was indeed convicted of at least one of the charges at trial.

Ms. Gemelli called both of Devon's codefendants as witnesses during the two-day trial. Charles went first. His account of Devon's involvement was relatively consistent with what Devon had admitted at the time of arrest. That is, that Devon had in the past received small amounts of drugs from Charles but that he was more or less just along for the ride on the night of the big bust. Ultimately, Charles testified that the drugs were all his, and that he took sole responsibility for the entire deal. He unequivocally told the jury that Devon had nothing to do with the drugs or the conspiracy. This testimony may explain why Ms. Gemelli never followed through on giving Charles a reduction in his sentence for providing assistance, since testifying at trial is normally worth quite a discount.[32]

Marina worked harder for the prosecution. She testified that Devon had helped count the money for Charles before they left, and that he had twice retrieved the drugs when Charles had ditched them out of fear of being followed—inconsistent with all of the other accounts and evidence. She also said that Devon held on to the drugs in the car, and that he made statements about how much money was lost once they were busted. On cross-examination, Devon's defense attorney was able to get her to admit that she herself had not implicated Devon when she initially gave statements to federal agents, and that she had indeed stated that Devon was not involved. He got her to admit to her own extensive involvement in Charles's drug business, including at least ten prior times she had rented a vehicle for him. He also had her admit that her prior drug bust, which was made by the very same trooper who stopped them on this case, was for actual sales made for Charles. So while she tried to deepen Devon's ties to Charles and his business through her testimony, it seemed evident by the end of her testimony that she herself was a significant player who had obtained a sweetheart deal for testifying.

Two DEA agents also testified against Devon; each tried to link Devon to the deal. The first testified that Devon told him, after the arrest, that he hoped to get some drugs or money from Charles for going on the trip. These statements were not included in the original interview notes. The second testified that during his surveillance he saw Charles meet up with Devon earlier in the day, trying to implicate him in a longer pattern of planning. The defense put on no witnesses of its own.

By midafternoon on day 2 of the trial, after arguments by both sides and instructions from the judge, the jury retired to deliberate. Four hours later, they had reached a verdict on both counts. Guilty on the first count, the conspiracy charge. Not guilty on count 2, the possession-with-intent charge. A bittersweet result, in that it confirmed that his case was indeed triable, as it looked from afar. But it would make no difference at sentencing, since only one of the convictions was needed to force the life sentence. Four months later, at his sentencing, Devon's lawyer tried one last time to undo the inevitable. He made a motion requesting a new trial based on the improper admission of evidence at trial. And he made a motion requesting the judge override the jury's verdict and issue an acquittal. Both were summarily denied. After hearing both sides' arguments for sentencing, which were functionally moot, the judge imposed the only sentence he was legally allowed to impose: "Imprisonment for a term of life, without release" plus a $100 special assessment, payable immediately, for court costs.

═ Chapter 5 ═

Drugs, Mules, and the Looming Border

O n my first day in Southwestern District, I got to sit in on an exceptionally rare event here: a drug trafficking trial. Out of nearly 3,100 drug defendants who were sentenced in the district that year, only 17 had been convicted at trial. This case was even more unusual than that, though. The star witness in the case was a cooperator, a rarer find in this district than in most.[1] A pervasive and credible fear of cooperating exists in this border district, because informers or their families could end up dead. This star witness, though, minimized his own risk of getting killed for talking. Rather than testify against a higher-up, he turned on his own nephew, twenty-five-year-old Abraham Rodríguez, whom he had sucked into his business to work as a "mechanized mule" to move 7 kilograms of methamphetamine across town. In this world, moving drugs is a segmented process, and multiple disconnected couriers and mules are put to work to transport illicit substances from Mexico to distribution sites north of the border.[2]

If Abraham was convicted, his sentencing exposure was significant. He did not have any drug priors but he did have enough of a criminal record that, with this kind of methamphetamine weight, he was likely going away for a long time. His guideline calculation would be in the range of twenty-four to thirty years, with a mandatory minimum of ten years. Because of his criminal history, he was not eligible for safety valve relief, so that mandatory minimum floor was solid. In short, the stakes were high for Abraham.

But if they were high for Abraham, they were even higher for his uncle. With multiple drug priors, the uncle was vulnerable to the double 851 enhanced sentence of life without parole. So he did what he had done on at least three prior occasions in order to lessen his own punishment. He informed, this time on Abraham.

In an effort to blunt an attack by Abraham's attorney on his credibility as a witness, the prosecutor walked Abraham's uncle through his history of drug dealing and informing.

Prosecutor: Tell us about your first conviction in this court.

Uncle: I pled guilty to marijuana distribution. I agreed to cooperate and testify against the driver of the truck and others involved.

Prosecutor: Why did you agree to cooperate?

Uncle: Honestly, to get less time in exchange for my cooperation. I got twelve months instead of three years. I did ten months.

The prosecutor then guided him through the rest of his twenty-year history dealing drugs. He reported getting right back into dealing after release from custody on a supervision violation.

Prosecutor: Why did you get back into dealing?

Uncle: It was difficult [to resist], being so close to the border, knowing the ins and outs of the whole valley. It was still so easy to get drugs into the country.

The uncle went on to describe his growing role in moving drugs across the border, and out to routes north and east. First, he was a guide car driver, making a thousand dollars a pop to direct the drivers of drug-filled vehicles over the border and to local stash houses. He then began to directly contract drivers on behalf of higher-ups in the organization to drive border crossing and outbound drug cars. He was authorized by his bosses to pay up to four thousand dollars to those drivers. That eventually led to his next federal conviction, when several of his drivers got caught and led law enforcement to him. He cooperated once again to reduce his sentence.

With the next bust, he exchanged informing on his local partner for a break on his sentence. He faced eighty-eight to one hundred months that time, and was able to get it to sixty-three months with the cooperation break. And he didn't even have to testify. Once back out, he reunited with his partner, who remained unaware of his betrayal. They teamed up once more to coordinate the movement of drugs across the border, to stash houses, and back out to distribution sites in other states. This time around, he brought his nephew into the business.

By all accounts, including the uncle's, the day they were busted was the first day on the job for Abraham. Abraham's job was to pick up a car parked in a nearby shopping center parking lot, and then follow his uncle to where the car had to be delivered, a local stash house. The uncle's understanding was that the car was being driven across the border, through a legal port of entry, by a Mexican man who held a border-crossing card.[3] That driver was paid to deliver the car to the parking lot, where he'd leave it, keys inside, before heading back over the border. Unbeknownst to anyone on either side of this deal, the drugs had been detected by border agents at the port of entry, and the driver had been taken into custody. Law enforcement delivered the car to the designated pickup spot in the shopping center, then monitored it for the pickup. Abraham's uncle drove him to the parking lot, and Abraham drove out of the lot, following his uncle. The agents swarmed the two cars and arrested the two men.

At issue was how much, if anything, Abraham knew about what he had gotten himself into. His uncle testified that Abraham basically pestered him into giving him a "job." Speaking with the authority of an expert, the uncle asserted that in drug parlance, a "job" is the equivalent of a "drug job," and that this is a "very common" usage of the word in that world. This was critical, since the other primary evidence offered by the prosecutor regarding Abraham's knowledge was a series of texts between the two men about whether the uncle had a job for Abraham, since he was out of work and needed money. The uncle did all that he could to sell to the jury that Abraham knew what he was getting into. Getting Abraham convicted would be advantageous for the uncle's own eventual substantial assistance departure at sentencing.

Abraham testified on his own behalf. His account, not surprisingly, diverged considerably from his uncle's. He admitted to knowing his uncle had been in trouble in the past for marijuana dealing, but he said that he thought the job he was doing was related to a car-buying deal. He testified that his uncle had a side business of buying, fixing up, and selling used cars, a fact that his uncle had also conceded on the stand. On cross-examination, Abraham was peppered with questions about how it would be impossible to grow up in their border town and *not* know the ins and outs of drug transportation. Since the car they were picking up had Mexican plates, the prosecutor insinuated, Abraham should have known that it was a drug car and that he was moving drugs by driving it. In this way, the prosecutor assigned guilt to Abraham by geographic association. Living on the border means drug trafficking is a way of life, and known to all. Transporting a car for a relative could not be an innocent act here; according to the prosecutor, it was willful ignorance to try to make that claim.

The jury wasn't so sure. After about five hours of deliberations in total, four of the jurors passed a handwritten note to the judge, asking, "What do we do if we are a hung jury?" About an hour later, after a last attempt at reaching a verdict, they sent out the verdict form saying they were not unanimous on any of the three charges. The judge declared a mistrial.

I spoke to one of the two trial prosecutors and to Abraham's court-appointed defense attorney during a break in the trial. Both men expressed discomfort with the uncertainty of going to trial, and especially with leaving so much of the outcome up to the word of a cooperator. The prosecutor told me this was only the second time he had ever put a cooperator on the stand to testify; the overwhelming norm in this district—if there was any cooperation at all—was that informers' identities remained secret and any weaknesses in their credibility remained unexposed. Nevertheless, this prosecutor shared that cooperators are "a good thing. We want people to tell on others who do bad things."

From the defense perspective, even with a successful cross-examination of a cooperator that reveals the high incentive to snitch and the serious credibility problems that most cooperators have (because of their own criminal records), dangers abound for defendants in situations like Abraham's. When any witness recounts specific details about illegal activities committed by the defendant, the fear is that jurors are inclined to think that even if the account is exaggerated, it is not made up out of whole cloth.[4]

In Abraham's case, the uncertainties generally worked in his favor. After the mistrial was declared, the prosecutor and defense settled on a negotiated guilty plea rather than giving it another go with a new jury. If Abraham pleaded guilty to illegal use of a communication facility—the same "phone count" offense that Devon Harrison's codefendant Marina pleaded to in Southeast District—he would get acceptance of responsibility credit and the maximum possible sentence he'd receive would be forty-eight months. Abraham agreed to plead.[5]

Things got better than that for Abraham. The judge in the case, not generally known for being generous to defendants in this court, did not apply any of the methamphetamine weight as relevant conduct, even though both the probation officer and the prosecutor urged him to do so. Because Abraham actually pleaded guilty to using the telephone to further a marijuana deal and never admitted to any crime related to the methamphetamine, the judge imposed a sentence of credit for time served and one year of supervised release. Abraham was freed from custody that day. His uncle received a sentence of ninety-seven months, nearly two years under the mandatory minimum and considerably better than what it would have been without informing on his nephew.[6]

In most drug cases in Southwestern District, the border looms large, as it did in this case. For Abraham's uncle, the border provided both opportunity and strong temptation to partake in the international drug trade. For Abraham—and for most low-level drug-movers who try to claim ignorance about what they are involved in—its very proximity insinuates knowledge about drug trafficking.

The border also helps define those who make up a large share of drug defendants in this district as outsiders who belong on its southern side. Indeed, the typical drug defendants in Southwestern District are not like Abraham or his uncle, citizens whose lives are well-established on the U.S. side; instead, they are immigrant men and some women who crossed the border carrying drugs as part of their payment to make a better life for themselves and their families. Drug dealing and immigration are enmeshed here, so the drug cases live blurred lives in court.

That blurring begins with how the vast majority of cases enter into the system in Southwestern District: via immigration enforcement. Day and night, American border patrol agents comb the vast desert that comprises hundreds of square miles of this border district. They look for covert human activity, indications of border crossings by those not officially authorized to be on the U.S. side of that line. At legal ports of entry and on the roadways near the border, customs officers scrutinize cars and drivers that fit their smuggler profile, who may be secreting people, cash, drugs, or other contraband into the country. And every day, border enforcement officers find what they are looking for. In just one enforcement sector within Southwestern District, nearly ninety thousand persons were apprehended in 2014, of whom forty thousand were criminally prosecuted. While the greatest number of those arrestees face charges of illegal entry or reentry,[7] the next largest number are charged with drug-related offenses. As a consequence, the majority of the drug defendants in this district have been brought to prosecutors by customs and border agents, after being caught in the stepped-up immigration enforcement of the border.

The single most common category of federal drug defendant in Southwestern District is the low-level courier or mule who is tied into the international transportation of drugs in the region. Some couriers, like the border-crossing driver in Abraham's case, are at the very bottom of the distribution ring and have no prior criminal history but face high sentencing exposure owing to the huge amounts of serious drugs, such as methamphetamine, that they are caught moving. Others are low-level across the board: they have no criminal record and carry marijuana on their backs across the border.

Those with the fewest roots in the United States typically get the best sentencing outcome, because they have negligible countable criminal history. This qualifies them for better plea offers and, in cases involving mandatory minimums, relief via the safety valve. Somewhat less common among the drug defendant population are arrestees like Abraham, who are at most mere couriers but who have criminal histories that preclude the safety valve. Defendants such as Abraham's uncle, who are more deeply involved in the drug trade, are fewer still; they make up an even smaller portion of the drug caseload in Southwestern District.

Rarest of all are the high-level traffickers who profit the most from the drug trade.

The looming border makes drug cases in Southwestern District quite distinct, in both form and process as to how they were adjudicated, from both Northeastern and Southeast Districts. Drug cases differed in important ways between Northeastern and Southeast Districts, but the modes of adjudicating cases bore some resemblance to each other. In both places, the prototypical drug defendant was deemed worthy of prosecution and punishment because of the risk posed by his or her illicit drug activities. Dealing itself posed a problem in need of federal intervention—for the defendants themselves and for the communities in which sales occurred. Beyond that, illicit drug activity was rhetorically linked to corollary criminal threats, so prosecutors and law enforcement characterized drug crimes as intimately tied to gangs, guns, and violence. Indeed, in both Northeastern District and Southeast District, a significant portion of the federal drug caseload was made up of small, street-level distribution cases that were "adopted" from state courts on just that kind of logic. And in both places, those targeted for prosecution have primarily been young men of color selected from highly policed minority communities.

In the non-border districts that I studied, even when noncitizens were prosecuted for drug offenses, prosecutors' arguments in support of harsh sentencing and judges' pronouncements often treated the immigration status of the defendant as an aggravator but not the core offense. In both Southeast and Northeastern Districts, I witnessed judges condemn noncitizen defendants at sentencing for coming into this country to "spread poison [drugs]" and "wreck lives of our citizens" when pronouncing sentence. Although the immigration status was not ignored, the real crime had to do with the drugs. In short, in the nonborder districts, drug cases were drug cases, and the adjudicatory narratives were built around what the drug offense meant as an act, whether it signified individual weakness or inherent evil, the ravages of poverty, gang and gun involvement, or social failures.

These narratives were much less prevalent in Southwestern District. Rather, even though many drug defendants' lives were ravaged by poverty, deprivation, and even violence, the courts in Southwestern District maintained a focus on efficient processing for future exclusion from the country. Three out of every four drug trafficking defendants here were noncitizens, so the predominant goal was to get them convicted and sentenced quickly so they could do their prison time and be removed from the country. And while the vast majority of defendants were also men of color here, it was often their citizenship status that essentially made them ripe for federal prosecution. Moreover, in Southwestern District there was virtually no practice of state adoption; rather, the thousands of drug cases came to federal prosecutors largely as a by-product of federal immigration policy and enforcement.

This was epitomized by the largest subset of mule cases, the so-called "backpackers," who are almost always unauthorized immigrants, arrested in the desert after covertly crossing into the United States with backpacks full of Mexican marijuana. Backpackers are typically apprehended in small groups, as are non-drug-carrying unauthorized border crossers. Their backpacks are filled with anywhere from twenty-one to twenty-eight kilograms of marijuana. Often they have transported the drugs as part of their payment to a "coyote" for being guided across the increasingly difficult-to-cross border.[8] Thus, many of the backpacker defendants are functionally similar to those who pay cash to coyotes for crossing assistance, or those who take on guide roles in exchange for getting across safely. Once across, the backpackers are met by drivers assigned to take the marijuana to nearby stash houses or directly out of state.

The backpacker drug cases, more than any other, are really immigration cases, and the prevailing adjudication narrative is foremost concerned with defendants' status as unauthorized outsiders.[9] These defendants usually have no legal way to enter the country and so take unauthorized routes over the border. Increased border enforcement has pushed crossers to riskier passages into the United States, which has fed the growth of the underground border-crossing enterprises. The migrant trail is dotted with payment stations—to drug dealers, to property owners, and to coyotes and guides—and through some routes, carrying marijuana is one of those payment alternatives.[10]

There has been astounding growth in the volume of backpacker cases in Southwestern District, especially since 2008, when border enforcement was significantly beefed up in the region, and criminal prosecutions became much more frequent (see figure 2.5, "Southwestern District Drug and Immigration Convictions, 1992 to 2014"). The crush of cases pushed the border courts in this district to adopt various early resolution programs to speed up the adjudication process. This was first limited to immigration cases but was later extended to drug cases as the volume exploded.

There are two potential routes to adjudication for both immigration and marijuana backpacker cases—either via a mass-processed mode or through an individualized mode. The mass-processing route includes assignment to what is known as "flip-flop court." Eligible cases for this court include illegal entry and reentry cases and the backpacking cases.[11] Key to the accelerated mass-processing adjudication scheme is that the defendant is charged with a "mixed complaint" that includes both a felony and a misdemeanor charge. The complaint comes with the opportunity for the defendant to bargain away the felony by taking a misdemeanor conviction and a specific sentence outcome, totaling less than 360 days of incarceration. In exchange, the defendant must immediately plead guilty prior to receiving discovery (the evidence controlled by the prosecutor), waive all her trial rights, and waive the full-blown sentencing procedure. Defendants who decline the offers are routed to the individualized process, and the opportunity to resolve the case with a misdemeanor plea generally disappears.

Not all immigration and backpacking drug defendants are offered a mass-processing option. Those who are not are funneled directly into the individualized adjudication route. In the border courts, the primary determinant of who gets sorted where is the defendant's criminal history, including his or her prior convictions in U.S. federal courts. Those priors are also often previous immigration or backpacking convictions.[12] Although the criteria appear to be somewhat malleable and can change over time, generally those with certain prior felony convictions are not eligible for misdemeanor offers, especially in the case of backpackers. Moreover, even though the schematic for these routing decisions is obscure, the pressure of case volume can and does expand eligibility for inclusion in mass processing.

This is precisely how marijuana backpackers became eligible for the mass-processing misdemeanor option in the first place. In 2012, the prosecutor's office in Southwestern District's border division issued a new policy that made marijuana backpackers eligible to participate in flip-flop court. The policy limited the opportunity to thirty defendants with no prior drug convictions per day but provided an exception to that daily cap if too many eligible backpacking defendants were picked up over the weekend. By 2013, the office had set a cap of forty per week on how many backpackers could be handled as felonies, thereby flipping the logic of exceptions for drug trafficking offenses. Thus, within a year of moving some cases that had exclusively been treated as felony trafficking cases to flip-flop court, the felony route became the exception and the treatment of backpackers as misdemeanants became the norm. The weight cap for flip-flop eligibility by this time was set at one hundred kilograms of marijuana, so even those who transported larger amounts by car could qualify.

The drug conviction profile of this district shifted quite dramatically as the exponential growth in drug cases overall was dealt with through the misdemeanor plea deal (see figure 5.1). By 2014, misdemeanor possession convictions, primarily backpackers, made up two-thirds of Southwestern District's total drug convictions. This district's possession convictions alone accounted for 83 percent of the nation's federal drug possession convictions, largely as a result of the flip-flop option for marijuana backpackers.

This policy had a dramatic impact on defendants as well. Prior to 2012, backpacker defendants with no records were offered a sentence

**Figure 5.1   Convictions for Drug Trafficking and Possession
in Southwestern District, 1992 to 2014**

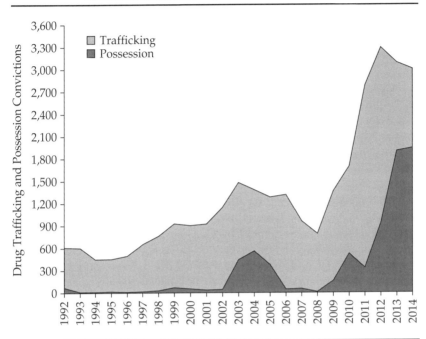

Source: Author's consolidated dataset of U.S. Sentencing Commission sentencing data.

of thirteen months and a day for pleading guilty to a felony trafficking charge. Such a sentence has significant collateral consequences for non-citizens. Any drug trafficking conviction resulting in a sentence of twelve months or longer is deemed an "aggravated felony," which bars non-U.S. citizens from legally entering or residing in the United States going forward. Those with legal status short of citizenship generally lose the opportunity to stay in the United States. The thirteen months and a day, therefore, ensured that the conviction would qualify as an aggravated felony. The sentence also has looming consequences for future illegal reentry convictions. Prior drug trafficking sentences longer than thirteen months increase the Sentencing Guidelines by sixteen levels for those subsequently convicted of illegal reentry.[13] Thus, the thirteen months and a day drug trafficking sentence is a particular construction for border districts, since it has unique punitive value in the immigration context.

The relocation of the backpackers to the mass-processed misdemeanor calendar made these defendants much more analogous to illegal immigration defendants. Flip-flop convictions have fewer immigration consequences since they are not felonies, and their terms are under a year. And in practice, these defendants are treated as part of a mass of unauthorized border crossers who happened to be carrying backpacks of marijuana, and the imperative driving their criminal adjudication is swift and efficient resolution to get them out of the system and out of the country.

Defendants get assigned to flip-flop court through a behind-the-scenes sorting process that happens soon after their arrest.[14] Every business day, this district receives dozens of men and women who have been arrested for border-related offenses. After being processed into formal custody by the U.S. Marshals Service, defendants are sent within seventy-two hours to a magistrate court for an initial appearance. By this point, the sorting into either a flip-flop offer or individualized treatment has happened, and the magistrate judge formalizes the assignment by announcing to each defendant his or her charges and the next step in the adjudication process.

The subsequent hearing for those heading to flip-flop court will take place within a week, by which time the defendant will have spoken to an attorney and been informed of the offer in exchange for pleading guilty. The sentence to be agreed upon is determined solely by the assistant U.S. attorney. It is not up for negotiation with the defense, and neither the judge nor the probation office has a say in its calculation. The written plea offer requires the defendant to sign off on waiving trial and appeal rights, and the right to a presentence investigation and report, which would normally be conducted by pretrial probation officers prior to sentencing.

I observed a number of flip-flop court sessions during my time in Southwestern District. In each one that I observed, marijuana backpackers made up the majority of the caseload. Here's a typical session that I attended: twenty-eight defendants, twenty-six men and two women, were present for the 9:30 a.m. calendar, filling the jury box and several rows of the spectator section of the courtroom. All wore jail-issued jumpsuits and all were shackled. All but three were monolingual Spanish speakers; each was provided with headphones to hear the interpreter seated in the witness box who was there to translate the mass-processing ceremony.

"Each of you is charged with a felony and a misdemeanor or petty offense. You are here to plead guilty to the lesser offense," the judge announced to open the session. She followed with the competency ritual: "Has any of you had drugs, alcohol or prescription medication that will affect your ability to understand? If so, please stand." No one stood. "Let the record reflect that no one is standing." The judge moved on to confirm that the members of the group understood the rights they were waiving by pleading guilty, including the right to remain silent, to confront and call witnesses, to force the government to prove its case beyond a reasonable doubt, and to appeal the judgment. Again, no one stood when the judge asked those who did not understand to stand.

The stage was thus set for taking guilty pleas and imposing the predetermined sentences. The judge called up the defendants and their appointed attorneys in small groups, organized by offense type. The defendants lined up at a row of microphones in front of the judge's elevated bench, with their attorneys at their side. Most defense counsel in the room represented more than one defendant. Indeed, one attorney represented three of the defendants in the first group of seven. This group, six men and one woman, was pleading guilty to a petty offense of illegal entry in exchange for the dismissal of the felony illegal reentry charge.

In each round of the small group processing, the attorneys were first asked to confirm that their clients had been advised and understood the legal process they were undergoing. The attorneys in each round answered in unison, "Yes, Your Honor." Each defendant was then asked a series of yes or no questions to establish the factual basis for the guilty plea and to confirm that the plea was voluntary. Finally, they had to announce their guilt: "How do you plead today?" "Culpable" was the correct response, or "Guilty" for those few who spoke English. Everyone in the first group of illegal entry defendants received a sentence of 180 days. As is the routine, the group was then marched out of the courtroom into the U.S. Marshals' holding pen; they all dropped their headphones in a portable cart on their way out.

A single defendant, the second of the two women, followed the illegal entry group. She pleaded guilty to the misdemeanor charge of possession of a false ID, for which she received ninety-five days. The remaining defendants, all men, were there to plead guilty to simple possession of marijuana in exchange for dismissal of the possession with intent to distribute felony charge.[15] They were called up in three groups of five and one group of four. One of the men had been caught driving a car with thirty-five kilograms of marijuana; all the others were accused of carrying backpacks filled with twenty-one to twenty-seven kilograms of marijuana. Despite the offenses' appearing nearly identical—many of those arraigned had been arrested with each other and all ostensibly had no prior drug convictions—the imposed sentences ranged from sixty to two hundred forty days. Indeed, the defendant with the most weight, driving the car, was the only defendant who received sixty days.

This day, there were two flies in the ointment in an otherwise rapid, routinized process. In the second-to-last group, a very old man, when asked if he pleaded guilty to carrying twenty-one kilograms of marijuana, insisted he had not carried anything but "I signed that thing [the plea offer] so I can get going already" (translated by the court interpreter from Spanish to English). The judge informed him, "I can't take your guilty plea if you did not carry marijuana." "But I want to go." The old man was asked to step out of the group to talk further with his attorney. After the group guilty pleas were completed, he was brought up again. He still asked to be sentenced but still insisted he had not carried any marijuana. For that, the AUSA pulled the misdemeanor offer and the defendant was calendared to go the individual route—facing a sole felony count of marijuana possession with intent to distribute.

The second complication was a lone defendant who remained uncalled and unclaimed by any defense attorney at the end of the process. It turned out he had been brought to court with the group by mistake and was scheduled for a hearing a week later, so he was taken back to lockup, which was several hours away. Such was the nature of the mass-processing route that defendants occasionally ended up without lawyers, or in front of the wrong judge, or in court on the wrong day. Defendants who ended up in the wrong place were just taken away, to be returned once their appropriate spot in the assembly-line was established.

This flip-flop session resembled the others I observed. In each, the formal charges nominally distinguished the defendants as either drug-carrying border crossers or noncarrying ones, but their treatment and the sentence outcomes were relatively uniform across offense types. All those sentenced that day received relatively similar sentences and would eventually be subject to similar proceedings for removal after serving their sentences. The most common backpacking sentence that I observed in flip-flop court was 180 days, which was also the most common for illegal entry. To be clear, the 180 days represented the lowest sentence for flip-flop backpacker convictions, whereas it represented the highest sentence for flip-flop illegal entry convictions, but in general it served as the default sentence for both types of cases in my observations.

In flip-flop court, the defendants' status as outsiders whose cases simply needed to be processed quickly was, at times, reinforced by their defense attorneys. Before formal proceedings began they'd counsel their clients on the sequence of "correct" answers to the plea and sentencing colloquy ("sí"; "sí"; "sí"; "no") to get them through the ritual and on their way. In one hearing I watched, the appointed attorney joked with his client, before the judge came out, that he'd covertly point to the correct answer, "sí" or "no," on paper if the client got confused on the ordering. Everyone in the room, including the marshals, laughed.

Not all backpackers got the misdemeanor, mass-processing option; the determinative factor lay not with criminal conduct but with criminal history. That meant that sentence exposure is typically much greater for backpacking defendants who are not routed through flip-flop court to a conviction. The individualized process came with much more attention to particularized procedure, so in that sense it more closely resembles how drug cases are procedurally managed in the other districts. As with cases in the other districts, the change-of-plea proceeding in the non-flip-flop drug cases includes a full discussion of the elements of the negotiated plea agreement and the likely outcome at sentencing, in addition to a more detailed discussion of the defendant's rights that will be waived by pleading guilty. The probation office participates more fully as well, completing a pretrial investigation and report for sentencing in these cases. The defendant is provided a full-blown sentencing proceeding, in which both sides can file sentencing memoranda and present arguments to the judge. But it differs from other districts in substance quite significantly.

Just as in flip-flop cases, in individualized cases efficiency prevails as the overriding driver of plea negotiations and sentencing. Most drug cases in Southwestern District, like immigration cases, are eligible for a "fast-track" option that is not routinely available in nonborder federal district courts. Under this program, both illegal reentry and drug trafficking defendants are awarded an additional four-level reduction from the recommended sentencing guidelines if they accept the plea offer by a date the prosecutor specifies (usually within a few weeks or a month of their initial appearance) and forego pretrial motions, in addition to the standard waiving of rights that attends plea offers. This means that even the individualized cases come and go relatively quickly in this district; it also contributes to the exceptionally high rate of guilty pleas here.

Efficiency is also achieved by a heavy reliance on binding pleas as to sentence in this district. So in practice, sentencing is much more constrained and streamlined than in the other districts I studied. Judges routinely worked within the stipulated sentencing ranges; if they did not, the entire plea was at risk of unraveling. On a handful of occasions, I did observe a couple of different judges ask to sentence below the bottom of the stipulated range before they actually imposed sentences. They first asked the AUSA on the case whether the lower sentence would prompt them to withdraw from the deal. No prosecutor ever backed out.[16] Perhaps as a consequence of the reliance on binding pleas, written sentencing memos were infrequently filed in drug cases by either the defense or the prosecution. Both sides typically made an oral pitch of some sort at the sentencing proceeding, but the sentencing process was generally more streamlined and less contested here.

In terms of the prevailing adjudication narrative, in most of the individualized backpacking cases the logic of immigration enforcement and the need for defendants to stay out of the United States still infused the adjudication process. For instance, I watched the sentencing of a backpacker, Julio Soto, who had entered into a binding plea agreement that specified a twenty-four-to-thirty-month prison sentence. The judge opened the hearing by reviewing the plea agreement with the parties. He turned to Mr. Soto to tell him, "Normally you'd get six months for backpacking, but this option is not available to you since you've been in trouble before." After the defense attorney, defendant, and prosecutor made their respective statements, the judge pronounced sentence.

The pronouncement revealed how much the case was about Mr. Soto's unauthorized immigration status rather than about the problem of drug trafficking. The judge told Mr. Soto, "You have been removed six times already. You cannot come back." He then posed a question for which there was clearly no correct answer: "What makes you think that coming back this time with marijuana would work out?" Mr. Soto tried to explain, "The situation is so bad in Mexico, I thought I could make some money." The judge then recited all of the time that Mr. Soto had already spent in custody. "How does that help your family? No matter how bad things are in Mexico, you make more there than when you are here in prison." Formal sentencing then ensued. The judge imposed a sentence of twenty-four months in prison, followed by a three-year period of supervision. He made clear to Mr. Soto how this sentence would affect his future should he ever be caught in the United States again. "You now have an aggravated felony, which means you will face ninety-two to one hundred fifteen months at the least if you come back here for *any* reason."

This sentence paved the way for a future of hard prison time for Mr. Soto if he is caught back in the country. Most sentencing judges counseled defendants about those future consequences as they warned against returning to the United States. I saw this same judge caution another backpacker, who had lived in the state for a long time with his wife and three children but who was now in a deportation-return-punishment-removal cycle, about what would happen to him the next time he came back. It was the defendant's second backpacking conviction, for which the judge had just imposed forty-three months. At the conclusion of the proceeding, the judge said that next time, "you will be a career offender, and could spend a lifetime in prison. You cannot come back."

The judge's threats are not idle. In a backpacker sentencing proceeding that took place the same week but in front of a different judge, the defendant, Adolfo Torres-Ortiz, had just pleaded guilty to a third backpacking offense, which exposed him to that lengthy career offender sentence. Mr. Torres-Ortiz, had been arrested by border patrol just on the U.S. side of the border in Southwestern District. He was one of four from a group of eight marijuana backpackers apprehended; the other four escaped but left behind their backpacks. This was Mr. Torres-Ortiz's third conviction for backpacking marijuana in ten years. Because his prior convictions had occurred before the flip-flop policy change, they served as predicate convictions under the career offender guidelines. So while Mr. Torres-Ortiz's codefendants in the case went to flip-flop court, where they likely received six-month sentences, he faced 188 to 235 months if sentenced as a career offender. Even with fast-track, the guideline sentence range was still 130 to 162 months, so he would have to serve nearly eleven years in prison if sentenced at the low end, prior to his removal from the country.

He also faced an additional 6 to 12 months for a supervision violation, since he came back this time while under supervised release. His sentence could potentially be twenty times that of each of his fellow backpackers, who were in flip-flop court.

This sentencing exposure was distressing to all sides—the defense, the prosecutor, and the judge—at the sentencing proceeding. The defense attorney began his argument speaking on behalf of his client and the prosecutor. He asserted that in constructing the binding plea agreement, "We *collectively* felt that the career offender guidelines overstate culpability in this case." He was brief in his comments, allowing the prosecutor to make the case for a sentence well below the guideline range.

The prosecutor began by saying he "echoes" the defense, and that he had never seen anything like this, which will lead to a "wildly disproportionate" result if the defendant is sentenced under the career offender enhancement. He asserted, "This is not what the career offender guideline was made for" and suggested to the judge that the sentencing guidelines should be calculated using straight criminal history rather than as enhanced criminal history. He explained that this is what the stipulated plea agreement set out to do, and urged the judge to accept the terms. He then talked about the mechanics of how the judge could make this plea agreement look appropriate on the record—whether the calculus proposed should be labeled a variance or whether it is a departure, since the criminal history "over-represents" culpability. Finally, he explained that since the defendant had pleaded guilty to conspiracy to traffic marijuana, the drug weight attributable to him is the total found in all eight backpacks, so 226 kilograms.

The judge was in full agreement with the attorneys. She accepted the plea agreement on the record but pointed out that owing to the drug quantity there was a five-year mandatory minimum below which she could not sentence Mr. Torres-Ortiz. With all agreeing that this was not a career offender case, the parties then proceeded to make the case for their respective recommendations on sentence. The defense requested a total of sixty-three to sixty-six months for the current offense and the supervision violation. The defendant then apologized to the court and explained that he came back to help his ailing mother, who is his last remaining parent: "I am very remorseful for what I did. I did it for my mother." The prosecutor asked that the supervised release violation sentence run consecutive to the sentence for the new conviction but reiterated that for "justice," the sentence should be below the calculated guidelines.

Now it was the judge's turn. She admonished the defendant: "You really messed up coming back here. You can expect to spend your adult life in prison if you keep doing this. It hurts you and your family." She pronounced a sentence of sixty-three months on the new conviction, and six months to be served consecutive to that for the supervised release violation, plus a *new* term of four years of supervised release to follow the incarceration.

For those defendants with some legal status in the country, the inter-woven logics of exclusion and punishment were often messier than for the undocumented. Among the noncitizen defendants, legal residents were often the most rooted on the U.S. side of the border and they had the most to lose as a result of drug felony convictions. They were also more likely to have enough generally low-level criminal history to preclude the mis-demeanor option that the flip-flop candidates received. Therefore, their convictions were more punitive in two ways: through the direct punish-ment that came with the conviction and through the stripping of opportu-nity to stay in the United States, where some had been for decades. Even those with border-crossing cards had amplified punishment, especially when they relied on their crossing rights for legally permitted business opportunities on this side of the border. Losing that privilege could have significant economic consequences for them and their families.

In general, these defendants were less likely to be backpackers and more likely to be mechanized mules, since their immigration status often allowed them to come and go through legal ports of entry and move around more openly on the U.S. side. A subset of mechanized mules were U.S.-born citizens, like Abraham, for whom the consequence of a drug conviction is limited to the criminal punishment and non-immigration-related collateral sanctions, since it does not impact their status as citizens. Otherwise, the majority of these couriers held a status for which the con-viction would potentially foreclose the possibility of ever legally reenter-ing or residing in the United States. And because they were transporting the illicit goods in vehicles, they were typically caught with much higher quantities of drugs than the backpackers, so mandatory minimums could be a significant factor at sentencing.

The felony calendars were littered with these kinds of defendants, who were low on the totem pole of the overall drug operation, but who poten-tially faced very long sentences. Typically these couriers reported that they were promised anywhere from five hundred to several thousand dollars for their participation in the drug trafficking offense.[17] Coming across the border seemed to generate higher pay than acting as a courier within the United States, but the risks of getting caught were there either way. At ports of entry, border enforcement has broad power to search people and vehicles passing through, so opportunities for detection of drugs are ample.[18] Those powers reach well into the interior of the coun-try too; immigration authorities have enforcement powers that extend one hundred miles in from the border. Border patrol routinely maintains "border checkpoints" on roadways within that hundred-mile zone, and many of the couriers I saw in court had been caught at these interior checkpoints. Drug-detecting dogs at ports of entry and checkpoints sniff out the contraband, which might be packed in the door panels, the gear-shift box, under the body of the vehicle, or in some other compartment of the car.

I watched thirty-five-year-old Ramiro Menéndez get sentenced for driving about 6 kilograms of methamphetamine through a border port of entry. Mr. Menéndez was not a citizen but had been in the United States since he was a child, and at the time of his bust he had legal status to be in the country. He was married to a U.S. citizen, and they had three U.S.-born kids, ranging in age from eight to eighteen. Despite his long history in the United States, he had no criminal record, which helped mitigate the terms of his punishment. But for him, the worst part was the near-inevitable deportation that would follow the criminal punishment. He ended up with a very generous plea agreement. He was given reductions for fast-track, safety valve, minimal role in the operation, and for providing substantial assistance, even though the prosecutor admitted this was more of a "pity" offering, since the defendant had been unable to produce any usable information for law enforcement.[19]

The sentencing hearing highlighted the punishing element of deportation for Mr. Menéndez. The prosecutor was the first to make this point. Arguing that the defendant deserved leniency at sentencing—he asked for a forty-one-month sentence—the AUSA described how the defendant had been in the country since he was a child, and was "integrated in American culture so deportation will be punitive, even though it is not a formal punishment." Mr. Menéndez's attorney fleshed out a picture of his client's family life in the United States. He argued that the criminal actions were aberrant and arose from a desperate financial crisis resulting from health problems faced by his client's wife and father. The defense attorney also pointed out the costs this conviction would exact from his family.

Mr. Menéndez's wife was then given an opportunity to speak. Through tears, she described her husband as an "awesome husband and father," a coach for the kids' sports teams, and a role model for his oldest daughter, who was about to graduate from high school. The judge interrupted to tell her, "No matter what sentence he gets, he *will* be deported." She responded by assuring the judge that she will move to the border, and work on the U.S. side while her husband stays on the Mexico side to live and work. Once it was his turn, Mr. Menéndez apologized to the court and to his family for the hurt he caused and begged for a second chance so that he could see his daughter graduate.

The judge then pronounced sentence. He first scolded Mr. Menéndez for smuggling that huge amount of methamphetamine into the country and for making the decision to destroy other people's families to help his own desperate financial situation. Nonetheless, he imposed only thirty-one months, which he said "is very much on the low end of what I have given. Only once have I given a lower sentence" for this kind of case. Perhaps recognizing that for Mr. Menéndez, deportation would be especially punishing, he calibrated down the formal punishment.

Some of these defendants adamantly denied knowing about the illicit substances packed in the cars they were driving. Others said they were told the contraband was marijuana, but their cars were instead packed with more serious drugs, like methamphetamine. But they had an uphill battle mounting a defense that they did not know what was in the car. The government readily attacked such claims as "willful ignorance," and a jury trial came with the risk of considerable exposure on sentencing. I was in court when a young woman who was a U.S. citizen, Amelia Flores, had a detention hearing after being arrested at a checkpoint while driving her aunt's car. Agents were alerted by the drug-detection dog at the checkpoint that the vehicle was suspicious. Upon searching it, the agents found a total of ninety-nine kilograms of marijuana taped to the undercarriage and hidden in the door panels. Although the amount of marijuana was below the threshold for flip-flop eligibility, Ms. Flores faced a felony because she had a record of low-level driving and drug possession misdemeanor priors.

At Ms. Flores's detention hearing, the judge agreed to release Ms. Flores to a drug treatment program while her case was pending. Later that afternoon she happened to be at the bus stop outside the courthouse, waiting to be picked up by the drug program, where I also waited. She told me that her aunt had lent her the car so she could go to a medical appointment in the city, fifty miles north of her border-adjacent town. She was furious with her aunt, who she felt had set her up as a blind mule to move the marijuana north. But, she told me, she would not go to trial because it was "too risky" on sentence. Her lawyer had assured her she would get a lenient sentence if she did well in the drug program, so she planned to plead guilty. Four months later, she pled guilty and was ultimately sentenced to thirteen months, significantly lower than the sixty-three months she potentially faced after trial.

For U.S. citizens convicted and sentenced for their part in moving drugs, the adjudication narratives more closely resembled drug cases in the non-border districts, in that the defendant's psychological deficiencies and needs were often debated. For Ms. Flores, her substance abuse was both recognized and addressed as part of the legal process. A sentencing I observed, of a 22-year-old man who was in the army and in uniform when he was caught driving 114 kilograms of marijuana across the border, is also illustrative. The defense attorney opened the discussion by referencing the developmental psychologist Erik Erikson, best known for his theory of psychosocial development. "My client is in Erik Erikson's 'moratorium stage,' where he is trying to figure himself out. He was in a bar off the base, and he was stressed. He owes $23,000 in federal loans and was baited into delivering more than 200 pounds of marijuana for a little extra cash."[20]

The judge, too, probed his psychology. "Why did you join the military?" The defendant said he had joined up to make a better life for himself and his family. He expressed his love for country, and his deep shame in disgracing it by transporting drugs while in uniform. The judge then turned to the prosecutor, "I am inclined to vary slightly [below the stipulated plea agreement] to twenty-four months. If I do, will you withdraw the plea agreement?" "No." With that, he was sentenced to twenty-four months.

The more robust concern with the citizen-defendant's personhood cut both ways, though. In a four-defendant case, the sentencing of the lead defendant more closely resembled those in Southeast District than peer cases within this district. The four young men involved were U.S.-born locals, all white men, who worked for a cartel to coordinate and orchestrate picking up the marijuana brought across the border by backpackers. Three of the four had previously been convicted in federal court, as codefendants, on fraud charges stemming from a theft ring they were involved in. Once released from prison, the three moved into the marijuana transportation business. The fourth defendant had been hired as a driver, so he was new to the group.

The ringleader of this subcontracting operation, twenty-five-year-old William Hopkins, was the relay person, who would direct drivers to the location of newly arrived backpackers when he got word from his bosses across the border as to where the backpackers were. The other three got their hands dirtier by renting and driving transport cars. Hopkins pleaded guilty first, and was to be sentenced by the same judge who had presided over his previous fraud conviction and supervised release violation. To facilitate the plea agreement in this case, the judge had authorized Mr. Hopkins's release from custody to "work" for the government as a cooperator. Instead of working, though, Mr. Hopkins got right back into the drug trafficking business. Needless to say, the opportunity for a sentence reduction disappeared. And the judge was not a fan.

Seeing the writing on the wall, Mr. Hopkins tried to withdraw his plea. He told the judge he thought that his plea agreement had a sixty-month cap, when in fact it specified that the sentence could fall anywhere from no time in prison to forty years maximum.[21] The judge did not believe him. "You are telling me, Mr. Hopkins, you didn't understand that agreement? When I let you out of prison per that plea agreement you are telling me this morning you don't understand it?" Denying both his request to withdraw his plea and his request to delay sentencing, the judge was more explicit about his assessment of Mr. Hopkins as he prepared to impose sentence.

Judge: Do you want to say anything regarding your sentence to be imposed?

Hopkins: Other than the fact I didn't understand the plea agreement? Your Honor, I made a lot of mistakes. You have seen me twice; you have seen me on my last previous case. I had every intention of doing good this time.

Judge: I have seen you enough, Mr. Hopkins, not to believe a word you say.

Hopkins: I also understand my credibility is shot in this courtroom. But I am—

Judge: Do you have something you would like to say regarding the sentence to be imposed?

Hopkins: As far as how much time?

Judge: Yes.

Hopkins: I would ask for the minimum [interlude with both attorneys and judge discussing terms].

Judge: Well, I am considering the guidelines as an advisory sentence, Mr. Hopkins, and then trying to determine whether there is a reason in the guidelines to depart from that range, and I can't identify any factor. . . . A criminal sentence must promote respect for the law; provide just punishment; provide a deterrence, not just to you but to others. . . . [It] must be a protection of the community. And I think that you are just a career offender. You cannot be trusted out in our community. I can't believe anything you say. You steal from people. This court releases you in a position of trust to cooperate in the prosecution of criminal activity and, of course, you go out and engage in criminal activity yourself for your own benefit and your own profit, so I think to protect the community you need to be incarcerated; you need to be locked up.

With that, the judge imposed a sentence of 210 months on Mr. Hopkins.[22] Notwithstanding Mr. Hopkins's very long sentence for his part in moving marijuana, Southwestern District looks like the friendliest one to drug defendants, at least in comparison to both Northeastern and Southeast. Prosecutors occasionally partner with defense attorneys to sell judges on below-guidelines stipulated sentences, fast-track discounts are unusual added breaks for drug defendants, and judges generally go along with the generous plea offers, and even sometimes push to go lower. Yet there are hidden costs here that make the fair-and-just adjudication calculus very different from the other districts'. Most significant—less apparent in open court but an ominous undercurrent of most drug cases in

Southwestern District—was the threat of violence by the major profiteers of the region's drug market: the cartels.

This threat worked in two ways: as a compelling force that brought many couriers and mules into the business in the first place, and to suppress cooperation with the government among those caught and prosecuted. Its presence meant that the cases as they appear on the books are not the same as how they actually develop and play out in the lives of many who get entangled in the drug trade here. From a distance, the large numbers of couriers in this district appeared to be making purely economic decisions to move drugs for cash or other benefits. To be sure, many couriers had life circumstances such as extreme financial pressures that pushed them into becoming one-shot or occasional drug couriers. Still, at first glance the drug business in the district looked like a market, with market-based wages based on calculated risks and commitments.[23]

But it was anything but for many of those who got involved. The choice to participate or not hardly resembled the legitimate labor market. Stories abounded about how people were coerced into participating, through threats of harm to loved ones, or tricked into transporting drugs through subterfuge. And once caught, most low-level defendants were under implicit or explicit threats of violence to plead guilty quickly and quietly and take their punishment, in order to avoid even the appearance of cooperation with the government. So snitching was relatively infrequent here, compared to the other districts. Put simply, cooperation came with lethal risks. A defender in the district shared a story that exemplified both sides of this pervasive undercurrent of violence:

> I've got a case right now that is just so heartbreaking. It's a lawful permanent resident, older guy, caught at the border, bunch of drugs. He says he was forced to do it. And I'm hearing that story more and more often, by the way. He was basically kidnapped, held for three days while they fixed up his car and hid it, loaded it in, and made him do it. And he didn't want to do it.
>
> He got caught at the border and subsequently, his wife and two young children were murdered. Grisly, just brutally executed. And we can't prove that it was connected to this, but the way they were killed—I mean, we've seen the death certificates and it's so clearly a cartel sending a message to somebody for something.[24]

The attorney tried hard to get the case dismissed, but the prosecutor refused. The defendant was afraid to go to trial because if convicted, a ten-year mandatory minimum (and even higher guidelines calculations) would kick in, and the safety valve and other reductions would disappear. The prosecutor was sympathetic and offered an additional reduction for "imperfect duress" as an acknowledgement of the circumstances, but the defendant would still be deported after completing his sentence. This was potentially a death sentence. "He's scared to death to go back to Mexico. He figures he's the last piece of the puzzle, you know? [That] they'll be looking for him next."

Several attorneys described for me the world in which their clients became involved in transporting drugs; those with border-crossing rights were especially vulnerable to duress. The threats were sometimes subtle, and the evidence supporting the defendants' accounts was often limited to their own word, so even if true, trials were risky. As one federal defender explained to me, their clients are typically dirt-poor, living in tightly knit communities that straddle the border. There is little way to escape when a cartel employee approaches and makes clear, "I know where you live. I know where your sixteen-year-old daughter goes to school. I know where your grandma gets her medical treatments. I can find you really easily."[25] Yet, she explained, juries had a hard time understanding the different world in which the defendants got roped in. "Do you want to take your shot with upper middle class, white, male retirees from [the suburbs]?"

Occasionally cooperation did happen in this district, but it was widely acknowledged by all the actors that the risks were great. As one defender put it, "It goes without saying that when you cooperate against these horrible organizations, you're basically putting your life on the line."[26] Another put it even more bluntly. "It's just common knowledge that the cartels kill. They'll kill everybody. They'll kill your whole family and you just to send a message."[27] The cartels could also enforce financial sanctions. For example, I observed several cases involving defendants with priors who had become involved again because, they said, they were forced to work to pay back the cartels for what they had lost on their earlier arrest. So not only did they face steeper penalties in court, their freedom once out was constrained by their financial debts to the cartels.

These pressures meant that cooperation patterns were somewhat bifurcated. Those who were citizens and whose families were in the United States were more likely to cooperate, since they had slightly better insulation and protection from the cartels. Those destined to be deported and those with families across the border were the least likely to cooperate, even if they had information to give. No matter what, the cartels' role ensured that, like Abraham's uncle, cooperators rolled on people below them before people above them. It was less risky, but ultimately it solidified the power structures that undergirded the entire illicit drug market at the border.

The second fundamental challenge to justice in this district was the efficiency imperative. There was immense pressure on defendants to resolve their cases quickly through a guilty plea, without the opportunity to fully vet the evidence against them, which is itself complicated by the fact that these cases live on both sides of the border. Prosecutors' biggest bargaining stick was the exploding offer, with the clock ticking for defendants to sign on the dotted line before the deal disappears. The most extreme form of this imperative was in the backpacker cases assigned to flip-flop court. Cases there had a lifespan of days rather than months. Defendants had to waive all procedures, including discovery and a presentence investigation, and they had to agree to plead guilty and be sentenced by the magistrate at the first proceeding after their initial appearance.

Even the individual fast-track offers here generally either implicitly or explicitly required defendants to waive rights to obtain evidence, pursue various hearing options, and access other basic requirements that are fundamental to adequate representation. Most of these offers came through the fast-track program, yet as a consequence of this structured norm, even cases outside of the program faced pressures to be resolved quickly and without defendants' pursuit of basic legal rights in order to get a beneficial outcome.

Indeed, in one of the offices in Southwestern District, prosecutors issued a contract that defenders were supposed to sign, requiring them to waive the probable cause hearing in order to receive discovery materials.[28] The contract allows the prosecution to hold back some evidence, and includes six additional conditions that the defense must meet in order to receive the materials without litigation. Failure to sign meant the defendant was excluded from participation in any expedited program, and it also meant the defense attorney had no evidence, prior to having the judge order its release, on which to assess the case and advise the client about whether to take the offer. In other words, it was a forced choice if defendants wanted to pursue early disposition offers, or even get a sense of the case in a timely manner. In the end, the cost of not going along quickly meant forfeiting the deep sentencing discounts associated with the expedited plea programs. And of course the high sentencing ceilings that are possible in drug cases ensured that all the punitive hammers could be pulled out of the toolkit for those defendants who did not accept the deals.

Finally, the proceedings detailed here highlight how the mandates of immigration enforcement undergird and shape adjudication practices in this border district. First, in the vast majority of individualized proceedings involving noncitizens, the in-court colloquies centered on the defendant's status as an excludable outsider. All parties focused in on the fact that the defendant had to stay out of the United States in order to be law-abiding in the future.[29] The sentences imposed on noncitizen drug trafficking defendants were justified as a deterrent to their returning (rather than to their transporting drugs), either this time around or, if the defendant came back, in future encounters. The message was reinforced by the use of special sentence terms, such as thirteen months and a day, which legally ensure sentenced defendants' future expulsion, exclusion, and enhanced punishment if they return.

Even in flip-flop court, where there was little to no individualized colloquy and where the sentences serve less as future deterrents, the practices marked the processed defendants as essentially of a single category of excludable subjects. Each was one of a flood of only nominally criminal border crossers who had to be dealt with as efficiently and expeditiously as possible so that they could do their assigned time in prison and then be removed from the country. The flip-flop backpackers carried illicit drugs but were otherwise indistinguishable from the other men and women picked up in the same desert. These defendants were nearly anonymous (even though identified by name in court) and could garner individualized engagement only when they went against the heavy pressure to plead and refused to take the deal.

Although the defendants here may have received what appear to be lenient sentences, at least relative to the sentences meted out for drug trafficking in the nonborder districts, this does not mean that these defendants' treatment was somehow more just or even too soft. Many of the cases at the nexus of immigration and drugs mask a whole host of globalized tragedies. Those caught at the border, with and without drugs, are all too often themselves victims of a number of punishing forces that attended their migration: the economic catastrophes in their home countries that pushed them north in the first place; the increased cost to safely make it across the border, including being compelled to carry drugs for coyotes and cartels; and the increasing incidence of families on both sides of the border being torn apart as a collateral consequence of the more recent American war on immigration.

═ Chapter 6 ═

Inducing the Plea:
Strategic Uses of Legal Power

According to the late legal scholar William Stuntz, the "collapse of criminal justice" in the United States is partly a consequence of our constitutional elevation of procedural limits on the government—primarily through our Fifth and Sixth Amendment rights in the criminal context—above limits to substantive criminal law. Stuntz observed, "Using procedures to defeat defendant-protective substantive law is difficult, but using substantive law to evade or nullify protective procedures is remarkably easy" for the government to do.[1] This paradox is no more evident than in the government's on-the-ground deployment of federal drug laws, as we saw in each of the districts I examined. The substantive law that prosecutors had at their disposal was wielded in distinct ways, but always with the force to nullify procedural protections along the way.

In this system, according to Kate Stith and Jose Cabranes, "[The] Sentencing Guidelines effectively function as an adjunct to the substantive criminal statutes enacted by Congress."[2] Indeed, a multitude of substantive legal weapons, some overlapping and multiplicative, can be used to overwhelm procedural rights. Defendants' ability to assess evidence, to challenge it, and to hold the government to its burden of proving guilt beyond a reasonable doubt can be obliterated by the sheer punitive force of the array of legal hammers in the prosecution's toolbox.

The power to punish is neither static nor autonomous from the humans who occupy the organizations that constitute the criminal justice system. The three case studies demonstrated the powerful and creative ways that statutes and guidelines can be deployed in pursuit of convictions and long sentences. In each site, the end goal was substantially the same—the defendant submits to a conviction—but the process to get there was shaped by localized norms and imperatives. The law's coercive power was activated and mobilized through socio-legal relations and could take multiple forms, depending on the particular circumstances of a given case, the particular configurations of legal actors, and the particular idiocultures—the "system[s] of knowledge, beliefs, behaviors, and customs"—that make up the local worlds in which these actors work.[3]

Therefore, the differential, and excessive, deployment of that power cannot and should not simply be understood as the actions of good or evil actors. To be sure, we all bring our own dispositions, personalities, viewpoints, and experiential knowledge to whatever roles we embody in our occupational and social lives. But the structures and contexts in which we operate also compel or constrain our action. A large body of social psychological research has demonstrated that situational forces often have more explanatory power than dispositional factors on social behavior.[4] For example, classic experimental studies have demonstrated the power of situational influences to induce conformity, even when the conformer knows he is agreeing to an incorrect conclusion; obedience, even when it appears to involve subjecting others to torture and harm; and helping (or declining to help) strangers in need of assistance.[5] Such studies have also demonstrated how social and institutional context can breed sustained abuses of power.[6]

In federal courts, the harms bred by the imbalance of power is hands-off, from a distance, and dressed in formal legal niceties. This makes them harder to recognize than the blood-and-guts brutality that comes with excessive use of force by police on the streets or by correctional officers behind bars. But it is no less troubling when the power to punish is wielded against defendants like Devon Harrison so that exercising their right to trial ends up costing them their freedom for the rest of their natural lives. The legal transformations of the 1980s produced conditions that allow for such power overindulgences to flourish, and those conditions then structured day-to-day practices in district courts around the nation.

National statistics—and the case specifics that I have detailed in the previous three chapters demonstrate that those changes pushed almost all federal drug defendants to enter guilty pleas to resolve their cases, even though they faced longer sentences than ever. In 1984, just before the introduction of the Sentencing Guidelines, approximately 75 percent of federal drug defendants whose cases were fully adjudicated forewent a trial and pleaded guilty. In 2013 more than 97 percent pleaded guilty to resolve their cases.[7] While trial rates increased for a few years at the beginning of the Guidelines era, over time fewer and fewer drug defendants have taken on the risk of going to trial, which generally exposed them to much harsher penalties if and when they were convicted (see figure 6.1).[8]

The so-called "trial penalty" became so extraordinarily high under the transformed legal regime that even those defendants with equivocal cases were discouraged from asserting this right.[9] In 2012, for instance, federal drug defendants who were convicted at trial received an average sentence of sixteen years, triple the average for drug defendants who

Figure 6.1   Percentage of All Adjudicated Drug Cases Resolved by Guilty
Plea, 1965 to 2013

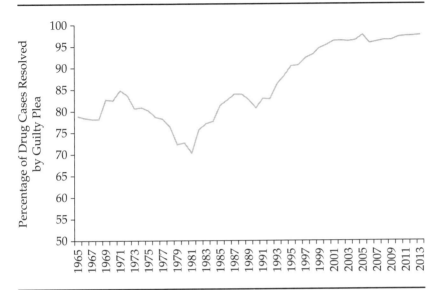

Source: Author's compilation. Data for 1965 to 2010 is based on University at Albany,
Sourcebook of Criminal Justice Statistics, table 5.37.2010. Data for 2011 to 2013 is based on
Federal Judicial Caseload Statistics, table D4.

pleaded guilty.[10] The chances of acquittal on drug charges are slim and
have diminished over time. About 88 percent of drug defendants who
have asserted their right to trial in the Sentencing Guidelines era have
been convicted (see figure 6.2). And it is not the case that drug defendants are offered particularly generous plea offers in exchange for their
guilty pleas; rather, prosecutors can make it so much worse for those, like
Devon Harrison, who do not go along with the offer made.

What the case specifics show as the statistics cannot are the micro-
mechanics as to *how* federal drug cases come to be resolved with a plea.
The answer to the "how" question lies in the multiple ways that federal prosecutors, especially in drug cases, wield their power to ratchet
up defendants' sentencing exposure and throw down the hammer when
defendants do not go along. In this system defendants face "an offer you
can't refuse," as a recent Human Rights Watch report put it.[11]

Central to any plea bargaining system is the notion of exchange.[12]
Prosecutors may alter or reduce the number of charges or agree to a discounted sentence in exchange for the certainty of the outcome that comes
with a guilty plea and for the assurance that there will be no appeal of the

Figure 6.2   Mode of Resolution for All Adjudicated Drug Cases, 1965 to 2013

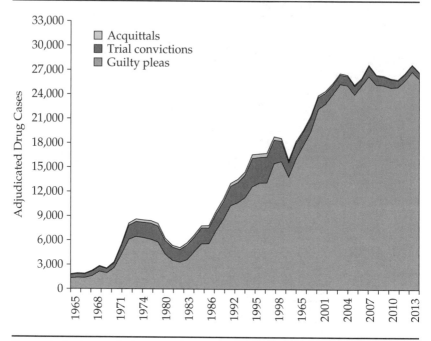

Source: Author's compilation. Data for 1965 to 2010 is based on University at Albany, Sourcebook of Criminal Justice Statistics, table 5.37.2010. Data for 2011 to 2013 is based on Federal Judicial Caseload Statistics, table D4.

resulting conviction. To benefit from the reduced charges or discounted sentence outcome the defendant typically waives all of his or her Fifth and Sixth Amendment rights, including the right to refrain from self-incrimination, to confront witnesses, call witnesses, testify, and appeal final judgment. In this way the decision resembles a cost-benefit analysis of the defendant's relative "exposure": What are the costs of rejecting a plea offer and proceeding to trial as compared to the chance of obtaining acquittal or other benefit that might come through litigation?

In state courts, defendants usually have two advantages in the nego-tiation process that are much rarer in federal court. First, sheer caseload pressure in typical state courts can produce plea offers in which the guilty plea discounts are significant, relative to the likely sentence on the original charges. In some sense, that helps explain the relatively generous offers in Southwestern District, where caseload pressure is so much higher than in most nonborder districts. In state court, the offers also tend to afford some certainty to the defendant since there are generally semi-standardized sentences for typical offenses, which removes some of the risk of pleading guilty. And in many state-level "courtroom workgroups," the crush of cases may lead judges, in routine cases, to actively pressure both the prosecutor and the defense to negotiate plea agreements.[13] This pressure further encourages conciliatory offers by prosecutors.[14]

Second, and at least as significant, is the matter of case quality. State courts process the bulk of cases that begin with local law enforcement arrests, and these cases are quite variable in the strength of their evidence. Criminal cases may fall out of the system at any number of points, including via an initial decision not to file charges or through prosecutor- or judge-initiated dismissals.[15] In those cases that do proceed defense attorneys can leverage weaknesses in the evidence to obtain better deals for their clients.[16] The defense attorney may well waive time and let cases drag out for strategic reasons, which can result in the loss of witnesses or decayed quality of witness accounts.[17] Defense attorneys may also impose on prosecutors' time (while also testing the quality of the evidence) through the filing of motions, demands for discovery, evidentiary hearings, and the like.

Finally, in state courts, once a guilty plea is rendered through negotiations, nonconvicted alleged criminal conduct typically disappears and has no influence on subsequent sentencing proceedings. In other words, if a defendant agrees to plead guilty, say, to a simple misdemeanor drug possession punishable by no more than a year in jail, the judge will not hold her accountable for the felony conduct underlying the original drug distribution charge once it has been bargained away.

These conditions are not typical of plea negotiations in most federal courts. First off, the caseload pressures in the federal system are much lighter than in the state system. The average judge in all state trial-level courts received 1,780 new nontraffic civil and criminal cases in 2010.[18] In federal courts, district court judges received an average of 523 new nonpetty civil and criminal cases.[19] Judges in the federal system also closely adhere to the prohibition on participating in plea negotiations; their role is limited to open-court formal plea acceptance or rejection.[20]

And because of the doubly discretionary nature of most federal drug prosecutions, the cases that assistant U.S. attorneys charge in federal court are typically ones with compelling evidence that prosecutors are motivated to pursue. Thus, defense efforts to test the evidence may not be as strategic in federal court. In short, federal prosecutors are not generally in the business of bringing weak cases. Rather, as a defender I interviewed said, they bring "the pick of the litter" cases. And since federal drug defendants are by and large detained in custody while their cases wind through the court process—more than three-quarters are locked up during this period—there is pressure on defendants to resolve the case and move on.[21] Thus, defense attorneys have fewer tools available to work with in negotiating favorable outcomes for their clients.

Moreover, because of the extreme imbalance in tools and techniques available in the federal system, the prosecutor's easiest course of action, non-action, is among the most powerful modes of obtaining a punitive outcome. The baseline charges and collateral relevant conduct, especially for those with prior records, will trigger long sentences under the guidelines, so without a negotiated plea, the starting point at sentencing will often reflect the worst-case scenario for the defendant. One defense attorney explained to me, "A big difference between state practice and federal practice is [that] in the state system . . . a lazy prosecutor was your best friend. The less they did the better, and the better for your client. In the federal system, in order to make something positive happen for your client, a prosecutor has to work harder. They have to be proactive. They have to go and convince somebody up the line that this is a good result."[22]

More fundamentally, prosecutors in the federal system have an exceptionally easy job of proving drug cases, given how the elements of the underlying charges are defined. Added to this is the case selection process in regard to so-called offender characteristics. Many defendants have come to federal court not because of the scope of the offense alone (or at all) but because of their prior criminal record, which, it turns out, adds a powerful tool for the prosecutor to wield in compelling a guilty plea.

Prosecutors also have a powerful weapon to obtain pleas in the form of "relevant conduct." Due to the construction of the federal sentencing guidelines, which is a modified "real-offense" sentencing system, alleged criminal conduct can be taken into account in sentenced defendants' guideline calculations, even when the conduct is not charged or has been acquitted.[23] In other words, defendants can be and are sentenced for behavior for which they did not plead guilty. Even in the context of a plea agreement, it can be exceptionally difficult to contain the impact of relevant conduct on the final sentence. Indeed, the U.S. Sentencing Commission estimated that over 60 percent of defendants sentenced in fiscal year 2012 were subject to adjustments to the Sentencing Guidelines range as a result of "relevant conduct" factors above and beyond the conviction offenses.[24]

All of this makes plea bargaining in federal drug cases a lopsided affair, and one filled with considerable uncertainty for the defendant as to what the actual sanction will be. Again, Southwestern was an outlier on this. There was the regular use of binding pleas in Southwestern District: the defense and prosecution agreed to specific facts and sentence outcome terms, which the judge then either accepted or rejected.[25] But outside Southwestern District, binding pleas were much less common and were almost always a deal with the devil from the defense's standpoint in that they frequently required agreeing to less favorable terms than might be possible to obtain if sentencing were left to the judge.

So "exposure" in federal drug cases is typically fraught with danger, made worse if the defendant does not go along with the prosecutor's imperatives. The risk of asserting rights in this system can be measured in years and sometimes even decades of added prison time. Ultimately, the answer to why almost all federal drug defendants plead guilty to charges that often result in very long prison sentences lies in the specific ways that prosecutors wield the multiple accumulated modes of power to dramatically increase defendant exposure. In fact, the same factors that have landed many drug defendants in federal court in the first place also propel negotiations around guilty pleas, including prior criminal record, "relevant conduct," and the assumed information that law enforcement expects to get out of the defendant.

The way these tools are wielded and the specific values that inhere in them varied among the distinct court settings I examined. Nonetheless, in each site they constitute the hammer and nails of the prosecutors' toolkit in the plea bargaining process. And in each site, the "exchange" that is central to the notion of negotiation is very one-sided: the prosecutor generally gives up little other than a promise not to make things even worse than they already stand for the defendant, whereas the defendant gives up a panoply of rights and submits to serious penalties at sentencing.

My interviews with multiple defense attorneys in the three districts shed additional light on the coercive tactics underlying the plea process. I asked defenders what each side gives up in plea negotiations. Across the board, the general consensus was that prosecutors gave up little in the exchange. For instance, in all three districts defendants had to agree to waive their right to appeal the conviction or sentence, but AUSAs did not give up their right to appeal: as a matter of course, prosecutors retained the right to appeal if they had a beef with the judge's sentence. A federal defender in Northeastern District told me, "I don't know that I've had prosecutors need to give up much of anything in drug cases."[26] A defender in Southeast District said, "Negotiation is almost a misnomer in federal court. . . . The deck is stacked too much against clients to take any risks in federal court. There's not that much to negotiate."[27] The prosecutors I spoke to concurred that what they typically gave up was the ability to make things even worse for the defendant, while acknowledging how much power they held even after the plea.

The exception to this extreme power imbalance was in Southwestern District, where the discounts offered in exchange for quick resolution are often significant. This is especially the case in the courts that process the bulk of border-related cases. Here, unlike the proactive quest to bring selected drug defendants into federal courts—the primary operational approach in the other districts in my study—drug cases often come to federal court in connection with immigration enforcement, and their discovery is often happenstance within the broader border enforcement regime. As a result, drug defendants in several typologies of cases in this district—especially the "backpackers"—receive offers that are relatively equivalent to those charged strictly with illegal reentry immigration violations. These cases have no real equivalent in the other districts, at least in terms of the guilty plea process and negotiated outcomes.

In many senses, then, the way cases are handled in Southwestern District has much more in common with state criminal courts than with nonborder federal courts. For instance, the plea offers in Southwestern's drug cases tend to be made in concrete sentence terms, so the uncertainty faced by most federal defendants is not such a concern here. In the lowest-level cases there is a waiver of the presentence probation report, and the judge simply ratifies the terms delineated by the prosecutor in the written plea agreement. This eliminates potential exposure on non-conviction-relevant conduct. The case is in essence closed when the agreement is reached and just needs to be formally signed off on by the judge.

Even so, the drug cases in Southwestern retain some unique features of federal cases that, similarly, make it very risky for defendants *not* to accept what is offered, so these negotiations are still very one-sided. And the general perception here was consistent with the other districts: that prosecutors hold the upper hand in negotiations. One defender told me, prosecutors "don't give up much really. . . . In some cases they're clearly giving up the ability to argue for a higher sentence. And that's about it."[28]

From the defense standpoint, two primary concerns motivate a guilty plea in federal drug cases: minimizing exposure on case facts and corollary "relevant conduct," and thwarting drug-related criminal-history-based enhancements and add-ons. These might be best characterized as damage control: the defense works to keep the case from getting even worse by agreeing to a plea. Part of this may involve working with the prosecutor, sometimes creatively, to box in what will be counted as relevant conduct when the pretrial probation officer prepares the presentence report and calculates the guideline range for sentencing.

For the prosecutor's part, she can and does go on the offensive to some degree to get something more than just the certainty of conviction in exchange for any promised breaks on sentence recommendations, or for not making the case worse. In the drug prosecution context, as exemplified by the practices in Southeast District, the most sought-after "something" is cooperation. The defendant may provide "historical" information about other criminal suspects or work as an active informant for federal agents in setting up others for potential arrests. The ratio of how much cooperation is rewarded at sentence varies considerably between districts, and even somewhat within districts. So, too, does the likelihood that cooperation is a component of the plea agreement. Prosecutors in Southeast District often included cooperation as a condition to favorably resolving drug cases, whereas cooperation was more an exception in Southwestern District's drug cases.

Another element frequently at the heart of the negotiation process is drug weight, since it drives both mandatory minimum thresholds and guideline offense levels. So just as weight thresholds drove the construction of a subset of federal drug cases to begin with, especially in Southeast District, the same thresholds can drive plea bargaining. The barter value for prosecutors comes with the indeterminacy of "weight" in some cases. My observations and interviews indicated that when actual drugs were seized that could be tested and weighed, weight was not a particularly fungible element in negotiations. Yet in the majority of conspiracies and especially in cases that involved confidential informants, the drug weight attributable to a given defendant was "soft," as several attorneys described it to me, and could grow exponentially if an appropriately constructed guilty plea was not rendered. To reiterate, this "historical weight" does not require anyone in law enforcement actually to have even seen any drugs of those or other quantities to count against the defendant. It can be established through hearsay or other questionable means and still be counted as relevant conduct.

From the start of a case, drug weight can propel sentencing by whether and how it is specifically charged in the indictment, especially to put mandatory minimums in play. For the purposes of guideline calculations, drug weight is critical to the bargaining stage, since its value as "relevant conduct" impacts offense level. Again, relevant conduct is especially easy to make stick because it does not need to be proven beyond a reasonable doubt to count against the defendant in the guideline calculations. In other words, defendants have much less ability to challenge weight that comes in as "relevant conduct" for sentencing purposes than as a charged element of the offense, even though it potentially has the same punitive impact on sentence outcome.

One bargaining tactic used by prosecutors against defendants was the threat that one or more confidential informants could testify to more deals with the defendant over a longer period of time, or that the defendant could be charged with additional participation in a conspiracy (a tactic called "widening the scope") in order to drive up weight-related relevant conduct. A defender in Northeastern District described how this worked as an incentive in conspiracy cases against going to trial and toward working out a plea agreement:

> If you're dealing with a larger-scale conspiracy, then the government can conceivably add drug weight. . . . We know what the client is charged with initially, but the relevant conduct that's involved in the case is so arbitrary sometimes depending on where the case goes. Depending on how many informants they have that can say, for instance, your client knew about

X amount of drugs or was involved with different transactions dating back, you know, to other periods of time. It just is a very ambiguous, dangerous place to be if you're thinking about taking it all the way in terms of a trial.[29]

Another attorney in Northeastern District told me about how her client's boastful attempt to convince the would-be buyer (who was actually setting up the arrest) of the product's quality was used by the prosecutor in an effort to increase attributable weight as relevant conduct at sentencing:

In one of the transactions which was recorded, my client made a comment about, you know, 'Oh, you know, this stuff is so popular I'm selling X amount a week.' Or 'X amount at a time.' And [the prosecutor] was arguing that that quantity should be used to up the weight even though there was no stuff there. My argument was that he was trying to placate a dissatisfied customer by telling him that the quality was so good. You know, just puffing.[30]

In Southeast District, historical weight as potential relevant conduct is wielded with even more force. As one defense attorney put it, "The relevant conduct game is played pretty serious here."[31] In cases in which the defendant had been brought into federal court via the so-called "interlude"—where federal agents pick up defendants from local custody after dismissal of state charges, then drive them around to get information before booking them federally—the information thus extracted is frequently used against the defendant during the plea negotiation process. These statements became the basis for historical weight that can be tagged to the defendant if he decides against accepting a plea offer. Not only is it used to compel a guilty plea; it is also leveraged to impel cooperation as *part* of the plea bargain. In many cases, no protections against "relevant conduct" were offered to a defendant for pleading guilty unless the defendant also provided cooperation.

And because of the pervasive use of confidential informants in Southeast District, it was common for historical weight to loom as relevant conduct in a high percentage of cases. The use of cooperation in Southeast District rippled out to bring in more and more people said to be involved in the drug trade. A federal defender in the southernmost division estimated that about 85 percent of the smaller historical weight cases that their office handled ultimately included cooperation as part of the agreement.

Thus, defendants in Southeast brought into federal court had frequently come to the attention of law enforcement in the first place through one or more other suspects' informing efforts. Opportunistic agents sometimes used the brief period prior to the appointment of counsel to get the arrestee to make incriminating comments that would later be used to increase pressure on the defendant to help dig himself out of that "relevant conduct" hole through cooperation. Finally, if the defendant chose not to succumb to the prosecution's conditions for a guilty plea, including any demands for cooperation, weight that could be built from informants' accounts was put forth as relevant conduct for sentencing purposes.

Even in the context of a plea deal, relevant conduct was hard to box in. The probation officers in Southeast District tended to do very law-enforcement-oriented independent investigations of relevant conduct that sometimes contradicted the prepared "statement of facts" that is part of the formal plea agreement. Therefore, when defense attorneys worked with prosecutors on the specific elements of the deal, a primary goal was to contain the risk level by curtailing the proverbial bleeding early on. The willingness of prosecutors to collaborate on this varied by prosecutor and by the circumstances of the case. One federal defender in Southeast District explained:

> Unfortunately, a lot of it depends on both your prosecutor and your proba-tion officer really. Because normally you do a statement of facts where the parties stipulate what the relevant conduct and the drug weight is. What happens is the probation officer then requests a copy of the prosecutor's file. So if you have a prosecutor who is on board with making sure this is how it's going to go, they will only turn over to the probation office [what's] in their file that supports that recommendation. That's not a problem. Where you run into problems is where the prosecutor is stipulating to something, but then they turn over a file that has all this other information. Then the question becomes, yeah, is there going to be an issue as to drug weight?[32]

Another defender described a case where his client sold ten painkillers from his own prescription of pills in a set-up arranged by a confidential informant. The prosecutor was not willing to limit the "relevant conduct" to the actual drug amount in the set-up in exchange for a guilty plea. He insisted that the defendant take responsibility for pills that the confiden-tial informant claimed to have previously bought from the defendant. The defender considered advising his client to reject the offer and plead "straight up" to the charges in the indictment and take his chances with the judge at sentencing. This would provide the opportunity to litigate the relevant conduct amount and would preserve the defendant's appeal rights. But the risk that historical weight would grow even larger, either through this confidential informant or additional ones, was too great. As he put it to me, "You want to kind of lock in your risk" with a plea agree-ment by closing off all the possible unknown information that might be traded by the web of cooperators in the district.[33]

Weight was not as much a bargaining issue in the courier and mule cases that were common in Southwestern District. In such cases the weight was actual rather than historical. And since most of these defendants were absolutely at the bottom rung of the enterprise and had little or no infor-mation about higher-ups involved, the offense-related negotiation often centered around whether the prosecutor would agree that the defendant be recommended for a mitigating role adjustment, the fast-track discount, and the "safety valve" provision to get under any mandatory minimum. This negotiation was critical, since the actual drug amounts could trigger mandatory minimums and very high guideline sentencing ranges for many defendants.

The other predominant offense-related negotiation in drug cases had to do with any guns present or used during the drug offense. Under a provision of the federal code, possession of a gun during the commission of a drug trafficking offense results in an additional five-year mandatory sentence that must run consecutive to the drug-trafficking sentence, with an additional twenty-five-year mandatory consecutive term for each additional conviction.[34] Guns are often carried for protection by parties involved in trafficking, but they are infrequently brandished or used. Nonetheless, if a gun is found in the defendant's possession or in the vicinity of the drugs or drug proceeds, such as in the same room, this enhancement, known colloquially as a 924(c), is potentially applicable. In such cases, defense attorneys will prioritize taking that added mandatory minimum off the table by negotiating for a lesser gun-related offense.

In Northeastern District and Southeast District, the 924(c) possibility prompted the elevation of some drug cases to federal court by the U.S. attorney's office in the first place; it subsequently became a vehicle for compelling guilty pleas. Prosecutors might offer to drop the 924(c) charge if defendants agreed to plead guilty to all other substantive charges. This would typically include a two-level increase in the offense level for the defendant, since the deal included a generic gun possession relevant conduct increase, but the full cost of the gun mandatory minimum was avoided. Trading the two-level "bump" on the offense level calculation for possession of a gun in exchange for removing the 924(c) from the picture was an accepted practice. Guns were less likely to be involved in drug cases in Southwestern District than in the other districts, but when they were, the prosecutor's strategy was to hold out the 924(c) filing as a threat if the defendant did not readily accept the offer put forth. The deal did not necessarily require a gun possession "bump"; rather, the imperative was to settle quickly and without fuss.

Criminal history is another potent and versatile weapon used by prosecutors against drug defendants with certain prior convictions. When those priors are drug felonies, they have the potential to dramatically enhance sentences through several mechanisms. Of course, like any other prior criminal conviction occurring within the time frames laid out in the guidelines, drug priors are calculated into the criminal history score, so they exert direct influence on the guideline calculation via the horizontal axis of the Sentencing Table (see figure 2.1). But that is only their first bite. As discussed in previous chapters, some drug defendants end up in federal court *because* of the exposure posed by their criminal history. So those defendants who were brought to federal court because of their eligibility for the career offender guideline or an 851 statutory enhancement will potentially have their drug priors bite twice or more at sentencing.

Although the career offender provision generally was not fodder for actual negotiations—attorneys I interviewed mentioned only isolated occasions where a plea deal would be constructed around keeping the career offender guidelines from applying at sentencing—they were still influential in the plea process.[35] This was especially the case in Northeastern and Southwestern Districts, because judges were often willing to sentence well below the career offender guideline sentences. For example, one defender in Northeastern told me that now that the guidelines are not binding, her strategy in some such cases, where prosecutors bring cases involving minute amounts of drugs because of the defendant's career offender exposure, is to plead straight up, without a plea agreement. She said that many judges do not approve of these cases being brought in federal court at all and will offer much more leniency in sentencing than anything offered by the prosecution:

> You can try to negotiate something, but it's usually not anything awesome. It's like maybe you can get them down [from fifteen years] to like eight or something like that. And a lot of times if you draw the right judge, a lot of the judges over there don't like those cases because they're not federal drug cases. You know, they don't think that they're important enough for their court. So it seems like sometimes you're better off without a plea agreement because this judge is going to treat your client better than the prosecutor's office ever would.[36]

The provision that influenced negotiations more than any other was the 851 enhancement, which doubled the mandatory minimums.[37] In every district, if the defendant was eligible, prosecutors threatened to file an 851 information if the defendant did not plead guilty. A defender in Northeastern District called it "the ultimate lever." Another in Northeastern said, "It's the bargaining chip that is the one most obviously used as a bargaining chip." This defender went on to say that the 851 filing is "a real threat. I mean some of our clients are looking at 851s that push them up to life. . . . I've had clients charged with that. They will move off that. In connection with a plea usually the 851s are negotiable. But for a price."[38]

It was the same story in Southeast District, where the 851 statutory enhancement was a credible threat made good if defendants did not plead guilty. A defender there shared her experience with this: "Up until the day of trial, two days before trial, they withhold the 851, but if you insist on going to trial, they file and, of course, it turns a five [-year mandatory minimum] to a ten, a ten to a twenty, which usually makes [the defendant] crumble. An 851 is a really good leverage tool to get our clients to plead."[39] In Southwestern District it was also used as a threat to dissuade defendants from going to trial. A defender there called it a "big stick." However, because so many of the drug cases involved people with little applicable criminal history, there were fewer such cases in which to make the threat.

This in itself created some stark disparities between codefendants, as illustrated by one defender's case in that district:

> I had one case [where] they caught these guys with this load in a U-Haul. . . . There were several codefendants. What was ironic to me was that my guy was the little mule who just did his friend a favor by going and finding this U-Haul with him. Now my guy got charged for all that quantity, and he was the one that had a prior. So they threatened the 851, and he's looking at ten years, when he played the smallest role.[40]

In Southeast District, at least in two of the divisions, when defendants had two eligible prior drug convictions, prosecutors routinely filed on the first prior and used the second as the leverage to force a plea. Thus, for a defendant who faced a ten-year mandatory minimum based on the offense itself, he would likely have to plead to a twenty-year mandatory in order to avoid receiving life without parole if convicted at trial. A prosecutor described the Southeast District's approach to the 851:

> Our office has a policy that, generally, one [prior] is forgivable but if they have two or more, that we're gonna have to file one. [We would] not file all of them, of course, because there would be no incentive for the defendant to plead guilty because two brings a life sentence, a mandatory life sentence. One brings a twenty-to-life sentence. . . . If there is just one, ordinarily, we could agree not to file the enhancement in a plea agreement. Of course, if the defendant goes to trial, all bets are off and we file the enhancements.[41]

The 851 is also used in conjunction with other criminal-history-based sentencing hammers, as a defender in Northeastern District explained to me. In that district, some prosecutors who charged very low-level drug defendants who qualified for career offenders sentences creatively used criminal history to try to maximize the potential sentence exposure during plea negotiations. So if a defendant was eligible for the career offender guideline but was not facing a mandatory minimum, an 851 filing would push the advisory sentence even higher than the career offender guideline alone, since the 851 also increases the statutory maximum. A defender gave me the following example from one of her current drug cases:

> The guy sold .29 grams of crack cocaine. If he were not a career offender, his guidelines range would still be incredibly high [because of his criminal history and relevant conduct]. Like five years. But because he has prior drug trafficking offenses, his guideline range as a career offender is up around

twelve or fourteen years. The prosecutor filed an 851. There's no minimum mandatory to double, but on the career offender grid that jacks him up to like eighteen years.[42]

A prosecutor in Southeast District told me that, since the guidelines are no longer mandatory, she will sometimes file the 851 in career offender cases to ensure that the doubled mandatory minimum will be the lowest a judge can sentence in the case. Similar to the practice in Northeastern District, she will also use the 851 in nonmandatory minimum cases to push up the career offender guideline.

Assistant U.S. Attorney Delacroix, in Southeast District, went even further: the 851 was used to prevent judges from departing from guidelines, now that they are advisory rather than mandatory. This, he said, was a common practice among prosecutors to constrain judicial discretion.

> In an effort to maintain some discipline in the sentencing process, we do file more enhancements. I don't think there's any question, if you were able to do a study—how often an 851 enhancement was filed before [*United States v.*] *Booker* and how often they're being filed now in 2013. . . . You see more of 'em filed because in the absence of a mandatory guidelines regime, the judge has enormous discretion to sentence a defendant between the mandatory minimum and the maximum. And sometimes, if we think that a case is serious enough based on the drug quantity, other aggravating factors in the case, or the defendant's serious criminal record, we think that, you know, a harsher sentence is justified, at least from the outset. And often times, these people are cooperating, so they'll ultimately get some sort of a benefit. But I would say that undoubtedly, we file more 851 enhancements now.[43]

The 851 was perhaps the most powerful tool that the prosecutor used to compel a plea agreement from defendants with eligible prior convictions, and those compelled agreements typically contained terms even more favorable to prosecutors than without the 851 eligibility. In each district, the withholding of an 851 was framed as a gift to the defendant, who then had to agree to worse plea conditions than would be the norm for a similar defendant who was not 851-eligible. Generally, prosecutors used it to get the defense to agree to take more time than the minimum mandatory or guideline minimum as the price for not filing the 851. In Southeast District it was used to get added time *and* cooperation. Thus, the 851 was more than a threat. It actually produced additional punishment for defendants, realized through the power of the threat about how much worse the prosecutor could make it. In the end, though, defense attorneys strongly advised their 851-eligible clients to settle because it would be much worse if they were convicted at trial.

The prosecutors used carrots as well as sticks in plea negotiations. The promise of sentence breaks for cooperation constituted the biggest concession. But even that had some pernicious aspects. Southeast District's plea negotiations in drug cases are largely built around snitching, which made it stand out from the other two districts. And in this district, cooperation was demanded more than requested, and there were costs for refusing. In the other districts, cooperation was fodder for bargaining, but the choice to participate, or not, was really the defendant's to make, and there were fewer consequences for declining. In Southwestern District, especially, cooperation was not discouraged by prosecutors, but defendants certainly were not pressured to do so, nor were they punished for declining the opportunity.

In all the districts the decision *to* cooperate included costs and risks for defendants. A defendant typically had to agree to plead guilty, waive appellate rights in addition to all the trial rights, and provide all information and other assistance as requested by law enforcement. Going in, a defendant did not know whether his information would be of any value to law enforcement, so there was always a chance that no benefit would be bestowed in exchange for the cooperation effort. Across districts, prosecutors never made any promises about whether a sentence break would be made, much less at what value. And there was generally no way out of the plea, once a cooperation agreement was made.

A defender in Northeastern District described the risk inherent in going the cooperation route: "It's really bitter because you don't always know going into it whether it's going to work out for you or not. So you're kind of forced, if you want to just jump off that cliff, to cooperate, hope for the best, and sign away your rights. And they'll make you plead out right away. You have to agree almost always to a very high guidelines range that it's your correct guideline range."[44] The case of Mr. Hopkins, the backpacker relay person in Southwestern District, is illustrative. He was initially offered a binding noncooperation plea that would result in a sentence of seventy-seven to ninety-six months. Once he agreed to cooperate, he was required to plead guilty with no limits on his potential sentence ceiling, except the statutory maximum of forty years. After he messed up his chance to cooperate, he received a sentence that was nearly triple the low end of his initial offer.

Despite the overarching consensus that the cooperation route required a leap of faith, there were significant differences in practice as to the valuations of what counted as cooperation and how much it was worth. First, in some places the opportunity to cooperate depended very much on the prosecutor and law enforcement agents. In Northeastern, for instance, the prosecution may make an overture to the defendant or defense attorney—or even make a hard sell—to get the defendant to cooperate, particularly if that is why he was brought to federal court in the first place. In other cases, there may be no offer to be had; the prosecutor just does not entertain the possibility of a cooperation reduction. Attorneys characterized this as a function of both the prosecutor and the client. Some prosecutors were "go home at five" bureaucrats who did not actively take part in the law enforcement side, so were reluctant to entertain cooperation offers by the defense. Conversely, some defendants were identified as being not particularly useful, so law enforcement had no interest in investing in them as cooperators.

In Southwestern District, across the board cooperation was less central to negotiations than in the other districts. Since so many of the cases there involved low-level couriers and mules who were purposely kept in the dark about the larger operation, they had little information to give. More critically, the risks that attend snitching, to them and to their families across the border, were quite real (as described in chapter 5). Numerous defenders in this district told me stories about clients' family members' being threatened with death as a way to preclude cooperation by the client. A defender told me, "Even my clients who do know stuff almost never want to cooperate. I've had a couple of cases where the assistant U.S. attorney has asked me, would your guy be interested in talking? And I'll bring it up and they'll almost always reject it, even before I finish explaining what it would mean. . . . As soon as I raise the topic, they're, like, no way. I have family. My family has already been threatened."[45]

Defendants' widely held reluctance influenced defense attorneys' opinions about cooperating as a negotiation strategy in Southwestern District. All whom I interviewed were keenly aware of the dangers for their clients, and some were hesitant to suggest it as an option. In fact, there was a clear split in philosophy among defense attorneys about this issue. Several made clear that it was their ethical duty to encourage cooperation as an option for clients who had no other way to escape mandatory minimums; others were uncomfortable with it and even actively discouraged it if there were other routes to sentence mitigation.

The distaste for cooperation among some defense attorneys was exacerbated by some bad experiences with the prosecutor. In light of the danger for their clients that comes with cooperating, some defenders refuse to deal with certain prosecutors who had previously "burned" their clients after getting them to talk. Either the prosecutor decided, after encouraging the defendant to talk, that the information had no value so refused to do anything, or the prosecutor made a motion for the 5K1.1 departure but then argued at sentencing for a higher sentence than was expected. The worst "burn" was when law enforcement then needlessly endangered the client's life. One defender described such a case:

[Our client] gave some information that was actionable, and they went and arrested this other person and this other person found out that [our client had] snitched, [and] made a death threat. That was captured on a jail call.

And we learned our client was subject to this death threat. She had to go into PC [protective custody]. She bought herself a couple years off and now she's on this hit list. And I learned then that the way she got found out was that the government accidentally gave up her name to that other defendant by not redacting her name out of the discovery that they gave that person. It was not on purpose. It was total accident. But wang, bang, she's facing a death threat and she hardly got anything out of it. My view now is discourage clients from cooperating unless they're going to face ten years and they're like, eighteen years old.[46]

Conversely, defenders in all of the districts mentioned the very rare but welcome times when prosecutors were willing to give credit for useless cooperation because the defendant was particularly sympathetic. In such cases the defense attorney was able to convince the prosecutor that the mandatory minimum was not appropriate, and so the defendant would give a "pity" proffer. The prosecutor would then recommend a small to moderate reduction under the mandatory minimum at sentencing. This was one of the few wins defendants got, but it was generally at the mercy of the prosecutor. This is not to say that the defense attorneys weren't excellent advocates or strategic in this regard. Central to their practice was working all angles, including pity, to mitigate the sentence.

Cooperation also gets tangled up in negotiating the application of the safety valve. The safety valve policy was enacted by Congress in 1994 to allow eligible defendants with little or no criminal history who are facing drug mandatory minimums a way out from under them. Its purpose was to provide relief from excessively long sentences for the least culpable defendants. But the fifth prong, that the defendant must provide "full and truthful disclosure" about the offense, could be a sticking point in negotiations.

That fifth prong requirement was at times used in Northeastern District, in particular, as another way to compel the defendant to do more than come clean. Several defenders described that fifth prong as the most common roadblock to getting the safety valve for their clients: prosecutors push defendants beyond a disclosure of their own behavior to disclose information about others. In the view of some defenders, this is potentially a more dangerous, less fruitful avenue to pursue than substantial assistance. Because no protection is built into the safety valve disclosure process against the information being used against the defendant as relevant conduct, some defenders simply had their clients go through the full cooperation proffer process so that the disclosed information could not be used against them at sentencing. In their view, since the prosecutors were basically making their clients snitch to qualify for the safety valve, it was worth getting the protection that comes with cooperation agreements as well as the added reduction at sentencing by having both provisions count.

The final major bargaining lever is time. Time works in plea negotiations in two distinct ways. First, it will often be factored into the offer in terms of how quickly and compliantly the defendant agrees to plead guilty, which can be rewarded with an additional offense level off for "acceptance of responsibility." In Northeastern and Southeast Districts this was generally a case-by-case negotiation and might include a requirement that the defense not file any motions or make any requests that would necessitate work by the prosecutor.

In Southwestern district, the time factor was central to negotiations in almost all cases. Most drug defendants, especially in flip-flop court, received exploding offers that disappeared if they did not accept within the timelines. Depending on the time of year and the day, a prosecutor in charge of the flip-flop calendar might dispose of as few as three and as many as thirty-five cases in a session; any number of those might be back-packing defendants.[47] The prosecutor's office imposed a sliding scale in valuating these cases, as a matter of both case pressure and internal office policy mandates. Up until 2012, drug cases were excluded completely from the flip-flop court option, and low-level defendants' best offer for those willing to plead quickly was a felony with a sentence of thirteen months and a day. The deals for backpackers and some mechanized mule cases got much better as more and more cases came into the district.

In felony cases, too, significant reductions and guaranteed sentence outcomes were traded for quick resolution. Defendants received up to four offense levels off, above and beyond "acceptance of responsibility," in return for pleading guilty quickly and for not pursuing basic procedural avenues. The work-up of these cases by the attorneys and the court was more substantial than in the flip-flop cases, but they still hinged on speedy, uncontested resolution. The U.S. attorney's division office distributed a chart to defenders with the standardized offer ranges, based on the weight of the drugs and the defendant's criminal history score, and those set the framework for each individual offer. This chart was periodically updated and redistributed, as case volume conditions shifted. There was little negotiation as to terms; the defendant usually either took what was offered by the prosecutor or declined and risked a much longer sentence. Although the judge had the final say on actual sentence—or as to whether to accept the stipulated sentence—defenders in these cases were generally precluded, as part of the agreement, from making arguments for terms below the specified range.

The other way time mattered to plea negotiations was in codefendant cases. The imperative to "rush to the door" to cooperate was present and indeed was encouraged by prosecutors. In a classic sales tactic, the prosecutor created the impression that there were more defendants than available credit for cooperation. A Northeastern District defender said: "[The] government will often in those cases say, 'Oh, you know. You better be the first one in. You want to be the first one in. Don't come back later. Blah, blah, blah.' So you know there's a lot of pressure, and the clients are all sort of watching each other to see who's gonna roll."[48]

In Southeast District, a defender suggested that the value of cooperation decreased with the cooperator's place in that line at the prosecutor's door:

> You want to be first in the door if your client's going to cooperate because the first guy in is gonna get the greatest reduction, and then the second guy in, his cooperation value is less because he can only give information to other people or people below him. . . . You end up with the first guy in can get a thirty or forty percent reduction, second guy in, just by the value of his information is twenty to thirty. And then the last guy in, it's like, well, he can say what he did but maybe he'll get a pity [reduction] of ten percent.[49]

Under these circumstances defendants felt considerable pressure to turn, quickly, on their codefendants. Those left without deals often saw the "evidence" against them grow more formidable with each additional guilty plea.

Taken together, the picture of negotiation in all three districts is that one side holds most of the cards and so can compel convictions through guilty pleas while dictating the parameters of potential outcomes. Those outcomes are often very punitive, especially in the nonborder districts and especially in comparison to what would have happened if the defendant had been prosecuted in state court. But it can get much worse. The costs of pushing back through the assertion of rights varied from district to district, but it was present in all.

Northeastern District, especially since the *Booker* decision, has enjoyed the best conditions for defendants who choose to litigate specific issues, although even there the trial penalty looms so large that relatively few drug defendants go to trial. Defense attorneys considered it to be appropriate and necessary practice to file motions on unconstitutional search or statement issues, and they were not routinely punished by prosecutors for doing so. Even at sentencing, there was robust litigation on sentencing issues. Much of this was due to the great increase in defendants choosing to plead straight up without a plea agreement since *Booker* made the guidelines advisory. The judges in this district have been very receptive to considering more individualized arguments about the particular defendants' circumstances, and they routinely vary from the guidelines when they deem it appropriate.

In both Southwestern and Southeast Districts, by contrast, there were considerable costs to defendants for asserting pretrial rights. In Southwestern District, the cost was the loss of deep discounts associated with the expedited plea programs. While the deals offered here were significantly better than what could be expected in the other districts, the pressure to plead quickly with little information was enormous. Since so many defendants here are noncitizens who do not speak English, they are often in an even more disadvantaged position in regard to knowing the ins and outs of their rights. But slowing down the process to spend meaningful time with their assigned attorneys to gain that understanding meant the sentencing stakes got much worse. The other major challenge was the cultural divide between defendants and the jury pool. Numerous defenders mentioned this impediment to taking triable cases to trial. Even when defense attorneys used expert witnesses to educate jurors about how the cartels operate and about the duress under which many defendants agree to move drugs, juries have not been as receptive to the defense.

Ultimately, though, in Southwestern District, pursuing pretrial rights did not typically inspire a piling on of additional enhancers or any other proactively punitive action by the prosecutor. That *was* the case, however, in Southeast District, which stood out in its aggressive approach to hammering drug defendants at every turn. Here the punishment also extended to basic procedural necessities for defendants to be able to even assess the contours of the case against them and test the evidence in order to make judgments on how to proceed.

In all three districts, the option of going to trial was viewed as the most risky of all, unless there really was nothing to lose, because so much time was looming in a given case. The cost of going to trial varied by district. There was a general consensus in Northeastern District that judges would not punish defendants for going to trial as long as there appeared to be a "good reason" to try the case. Thus, defenders in this district expressed some willingness to consider a trial as an option in select cases. Conversely, defenders in Southeast District were loath to recommend a trial except in cases where things could get no worse for the client.

I asked the defenders in each district to describe what cases went to trial and got two notable types of responses. First, most said they just don't take drug cases to trial because of how bad it is for their clients. Second, the times they went to trial were generally chalked up to unrealistic clients. A defender in Northeastern District told me, "The cases that don't settle are cases where the client just can't accept the amount of time."[50] A Southwestern District defender, too, told me that a lot of the decision to go to trial "is going to be driven by the client."[51] Some of these decisions by clients were characterized as "a kamikaze mission."

Devon Harrison's case is an extreme illustration of the costs associated with pursuing trial rights in the federal system and declining to submit to the prosecutor's offer in exchange for a guilty plea. For Devon, who sold tiny amounts of drugs to support his own habit, being brought into federal court was only the start of the bad turn of events. It set into motion a process that was destined to end with a long prison sentence no matter what decisions he made about how to proceed. A sentence of life with no chance of release, though, for a defendant such as Devon does not seem conceivable under a system that purportedly aims for fairness and consistency. The sentence he received—which the judge was obliged by law to impose—was mandated *because* he exercised his Sixth Amendment rights, not in spite of this. Devon demonstrated enormous fortitude in holding out against the pressure to plead. His prosecutor, Linda Gemelli, succumbed to the seductions of power.

= Chapter 7 =

Taming the Power to Punish?

The confluence of tough-on-crime politics, sentencing reform, and jurisdictional expansion in the 1970s and 1980s opened up a world of opportunity for federal prosecutors. They seized, with gusto, the opportunity to join the national crime-fighting bonanza. The transformation of the federal crime control role was especially evident in the world of drug law enforcement. Local drug cases became potential federal matters, and the power to charge federally became, in and of itself, a new strategic tool. In both Northeastern and Southeast Districts, that power to federally charge local drug defendants was explicitly deployed to deal with problems of violence, but it then took on a life of its own. Federal prosecutions were initiated for a variety of strategic reasons—to get information, to more easily obtain convictions, and to punish more severely than the state would.[1] As a consequence, in both of these districts the small, state-type cases grew to constitute a sizable share of the federal drug caseload.

Once brought into federal court, drug defendants, in most jurisdictions, are assured much more punitive treatment than they would have received if they had been left in their local courts. If they do not accept this inevitability, things generally just get worse for them. Statutes such as 21 U.S.C. § 851 lurk, available to be deployed as soon as eligible defendants do not succumb to the will of the prosecutor. And although the attorney general can issue directives in an effort to tame discretionary abuses, in the heat of the case, when a given prosecutor is facing down a given defendant, there's a good chance that all legal tools *will* be utilized.[2] The rules of power relations nearly compel it. The micro-dynamics of legitimacy—that threats will be made realities when defendants don't comply—trump the broader assault on the law's legitimacy that result from the abuse of legal discretion. Again, the very nature of social power ensures this outcome, since the tool's force will evaporate if its wielder is unwilling to use it.

The fundamental nature of social relations also ensures that the more rules are promulgated to direct and constrain power, the more creative human actors will be in finding ways to thwart them and reappropriate them for their own ends. Ironically, the core assumption underlying the legal changes of the 1980s was that decisionmakers' discretionary power should and could be tamed and controlled by a set of rules. Sentencing reformers operationalized the goal of achieving honesty, uniformity, and proportionality by developing an intricate set of rules to meet that mission.[3]

"Honesty" was to be achieved through the abolition of parole and through the modified "real-offense" approach whereby all conduct relevant to the offense charged would be quantified.[4] Uniformity was purportedly achievable through the intricate calculations of offense characteristics and defendants' criminal history, which then dictated the sentence range. Proportionality, too, was to be achieved through the same process, since in the ideal version, like defendants would be sentenced alike and dissimilar defendants would receive different sentences.

Yet all of these imperatives relied upon human actors to interpret meanings and put the rules into action. Ultimately, there is a fundamental struggle between the idealized version of a sentencing system that would be implemented in a wholly orthodox manner and the on-the-ground realities whereby myriad actors assess and negotiate the meaning of individual case elements to convert them into the numeric system that corresponds to the Sentencing Table. Legal actors could be constrained and redirected by the increasingly detailed body of rules that constituted the Sentencing Guidelines but not wholly converted into "operator[s] of a machine designed and built by legislators."[5] They would impose their own sets of values and imperatives—partly shaped by the local legal cultures in which they worked, and partly shaped by the interpersonal power dynamics of the adversarial process.

Not surprisingly, actors quickly learned how to formally comply with the guidelines' dictates and to make things look, on the record, as though the guidelines were being appropriately applied. One former prosecutor told me that getting around the guidelines to arrive at where they wanted to be "became an art in and of itself: How to massage the guidelines."[6] That "art" varies depending upon the case, the actors, and the local norms and constraints. Further policy fixes, such as the safety valve, which was introduced to mitigate sentences of the least culpable and help ensure proportionality, easily became under some circumstances yet another tool for obtaining cooperation in the game of adjudication.

The most ardent attempt by Congress to control sentencing discretion since the Guidelines' implementation in itself reveals the irreconcilability of this struggle. In April 2003, yet another crime control bill, the PROTECT ("Prosecutorial Remedies and Tools to end the Exploitation of Children Today") Act, was passed by Congress.[7] It contained an amendment that aimed to further limit judges' ability to downwardly depart from the mandatory guidelines in a subset of cases.[8] It also institutionalized a surveillance mechanism over judges by mandating that prosecutors report when judges granted downward departures over the government's objections. And it changed the standard of appellate review of sentences to a de novo standard whereby trial judges' determinations were given no presumption of reasonableness in the sentences they imposed.[9] This policy was in place for a period of twenty months, before the ruling in *United States v. Booker* essentially vacated it.

Rather than further rationalizing the system to ensure uniformity, the PROTECT Act emboldened prosecutors even more. A longtime defender in Northeastern District told me that this twenty-month period "was really bad. . . . There was a sort of a Know-Nothing response [by prosecutors] to any argument that suggested that there shouldn't be a massive penal response to any crime. There was no bending on 851s. . . . There was an attempt on the part of the U.S. Attorneys Office to propel sentences up as high as they could possibly get."[10] And when judges tried to intervene by granting any departures in this district, prosecutors regularly appealed the sentence to keep "judges in line."[11] A career defender in Southwestern District told me that during this period, her role had been reduced to, effectively "delivering a message" from the prosecutor to her clients about how bad the punishment would be.[12]

Ultimately, what all the efforts to constrain judicial sentencing did was to move the location of discretionary power away from judges to prosecutors. So not only do prosecutors have ultimate power at the front end of the system to decide whom to charge in federal court, and with what charges, they have gained considerably more power at the tail end of the adjudication process. In the drug case context, that power is all the more formidable because of the extremely long punishments that are possible under the mix of legal provisions in play.

Prosecutors also hold substantial discretionary power for granting relief from those harsh punishments via substantial assistance departures and via their role in affirming compliance for the "safety valve" relief.[13] To be sure, some prosecutors have, over the course of the guidelines regime, used their power to mitigate punitive sentences (for example, with "pity 5K1.1 departures"). Nevertheless, and paradoxically, the fact that so much power to grant mercy rests with prosecutors has reinforced its effectiveness in obtaining compliance.[14]

In the contemporary sentencing regime, prosecutors have become the conductors and primary navigators of case outcomes from inception through resolution, catalyzing cooperation even when it comes with heady risks, discouraging pretrial litigation and challenges to evidence, and compelling guilty pleas at exceptionally high rates. As judges lost their power to shape outcomes in the guidelines regime, defense attorneys' advocacy efforts became even more focused on early-stage negotiations with the prosecutor. Under the worst conditions in this system, the sentencing proceeding became more a formality than robust litigation. Concessions to be won—or losses to be minimized—had to be managed well before a guilty plea was entered, much less before a pretrial report was drafted and a sentencing hearing scheduled. Consequently, the adversarial process moved even more behind closed doors, away from open court and court reporters and out of earshot of the judge.

The adversarial process also became more lopsided than ever. The shift in power and the extreme imbalance in its distribution explains why and how drug case numbers shot up, guilty plea rates increased, and sentences grew significantly longer. Convictions, first and foremost, and lengthy sentences, under most circumstances, count as wins for the side with the power to make them happen. Because drug convictions became easy wins to achieve under the prevailing rules, there has been little downside to prosecutors for pursuing these cases. With the entire system of metrics pushed so high by the guidelines and statutes, sentences that look from the outside to be unreasonably long came to be viewed as reasonable outcomes in the insular worlds of local district courts.

But why even bring a defendant such as Aaron Crenshaw, in Northeastern District, to federal court in the first place? Or Franklin Samuels, in Southeast District, who helped his son sell a single gram of heroin? In the longer view, why did drugs become such a priority for the federal criminal justice system? The deployment of criminal law is "a form of power which subjugates and makes subject to."[15] It is not surprising that the most forceful legal tools have been invented and reinvented to subjugate and control those with the least power in society, especially people of color and the poor. These choices are justified by multiple long-standing rhetorics to the effect that the state's power is needed to discipline, teach respect, incapacitate, or even save the subject from himself and his community. No matter the justification, though, the aim is primarily directed at those at the bottom.

When I was back in Southeast District eight months after my extended period of research there, I attended the arraignment of three young African American men, all from one of the same neighborhoods as most of the drug defendants in this court. Each was charged with heroin trafficking and conspiracy, after collectively selling less than half a gram to a confidential informant. The prosecutor told me, after the proceeding, that the region had a new and growing problem with heroin and that there had been a rash of overdoses, some fatal. These defendants had been arrested in response to the growing problem.

It turns out that much of the "new" heroin problem was in a wealthier white community, including in a high school where students themselves dealt the drug to their peers. But those students and their customers were characterized as victims, while the poor young men of color from up the road were labeled the problem that deserved federal intervention. A defender sardonically said, "None of the kids at these high schools have been prosecuted. . . . They're 'victims.' At most they've been getting first offender treatment [in state court]. 'Because we don't want to ruin their college opportunities.'"[16] This is a pattern already familiar from Harry J. Anslinger's first war on drugs in the mid-twentieth century and going forward.[17] Indeed, it is practically hard-wired into the production of power relations that status markers such as race and economic standing enter into the calculus. Dominance and control is easier and more easily justified when imposed upon socially derogated "others" who can be blamed and punished for society's ills.[18]

In the federal criminal context, these practices have come at considerable cost, especially to those who have been effectively steamrolled into prison by swamping their fundamental rights with massively powerful substantive law. So reinvigorating procedural rights for criminal defendants is a necessary step for fixing this out-of-whack system, if only to be truer to our legal institutions' stated values. But we also must shrink the substantive law itself. This is not an either-or choice. As I have demonstrated, the process and substance of law are tightly coupled in practice, and must be treated as such when considering reform.

This is not to say that things haven't improved in recent years. The *Booker* decision, which directly concerned Sixth Amendment procedural rights, released a lot of collective pent-up desire, especially in the judiciary, to move away from the harsh and rigid mandatory guidelines system. In places like Northeastern District, for example, defendants have more and more been able to side-step the whole plea negotiation process to plead straight up and leave the sentencing determination to the judge. But it could not and did not get rid of those Hendley-type cases, which even if done for all the right reasons, and even if sentenced well below the potential guidelines sentence, kept coming and remain very troubling.

And *Booker* hardly made a dent at all in places like Southeast District, where judges remain loyal to the guidelines and where probation has been more law enforcement oriented. Because the local norms did not conflict with the guidelines, prosecutors still reign supreme in directing case outcomes. One defense attorney in Southeast told me, "After *Booker* everyone got really reenergized, that all of a sudden we were really going to go to individualized sentencing. . . . and there was going to be a lot more leniency in sentencing, and I think the reality is that it hasn't done anything."

In fact, some prosecutors have perceived *Booker* as a threat to their power and have taken steps to redress the balance in their favor. Assistant U.S. Attorney Adam Delacroix, from Southeast District, told me:

> The mandatory guideline regime certainly did give defendants an enormous incentive to cooperate. Now, a defendant can plead guilty, sign a

cooperation agreement and his plea agreement with the government, and then perhaps drag his feet on cooperation. See what sentence he ends up getting from the judge. If the judge sentences him to a low sentence, you know, below-guideline sentence or [at the] mandatory minimum sentence, I think that's obviously because the guidelines are now discretionary or advisory, [and] the defendant, I think, feels less of a compulsion to cooperate.

As a consequence of this perceived loss of power, one way prosecutors imposed "discipline" on both judges and defendants was to file more 851 enhancements to keep the cooperation incentive high and the final punishment long. The places where sentences were the harshest at the height of the war on drugs have endeavored to stay that way. They just get there in new ways, as the rules of the game have shifted.

Delacroix's concern about losing discretionary power echoes the national efforts that a group of more conservative assistant U.S. attorneys have made to derail current sentencing reform proposals. In July 2015, the National Association of Assistant United States Attorneys, which claims a membership of about 30 percent of the nation's AUSAs, released a white paper that directly attacked a pending piece of bipartisan legislation, the Smarter Sentencing Act.[19] Titled "The Dangerous Myths of Drug Sentencing 'Reform,'" the paper relies on the old-style fear-mongering that propelled the punitive laws in the first place.[20] The paper sets forth so-called myths that are basically straw men set up to be debunked in order to justify maintaining the status quo: to protect prosecutors' most powerful weapon, lengthy mandatory minimums, and all that comes with them.

The white paper relies on the same set of tropes used by Anslinger sixty-five years ago to advocate for the first real drug mandatories. To counter the "myth" that drug crimes are nonviolent, the authors assert as fact that "it is well established that drug trafficking is inherently violent and that all drug dealing is dangerous, taking the lives of thousands of Americans, destroying families, and undermining the moral fabric of our communities."[21] It also engages in subtle race baiting. In its effort to debunk "Myth Five: Minimum sentences for drug dealers should be reduced because drug sentences have a disparate impact on minorities," the authors come right out and say that "minority males are convicted and incarcerated at a higher rate than their relative numbers in the general population" as a result of minority males' disproportionate involvement in high-level drug trafficking—not law enforcement or prosecutorial bias. The implication is that reforms that would reduce mandatory minimums will simply release "dangerous" minority drug predators to the communities upon which they "prey."[22]

The anxiety about losing power is made explicit in the debunking of the fourth putative myth: mandatory minimum sentences are arbitrary and reforming them will promote fairness and public safety. Rather than defending the current mandatories on the grounds of justice, the authors reveal their real fear: "many drug trafficking defendants will be less inclined to cooperate and share information if their minimum sentencing exposure is substantially reduced."[23]

The white paper's talking points have been adopted by some law-makers, who are trying to maintain the status quo, both by actively lob-bying against reform efforts within Congress and by broadcasting the messages to their constituents and the general public in media forums. For instance, Senator Tom Cotton, a Republican from Arkansas, credits man-datory minimums for the national drop in crime and asserts that reforms to those mandatories would be a "massive experiment in criminal leni-ency" that would undo all of those public safety gains.[24] He and several colleagues play up the dangers of making any changes to current drug laws. Although their efforts may not completely thwart impending sen-tencing reform, they almost guarantee that the political process will water down the provisions as a compromise for passage of reform legislation.

Legal power of the sort I have examined is difficult to tame and restrain; it is even more difficult to rescind once bestowed. This conundrum extends beyond the federal system, as jurisdictions across the nation come to terms with the unsustainability of the mass incarceration binge of the past four decades.[25] What would it take to retrench from these punitive excesses? First, the substantive law must be tamed so that it no longer overwhelms the procedural rights of defendants by authorizing outrageously high sentences. In the federal context, that means a major overhaul of both the criminal code and the Sentencing Guidelines. Since the 1980s, Congress has primarily policed the floor of drug sentencing to ensure that imposed drug sentences do not fall below an imagined ideal punishment. It has done so most directly through the enactment of drug mandatory mini-mums, and less directly through the other punitive tools that are available to prosecutors. The Sentencing Commission, too, translated its congres-sional mandate to achieve uniformity and proportionality by constructing the drug guidelines around those mandatory minimums. Thus, it too has primarily patrolled the floor. But Congress has done little to patrol the ceiling. This is ironic in light of the original impetus for sentencing reform, which was that disadvantaged defendants, including minorities and the poor, were overpunished relative to advantaged others. While leniency is the flip side of punitiveness, and so-called "unwarranted disparities" can occur on either side of that coin, Senator Kennedy's concerns in the 1970s were squarely with the disadvantaged, who got too much punishment.[26]

The statutory maximum penalties under the federal drug laws are now so high that the headroom, as it were, reinforces the power of the prosecutor. The base maximum sentence for trafficking most substances (besides marijuana and certain prescription drugs) at the lowest quantities is twenty years, and it goes up from there, to life without parole, as a function of drug quantity and criminal history.[27] As a result, prosecutors have much leeway to push up sentences when they do not get their way. Reforms that aim to rescind drug mandatory minimums are critical first steps to lowering the sentencing floor and allowing for reasonable people to work out reasonable sentences in all cases, with less draconian constraints imposed by mandatory sentences. Without also bringing down the ceilings, though, the power to hammer defendants remains at the ready, to be wielded by individual prosecutors or judges when they choose to do so in the heat of a case or as a matter of personal preference.

Thus, the statutory maximums need to be significantly reduced for each subcategory of drug offense to structurally contain that potential. Doing so will better achieve the goals of proportionality and uniformity by protecting against over-the-top sentences for sporadic defendants. It will also mitigate the damage to legal principles done by prosecutors who use the drug laws—for the ease of convictions and the sheer force of punitive potential—as a proxy in the kind of "Al Capone" strategy that Assistant U.S. Attorney Tom Hendley used in Northeastern District. Under certain circumstances, this strategy of using drug laws to prosecute and convict those suspected of other criminal acts may have value for public safety, but it comes with the substantial risk of sweeping up too many people who are neither the public menace they are claimed to be, nor legally guilty of the acts they are suspected of but for which they have *not* been arrested, much less convicted. Such a strategy is by its very nature an assault on core due process principles.

In addition, the multitude of hammers that can be used to ratchet up sentences must also be revisited. Mandatory minimums are only the starting point for dictating lengthy prison sentences. Criminal history calculations, career offender guidelines, 851s, offender-related role adjustments, protected zone enhancements, "historical weight," and other ephemeral relevant conduct are all deployed in a variety of ways to ratchet up drug defendants' sentences when there is the will to do so.

Some of these tools, like the 851 enhancement, which only applies in drug cases, are clearly ready to be retired as relics of our fading drug war. The career offender guidelines, too, provide too much punitive potential in low-level cases to be considered sustainable. The guidelines themselves already take into account the prior convictions of all sentenced defendants, so these pile-on enhancements for drug defendants are hard to justify on empirical or penological grounds. "Historical weight," especially that which is produced by confidential informants who are themselves benefitting from naming names and drug amounts, is another tool that may be worth scrapping. As we saw in Southeast District, phantom drug weight produced by informants has accounted for adding centuries more to defendants' prison time, collectively, when it is calculated as relevant conduct at sentencing. Using law enforcement resources to build "historical weight" cases does little to address public safety, since no drugs are actually seized and destroyed, and it is produced in such a way as to make it especially unreliable as evidence.[28] Indeed, relevant conduct itself is ripe for extinction. Introduced by the Sentencing Commission to thwart prosecutorial circumvention of the guidelines in plea bargaining, it has itself become a powerful tool to compel guilty pleas. More fundamentally, its very use erodes the legitimacy of the system by sidestepping the due process rules that attend criminal law.[29]

Finally, the vast discretion that prosecutors hold as to who will be brought into this system to face federal drug charges is due for some scrutiny and, ideally, regulation. Given the statutes on the books, federal prosecutors can pluck the most piddling drug defendants out of state court, or off the street after they have been targeted in buy-busts. As we saw in Northeastern and Southeast Districts, the targeted defendants were almost always persons of color, whose overexposure to local police in their neighborhoods elevates their visibility and hence their vulnerability to federal prosecution. These kinds of cases fuel the extreme racial disparities that characterize some districts' drug caseloads.

Many of these defendants' vulnerability to federal prosecution comes from criminal records that are themselves produced by years of overpolicing. In particular, as a result of selective drug law enforcement practices in local jurisdictions across the country, those with drug offense records are racially and spatially concentrated in a pattern that does not accurately reflect actual drug crime.[30] And those drug priors are among the most potent forms of criminal history in the federal system, elevating sentencing exposure in multiple ways.[31]

These kinds of cases can also serve as a near endless supply of low-hanging fruit that helps keep case numbers up and the institutional machinery intact, and which require fewer resources and less effort to prosecute than the more traditional federal drug cases—to say nothing of complex fraud or other white-collar crime. As a result, they became more common over time in jurisdictions like Northeastern, displacing the higher-cost, more complex large-scale drug conspiracies that we imagine as federal cases. Because many of those brought in for very low-level offense conduct are vulnerable to the uniquely punitive federal criminal history enhancements, huge disparities are produced between those who get to stay in state court and those subject to federal prosecution.

Yet the prosecutor's charging power is nearly inviolate in the American legal tradition.[32] That means the prospects for change to the front end of the process as to who gets charged are the least promising, absent a major revision of the criminal statute to more narrowly define what constitutes a federal drug offense. Changing local practices as to norms and perceptions about prosecution-worthy cases will not be achieved simply through a top-down policy mandate. There remains considerable allure to these small cases, especially in light of the low time investment and high conviction yields that these cases bring. And in any case, policing local U.S. attorney's offices on their charging decisions is not sustainable as a policy fix.

Meaningful retrenchment will be hard work, given that well-established norms and practices within trial-level court communities present a formidable barrier to efforts aimed at reducing the racially unequal, punitive reach of this system. Because actors across districts adapt to changing policies in light of local norms, motivations, and logics, policy interventions that aim to roll back the force of these laws will need to account for the multiple forms of resistance that have already emerged from frontline institutional actors.

Numerous reform efforts—including the very one that created the Sentencing Reform Act of 1984—have demonstrated that the best intentions can sometimes be the ripest for perversion. This means that extreme vigilance is required vis-à-vis the minutia of the policy processes that purport to fix this broken system. Otherwise, we will witness a deepening divide between the locales that are ready to move away from the punitive drug war and those that cling to the old punishing rhetoric and practices. At the very least, we must take a stand that there must be no more Devons, punished with "life-trashing sentences" as a consequence of a failed war.[33]

= Epilogue =

Some Hope and More Despair

In September 2014, Devon Harrison received a letter that gave him more hope than he had experienced in over a decade. Back in 2004, when he had been prosecuted and convicted in Southeast District, the conditions for federal defendants were the worst they had ever been in the guidelines era. A month after Devon's jury had returned its verdict, the United States Supreme Court issued its ruling in *United States v. Booker*, which implicitly repudiated the extreme constraints that had been imposed on judges by the Feeney Amendment of the PROTECT Act. This would not matter for Devon, though. While *Booker* made the Guidelines advisory and allowed judges to exercise much more sentencing discretion, it did not invalidate the mandatory minimum statutes or the "851" statutory enhancement that had dictated Devon's life sentence.

From his prison cell Devon also watched as his peers, including his friend and codefendant, Charles, got the benefit of sentence reductions and early releases under the crack retroactivity policies following crack sentencing reforms.[1] But none of these resentencing options applied to him. With the drug weight involved in his case and the 851 enhancements, his life-without-parole sentence stood because it remained a legally valid mandatory minimum.

His appeals also went nowhere. There had been some troubling aspects to his case, above and beyond the extreme sentencing exposure he faced under the double 851. The judge had allowed the prosecutor to present evidence that Devon had a small amount of heroin on him for his own personal use, even though he had not been charged with its possession. When the prosecutor failed to make the connection to the case at hand, the judge's "corrective"—an instruction to the jury that the evidence should not have come in so they should ignore it after all—could hardly undo its impact.

More troubling was the fact that, just months after Devon's sentencing, one of the two DEA witnesses who had testified against him came under investigation for coercing a cooperator in another drug case to sleep with him in order to obtain leniency. The agent pleaded guilty to a felony charge of providing false statements to federal officers. The very same judge who had presided over Devon's case was assigned to the DEA agent's case.[2] Given the plea deal obtained by Devon's codefendant, Marina, one has to wonder how her "star" testimony may have been shaped by her interactions with this agent. The credibility of the agent himself, whose testimony was relied upon to obtain Devon's conspiracy conviction, was surely suspect. Yet this, too, triggered no reassessment of Devon's conviction on legal or ethical grounds.

By spring 2013, Devon's appeal efforts had been shut down for the final time. Citing the Clinton-era Anti-Terrorism and Effective Death Penalty Act, his trial judge declared his last attempt at relief "an unauthorized successive motion," so it would not be considered.[3] With his legal options exhausted, Devon had to come to grips with never getting out. And with that came the realization that he'd never see his mother again, who was too infirm to travel the eight or so hours by car to visit him.

The letter of hope came from Clemency Project 2014, informing Devon that he potentially qualified for the new clemency initiative instituted by President Obama and Attorney General Eric Holder. The federal defenders in Southeast District had flagged his case for the project as one that should be at the top of the pile. Over the following year, Devon's assigned clemency lawyer worked up the petition, a process that requires navigating the communications challenges that come with imprisoned clients and that must rely upon the cooperation of prison officials to provide necessary documentation. It was filed in December 2015.

Devon's emotional world has become topsy-turvy ever since he got that letter. With the hope for a way out of prison before he dies comes a rush of anxiety that this hope, too, can be dashed. After someone has been locked up for more than a decade, it is hard to come up with a viable release plan, a requirement of the petition. This is made harder by the fact that lifers in prison have lowest priority for vocational and educational programs inside, so coming up with a narrative about preparation for the free world is difficult. As of this writing, Devon's petition is still pending.

There are tens of thousands of men and women like Devon, whose hopes for relief from long drug sentences are pinned to the Obama clemency initiative. So far, only several hundred have had their hopes realized. Nonetheless, the clemency initiative is a genuine, tangible rollback of the War on Drug's excesses. The initiative has been framed in just those terms: like Devon, the men and women who have benefitted had received sentences that were disproportionately punitive by most objective measures.[4]

Signs that the War on Drugs is receding can be seen elsewhere, as well. For instance, in 2012 U.S. District Court Judge John Gleeson helped establish a diversion program for drug-involved federal defendants in the Eastern District of New York. The Pretrial Opportunity Program (POP) allows substance-abusing defendants a path to treatment and a stable life without their ever going to prison. Gleeson, a former federal prosecutor himself, had become one of the most outspoken critics of the hard edge of the federal drug war, especially the use of 851s.[5] This diversion program was a way to actually blaze a new trail for defendants, like Devon, whose criminal involvement stems from personal drug problems. If only Devon's case had appeared on the docket hundreds of miles north and a decade later, he, too, would have had the chance to deal with his addiction and get his life back on track in the POP program, perhaps without ever going to prison.

But just when Devon Harrison had finally gotten a glimmer of optimism via Clemency Project 2014's letter, and just as Judge Gleeson was presiding over more and more milestone celebrations and successful diversions in the POP program,[6] yet another young black man saw his hope crushed that he could ever be free again. On August 28, 2014, twenty-five-year-old Chris Young (his actual name) was about to be sentenced. He had been convicted a year earlier in federal court in Nashville for his part in a crack conspiracy. Like Devon, Chris had gone to trial.[7] And like the AUSA in Devon's case, Chris's prosecutor filed the double 851 after Chris turned down a fourteen-year plea offer and proceeded to trial.[8]

It had been a long, complicated road for Chris to get to this day. Ultimately, Chris knew, Chris's lawyer knew, the prosecutor knew, and the judge knew that this sentencing proceeding was a mere formality, required by law. Nothing that Chris or his lawyer said or did could change what was going to be imposed at the end of it. But Chris had something to say before he was thrown in federal prison for the remainder of his natural life.

His speech was compelling. And it is heartbreaking. It is heartbreaking for familiar reasons. He spoke of the exceptionally challenging conditions of his childhood. It is even more heartbreaking because it so clearly and tragically revealed the human potential that the government was about to lock up forever. He opened by tacitly acknowledging the futility of his allocution in light of the inevitable life sentence to be imposed:

> I had planned on coming here impressing you, Judge Sharp, leaving you disposed to me, showing you that these four years I've been incarcerated I've been studious with my time taking copious notes. To accomplish this, I was going to speak on a variety of topics, one of which being American history.
>
> I'm familiar that William Penn purchased Pennsylvania from the Delaware Native Americans, how Washington disbanded the troops in 1783, how March 16th, 1783, Washington delivered the speech that made the troops avert their plans.

Chris moved through American history from the nation's establishment to the famous and arcane events of the twentieth century—the establishment of the Federal Reserve in 1913, Nixon and Watergate in the 1970s, and Reagan's meeting of the minds with Margaret Thatcher on the appropriate role of government in society in the 1980s. He spoke of the most minute details about the Declaration of Independence and mentioned that he had memorized all of the amendments to the Constitution.

He named the many philosophers he would have spoken about to show Judge Sharp how much he had learned. Then on to the famous financiers and economists: "Andrew Carnegie, whose philanthropic activities account for opening over 2,500 libraries in Canada, America, and Europe and also for donating up to $300 million . . . John Maynard Keynes, whose economic philosophy and doctrines have been the foundation for the IMF." He told Judge Sharp about how he would have talked about his "love for financials" and his dream of working in wealth management and how he keeps up on the news of all the major CEOs and stock funds and international currency markets.

And this leads me to speak on different surveys and polls that have been conducted that show[s] the recidivism rate is higher amongst individuals that have been incarcerated for long periods of time and how even I myself do not believe that it takes thirty, twenty, fifteen, or even ten years for a person to realize he done something wrong and he need[s] to find a more decorous way to go about it.

Your Honorable Judge Sharp, as you know, I stand before you today facing a life sentence based on two prior felony convictions I obtained at the young tender age of eighteen . . . one of which was the simple possession of less than .5 grams, less than .5 grams. Your Honorable Judge Sharp, you've seen enough drugs in your day to know that's barely enough for an addict or user to strike their lighter once and it's gone.

Speaking of addicts and users, if you don't mind, I'd like to take this time to reflect on my childhood real quick, Your Honor. . . .

As you know and I've spoke on before, I have a disease called sickle cell anemia. It's a blood condition you have to be born with, which takes your blood cells from the normal shape to a sickle shape, which makes you rheumatic and locks your body up and causes excruciating pain. So when I was a child, I spent a lot of time in the hospital and up under my mother, which in so many ways and words made me a mother's boy, which also can help you imagine the pain I felt watching her struggle with her addiction and domestic violence in her various relationships. . . .

Like I've hinted and like you know, my mother had a very extreme addiction to crack cocaine, which led her to raising us in some of the severe and most critical conditions a child should be raised in in America. We spent a significant amount of time living with no lights and water. When it was wintertime, she heated the house with kerosene. When it was nighttime, she lit the house with candles.

So then just try to imagine two young kids, one of which almost a teenager, my brother, going to school with holes in our shoes, their skin smelling like musk and grass from playing outside the day before, their clothes too small or in my case too big because most of the time I was trying to wear my brother's clothes, and the clothes smelling like kerosene from being in the house. Combine these two scents and imagine the malodorous smell we was carrying to school with us each and every day. Imagine what your opinion would be upon first meeting us.

Imagine the emotion and anguish that me and my brother dealt with at a young tender age, more so my brother because most of the time I did not have the appropriate meal unless my brother came upon some money and went to one of the local neighborhood restaurants or stores and bought something and came home and shared it. A lot of times I didn't bathe unless my brother sucked up his pride and asked one of his friends in the neighborhood could we bathe at their house or asked one of the neighbors could we bathe at their house.

Chris went on to recount how he got into the drug business, how he wanted money and was too young to get hired at the few jobs available, and how he was good at drug sales. He shared how much he hated drugs, which made him good in the business. He saved his money, and got training in acting and modeling and music. He was an aspiring rap artist. Then he shared the tragedy of his older brother's death, the only person who had ever loved him unconditionally. He asked to "fast forward" to the present, to talk about how he was tutoring other inmates in math within his jail pod, and how he was being rehabilitated and could do good if ever given a chance to be in the community again, while recognizing it was not a real possibility.

All I'm asking, Your Honor, is that you please acknowledge my ambition, my order, and my potential, and that if I was given a chance to be released back into society within a reasonable amount of time, I could accomplish and achieve my aspirations and hopefully go down in the ranks with some of the men I admire the most.

The speech wound down, and Chris thanked Judge Sharp for letting him speak and "for treating me like a man and looking at me like a man because some people, they naturally look at us like we're something else just because we've made mistakes and we've ended up on the other side of the law." At the conclusion, Judge Sharp engaged with Chris about some of the many topics he had raised, and recommended some further readings on C. P. Snow and Genghis Khan, both of whom had been mentioned by Chris. He thanked Chris for speaking and turned the proceeding back over to the lawyers.

In the end, Judge Sharp did what he had to do. He imposed a sentence of life without the possibility of parole, plus five more years, consecutive, on top of that for a 924(c) gun conviction, followed by five years of supervised release.[9]

= Appendix A =

Background, Methods, and Overview of the Study

This book is based on a comparative qualitative field study that I conducted from December 2012 through July 2014. The study was conducted in four federal districts, with additional interviews conducted in two more districts. In this book I focus on three distinctive districts to illustrate the varieties of ways in which the same law is differentially deployed. My fourth main district was a rural one with a small criminal caseload overall, and a small drug caseload.[1]

The study was designed to analyze the interplay between localized norms and imperatives in how drug laws are implemented, and the larger legal structure in which local courts are situated. It was the second part of a larger, multimethodological research program concerning the impact of formal legal change on federal criminal drug trafficking cases. The first component of the project used longitudinal multilevel regression analyses to examine the influence, over time, of local context on variations in sentencing. In that project, funded by the National Institute of Justice (NIJ), Marisa Omori and I examined federal sentencing patterns in drug trafficking cases from 1992 to 2009, individually and by district.[2]

We found that districts appear to maintain stability over time in the kinds of trafficking cases that get prosecuted and sentenced, and in the lengths of sentences imposed. Ultimately, districts looked like themselves over time, while consistently varying from each other, suggesting district-level legal culture is both enduring and important to case processing, above and beyond the changes brought by *United States v. Booker* and other such top-down legal mandates.

We also found that although districts tended to look like themselves over time, the mechanisms used to maintain that stasis changed as a function of policy period. Therefore, it appeared that court actors adapted adjudication practices to meet the demands of policy mandates while simultaneously maintaining their local case norms for actual sentence outcomes.[3] And districts that prosecuted more mandatory-minimum cases, compared to low-mandatory-minimum districts, were especially likely to have racially disparate outcomes, disadvantaging black defendants in particular. This suggested to us that the more power imbalances favored prosecutors, the more likely bias was able to flourish.

The qualitative field research reported on in this book was designed to follow up on some of our findings by specifically exploring phenomena that are not easily examined through official data sources.[4] For instance, we found that drug trafficking caseloads differed considerably by district in ways that are not adequately explained by regional patterns of drug offending. Yet the data could not speak to how, from the universe of potential federal defendants, those selected defendants ended up being prosecuted federally. This problem is particularly notable with drug trafficking because many of those federal cases could have been handled in state court, and conversely, many or most felony drug sales, manufacturing, and transportation cases handled in state courts could conceivably qualify for federal prosecution under contemporary drug trafficking statutes. Because the caseload composition in a given district shapes how the work group members in that district manage cases, the qualitative project was designed to explore this phenomenon.[5]

The qualitative field research was also designed to examine how legal actors in distinct locales appear to shape case outcomes both individually and collectively. This kind of examination is not possible using official case data, since the courtroom actors assigned to any given case—judges, prosecutors, defense attorneys, and pretrial probation officers—are not made publicly available in the federal data sets. At present, given the omission of court actor data, it is difficult to directly determine from the USSC or federal court datasets whether judges, prosecutors, or defense attorneys are behaving differently in the wake of *Booker*, and whether those work group members' relative influence on sentence outcome has changed. More fundamentally, even if individual legal actor data were available, there is a dearth of research on how those actors understand and categorize cases, including how they perceive their own role in producing case outcomes.

This project also aimed to explore how cases with multiple defendants are managed. The USSC does not code for codefendant cases, which makes impossible analyses that could identify and quantify a potentially huge source of "unwarranted" or at least unjust disparity both pre- and post-*Booker*. The USSC's 2009 regional hearings include compelling testimony from practitioners about serious injustices that arise in codefendant cases, particularly around the issue of cooperation.[6] This is particularly problematic in drug trafficking cases, which often involve codefendants, and where both mandatory minimums and 5K1.1 departure motions for "substantial assistance" to the government are widely used.[7] For these reasons I designed the qualitative project to assess the impact of codefendants on prosecutorial, judicial, and defense adjudication strategies.

I also aimed to unpack and tease out some of the complexities of changing policy and practice that are co-occurring with *Booker*-related and other policy reforms in the design of this project. There are multiple moving parts both within the federal criminal justice system and in the larger social, political and governmental realms that can potentially shape sentence outcomes, rendering it difficult, if not impossible, to isolate the impact of specific legal changes in quantitative models. In that regard, there are numerous policy changes that have been in play in recent years.

For instance, the Fair Sentencing Act of 2010, which increased the weight thresholds for mandatory minimum penalties in crack cocaine cases, directly impacted sentence outcomes and may well have influenced how prosecutors charge and negotiate crack cases, in the period leading up to and subsequent to the enactment of the legislation.[8] Additionally, Attorney General Eric Holder issued a memorandum in 2010 giving more discretion to individual U.S. attorneys' offices on charging and plea bargaining.[9] The Holder memo reflected a significant change from the Department of Justice policy previously in place, which required assistant U.S. attorneys to pursue the most serious charges that are readily provable and seek the maximum possible sentence allowed. These kinds of structural influences were explored in the field research project, especially in the in-depth interviews.[10]

This research also explored some of the tensions between unwarranted differential treatment and "unwarranted uniformity"[11] that have plagued guidelines-based sentencing pre- and post-*Booker*. Within this, I aimed to explicate the degree to which the very measures that come to represent "warranted" and "unwarranted" sentencing considerations are contextually specific in their construction and application, since much of this tension hinges on the question of official measurement and what it represents in terms of disparity.[12] Finally, the research explored how "legitimate" sentencing factors, such as 5K1.1 "substantial assistance" departure motions, actually get deployed in cases as a function of office and courtroom work group members, in order to better understand and explain differences in formal outcomes across locales.[13]

In sum, this research revisited some of the larger underlying questions about how criminal case adjudication and sentencing work in practice, for which there has been a relative dearth of field data since the early days of the guidelines. It also focused on the mechanisms of legal policy change and how they get put into effect to provide a fuller, more contextualized picture of how cases are negotiated and sentenced in a period of policy transformation. To that extent, the research ideally functions as a bookend to the mixed-methods, multidistrict research conducted by Irene Nagel and Stephen Schulhofer when the guidelines were initially implemented to assess how the new policy was absorbed and put into action by district courts.[14]

I had several specific research purposes with this project. First, I sought to develop a narrative account of how the data points that end up in the

USSC database are differentially derived as a function of local setting. Within this, I examined the degree to which "similarly situated" sentenced defendants, according to that dataset, may well differ on culpability and other such determinations, as a result of the differences in how cases are processed in different locales (and vice versa).

Second, through a set of interviews with federal defenders and other court actors, I sought to explicate, in rich detail, how plea negotiations and sentencing are and have been done in each district. Within that, I assessed interviewees' perceptions of the degree to which *Booker* and *Gall v. United States* (as well as other changes and policy reforms) have altered the sentencing process in the given district.

Third, I sought to tease out the tension between the ideal of uniformity (often emphasized by the USSC) and more individualized sentencing to assess the costs and benefits for justice under each model, as it actually plays out in criminal adjudication.

I selected the four districts in the study to differ from each other on several key dimensions: overall size, size of criminal caseload, size of drug trafficking caseload, demonstrated rate and type of sentence outcome variations post–*Kimbrough* and *Gall*, and geographic location. I obtained initial access to the district-level federal defenders' offices with the assistance of the National Sentencing Resource Counsel, which serves as an expert litigation, research, and policy analysis body for the myriad federal defenders' offices that represent clients in U.S. district courts.[15] Once I gained access and began to spend time in each district, I developed contacts with other court actors and sought formal and informal interviews with them outside the federal defenders' offices. These actors included private and panel defense attorneys, former and active prosecutors, judges, and several federal law enforcement agents. In accordance with prevailing ethical standards for conducting social science research with human subjects, all of the attorneys, judges, defendants, and others I discuss in this book are given pseudonyms to protect their privacy. The districts are also given pseudonyms to ensure that privacy and confidentiality.

I entered the field through federal defenders' offices for both strategic and accessibility reasons. Federal defenders provide representation to federally charged indigent clients in their respective districts; there is also a panel of attorneys in each court who are appointed to represent indigent defendants. Because over 97 percent of federally sentenced drug trafficking cases are resolved through a plea of guilt rather than a trial, uncovering how those defendants come to decide or are incentivized to plead guilty is central to understanding contemporary federal sentencing.[16] Therefore, in order to directly observe how criminal case adjudication happens, access to attorneys whose negotiations primarily occur outside of open court was optimal for achieving this study's goals.

An alternate approach would have been to gain primary access through district-level U.S. attorneys' offices, but access to those offices for observational field research is notoriously difficult to obtain, if not impossible.[17] Even for those with the authority to collect data from prosecutors, access is limited for key parts of the adjudication process, owing to the secrecy of the grand jury indictment process. The difficulty of gaining access to prosecutors' offices in general—and the resulting inability of researchers to fully analyze the prosecutorial role—has been the subject of much commentary and lament.[18] But even if this had been a viable alternative, there are compelling reasons to begin with the defense.

Situating an observational study of how cases are processed prior to formal sentencing within federal defender's offices allows the researcher to see how cases proceed from the early stage through resolution, since defenders are generally appointed at the charging and arraignment stage. The researcher is privy not only to what is offered in negotiations but also to how "good" or "bad" offers are construed, and accepted or rejected. In addition, this access allows for a contextually rich account of criminal defense work within the analysis of how cases are dealt with in the federal system. Accounts of criminal defense lawyering are largely absent in the contemporary empirical federal sentencing literature and are sparse in state court literature.[19]

I took a comparative case analytic approach to examining the negotiations, conflicts, compromises, and resolutions that occur in federal criminal cases. By "case analytic approach," I mean that I followed a set of individual drug cases through to their adjudication in each of the four districts. My observations were of the people and processes involved in resolving cases, but my units of analysis for this component of the study were the individual cases themselves. My own "case" observations were supplemented by data from case files. Although I was not able to directly witness most behind-the-scenes negotiations, I was able to obtain accounts of the process from the attorneys involved.

The direct observations and case materials were also coupled with both shorter informal interviews and structured, in-depth interviews with willing courtroom work group members in each district. I conducted sixty-three formal interviews and an additional twelve shorter, informal (often impromptu) interviews. The average formal interview was just over an hour long and ranged from about twenty minutes to over two and a half hours.

The formal interviews were structured to cover four broad areas of interest:

1. The norms of case processing and negotiating outside court, both generally and specific to drug trafficking cases
2. The changing nature of case negotiations over time, and the relative influence of different kinds of legal, political, and organizational change

3. The working relationship between attorneys, pretrial probation officers, and sentencing judges, and complications posed by each set of courtroom actors, as well as by codefendants and their co-counsel, in the adjudication process

4. Perceptions about disparities in sentencing patterns, the meaning of "uniformity" in sentencing, and broader justice challenges that face the federal criminal justice system

I also used longitudinal data pertaining to case processing in each district, obtained from the Executive Office for U.S. Attorneys, Administrative Office of the U.S. Courts, and the USSC. These data were used to develop longitudinal district-specific "portraits" of the four distinct districts as a contextual backdrop to the qualitative observational findings.

I chose to continue to focus on drug trafficking cases in the field portion of the study for several reasons. First, federal drug cases have engendered the most policy debate since the inception of the guidelines and are a major category of primary sentenced offense. Although the number of immigration offenses equaled drug trafficking offenses by 2009, and they have since surpassed drugs as the largest category of federal convictions, drug trafficking remains a large and important component of the federal criminal caseload. Moreover, the major Supreme Court cases themselves that have substantially changed federal sentencing (*Booker, Gall, Kimbrough*) involved drug trafficking convictions, so the decisions have direct relevance to sentencing issues pertaining to drug trafficking defendants.

Second, since a significant subset of drug trafficking offenses is also subject to mandatory minimum statutes, this project was able to disentangle the complexities of sentencing in drug cases that are subject to mandatory minimums as well as the guidelines, by exploring how exposure to mandatory minimums shapes plea negotiations and final sentences. Thus, the project contributes to our understanding of how complex and competing bodies of law get interpreted and applied in the real world by looking holistically at the sentencing process in this evolving system.

Finally, as previously noted, the federal drug trafficking caseload is arguably the most discretionary of the criminal caseloads in the federal system. As such, federal drug cases provide an especially clear window into the role of discretion in legal processing and provide insight into whether, why, and how factors such as defendant demographics—a central concern of sentencing and mass incarceration research—shape case selection, negotiations, and outcomes.[20]

= Appendix B =

Portraits of the Three Districts

I examine three distinct federal districts in this book to highlight how the law lives differently as a function of the localized conditions and socio-legal dynamics of distinct courthouses. This appendix provides more contextual detail for each of those three districts: Northeastern, Southeast, and Southwestern.

Chapter 3 is set in Northeastern District. In this district, most of the criminal caseload originates in the Urban division, based in the major metropolitan area of the state. The federal courthouses in this district are lightly used, especially relative to the state courts in the region. No matter the time of day, the hallways are relatively empty and the sounds of life mainly come from the first floor, where the marshals assigned to security duty banter. The main courthouse in the Urban division is a beautiful, modern building; each courtroom inside is finished out with high-end tiger oak furnishings and wall paneling. Security is thorough in this courthouse. Visitors are screened upon entering and are prohibited from bringing in any electronics, including cameras, computers, and cell phones. Nonetheless, as a courtesy to those who arrive with such items, the marshals have set up a system at the entry, like a coat check, for visitors to stow devices while inside.

Approximately 86 percent of the drug trafficking convictions from 1992 to 2012 took place in the Urban division of Northeastern District; the remainder happened in the two small divisions that serve the rest of the district.[1] Each of those smaller courts is staffed by a single active district court judge and one or two magistrates, whereas the Urban division has about two dozen district judges and magistrates hearing cases. Few if any federal drug possession cases are pursued in this district in any given year; however, there is a substantial caseload of very small, street-level drug distribution cases that are adjudicated here. As I explore in detail in chapter 3, the low-level drug defendants brought to federal court were overwhelmingly African Americans, who often had criminal records that qualified them for greatly enhanced sentences under both the guidelines and via statutory enhancements. As a consequence, sentences for African American defendants, particularly in the pre-*Booker* era, were significantly longer than those for white drug defendants, even when the black defendants' drug amounts were lower.

My second site, Southeast District, is best understood as comprising three major, autonomous divisions—what I call North division, Middle division, and South division. Each has norms and practices of its own.[2] The courthouses in each of the divisions were the least friendly to the public of all federal courts I visited. Middle division's courthouse was the most modern of the three, and the most technologically advanced in its security. For example, stairwells were traps—if visitors tried to take the stairs to access courtrooms on different floors, they found themselves locked out and stuck. This was part of the security design, I was told, to prevent terrorists or other intruders from being able to move between floors outside of the elevator system. South division's courthouse, though, was the least user-friendly. Housed in a Depression-era art deco federal building, its security staging area was cramped inside a small entry that was never intended to be used for anything besides ingress and egress. Marshals here inquired about visitors' purposes for entering the building, less to be helpful than out of suspicion of visitors' motives.

Like the courthouses in Northeastern District, none of the three here allow any electronic devices, and all require entrants to show government-issued identification. But unlike in Northeastern, visitors were stuck if they had cell phones or other barred items on them. Marshals offered no place to hold them and simply turned away those who possessed such items. More than once I met family members of defendants who, sometimes after traveling for hours by car or bus, were told they could not enter since they had cell phones on them. An elderly woman, there for her son's initial appearance after being taken into custody, told me that she ended up hiding her cell phone in a planter box outside of the court since she had come a long distance on the bus. She worried that it might be gone by the time she was able to retrieve it, but her priority was to be in court for her son. Even lawyers in this district were only allowed to bring their laptops into court if they received prior approval from the judge presiding in their case.

Most striking in Southeast District was the opacity of what was actually happening inside the courtrooms. Federal districts almost uniformly post court schedules online, which are generally available up to a week before some proceedings, and which are often updated on a daily basis as calendars change. At the actual courthouses, there is usually a system to see what cases are on the calendar that day, at what time, and in which courtroom. The urban courthouse at Northeastern District had full copies of the day's calendar available at the security area, and each courtroom's calendar was posted outside its doors. In Southwestern District, every floor had a large, scrolling electronic board announcing the calendars for each courtroom.

But in Southeast District, accurate calendars were hard to come by. In Middle division, if one did not check online before coming, the only way to find out was to go to the court clerk's office, on the top floor of the building, and ask the desk clerk to check on a given case or judge. South division was the most troubling. Each judge was supposed to post her schedule on a bulletin board behind glass on the first floor, but compliance was spotty at best. The chief judge refused to post a schedule at all, on the bulletin board or online, so there was no way for an outsider to find out what was scheduled in that court. It was hit or miss with other judges. Some clerks posted handwritten notes for their judges that all too often were out of date or incomplete; others were complete and up to date. All in all, the problem was pervasive enough here that even the most diligent visitor ran a high risk of not being able to access full and accurate information about public court business.

In terms of case norms, the North division has traditionally been less punitive in its sentencing practices than the Middle and South divisions. Its drug caseload is also both smaller and more varied than that of the other two divisions. Conversely, Middle division has had the highest proportion of its criminal caseload devoted to drug cases; four out of ten criminal cases over the period from 1992 to 2012 were drug trafficking cases, and the vast majority of the defendants in those cases were African American. Specifically, from 1992 to 2012, 83 percent of drug defendants in Middle division were African American, whereas 75 percent in South division and 52 percent in North division were African American.

Middle division has also been a national leader in its number and rate of crack prosecutions, which correlates with its exceptionally high rate of black defendants. More than 65 percent of all drug trafficking defendants there were charged with crack offenses over the years from 1992 to 2012, compared to 39 percent for North division and 50 percent for South division.[3] This division was also especially harsh relative to the other divisions and to the rest of the nation. Sentences meted out in Middle division were on average 6 percent above the guideline minimums, whereas in the rest of the district, they were 4 percent below the guideline minimum. In essence, the Middle division of Southeast District exemplifies the most punitive implementation of the federal war on drugs.

Southwestern District, my third site, located on the U.S.-Mexico border, has two major urban divisions, which I will call Urban division and Border division, with several outpost courts that are each staffed by a magistrate. Given its location on the border, the district faces a crush of drug and immigration cases, which constitute the bulk of the criminal caseload. The Border division, which handles more than 80 percent of the entire district's criminal cases, is the busiest court, and in some ways functions more like an overburdened state court than a prototypical federal court.

The drug defendants in Southwestern District differ substantially from the typical drug defendant in both the Northeastern and Southeast Districts. Here, the vast majority of sentenced drug defendants are Latino, and as of 2012, approximately three-quarters of those sentenced for drug trafficking crimes were noncitizens (see table B.1).[4]

The courthouses in this district are also more publicly accessible than those in the other two districts. Although the courts here, too, prohibit bringing in cameras and recording devices, they do allow visitors to enter with their cell phones, smartphones, and even laptop computers. The two main courthouses, those in Urban division and Border division, were bustling compared to the courthouses in Northeastern and Southeast Districts. The stand-alone magistrate court along the border, too, felt more like a local municipal court (though less busy) than like a staid federal courthouse.

The physical structures of the courthouses here were modern and well appointed, white and light in construction with light wood accents. The courtrooms in the Urban division were finished out in spare, clean-lined, high-end maple décor. A striking feature of many of Southwestern District's courtrooms was the prominence of the guidelines' Sentencing Table permanently displayed somewhere. In some courtrooms, a large poster-sized version stood on a display easel, angled toward the podium where the defendant stood for proceedings. In others, it was taped across one of the outdated computer monitors that occupied space on podia, tables, and counsel desks. Its visual prominence seemed incongruent here, since this district has among the most generous "fast track" programs in the nation, which offer significantly reduced sentences to defendants who plead guilty quickly to immigration and drug charges. This is all to be able to efficiently process the crush of cases here.

Table B.1   Drug Defendant Characteristics in Three Case Study Districts, 2012

District[a]	Race or Ethnicity			Gender		Mean Criminal History Points	Mean Offense Level	Guilty Plea Rate
	White	Black	Latino	Men	Women			
Northeastern district	23%	34%	41%	95%	5%	4.2	24.3	93%
Southeast district	17	63	18	87	13	3.8	26.2	96
Southwestern district	6	2	89	88	12	1.2	17.4[b]	99

Source: Author's consolidated dataset of U.S. Sentencing Commission sentencing data.

[a]Northeastern population demographics: 75 percent white, 8 percent black, 11 percent Latino; Southeast population demographics: 62 percent white, 21 percent black, 9 percent Latino; Southwestern population demographics: 57 percent white, 5 percent black, 30 percent Latino.

[b]Driven down by drug fast-track program in this district, which adds a four-level reduction.

═══ Notes ═══

Introduction

1. I use pseudonyms for all of the defendants, lawyers, judges, and other legal actors whom I observed or communicated with in conducting this research. This is part of my ethical commitment to maintaining confidentiality, which is a standard requirement for all social science research that does not involve well-known public figures. In order to ensure the research participants' confidentiality, I also use pseudonyms for the locations where my research took place. For a full discussion of requirements and duties for conducting ethical social science research see Sieber and Tolich 2012.

2. Devon's girlfriend was spared federal prosecution in this case for reasons only the U.S. attorney really knows; she was also not charged in state court with any crimes related to this incident.

3. These conditions have also changed in state criminal justice systems over the same time period. See, for example, Zimring and Hawkins 1993; Tonry 1996; Garland 2002. However, the federal system's overhaul remains among the most dramatic and controversial. For a comparative assessment, see Frase 1999.

4. Public Law 98-473, § 212(a)(2) 98 Stat. 1837 (1984), codified at 18 U.S.C. §§ 3551–3742 and 28 U.S.C. §§ 991–98 (1994).

5. Over time, Congress also dramatically increased the punishments for methamphetamine, which now triggers the harshest sentences under the drug trafficking statute.

6. Kate Stith and Jose Cabranes (1998) provide a detailed analysis of the impact of federal sentencing reform on judging.

7. Barkow 2008, 878.

8. Office of the U.S. Attorneys (website), "Annual Statistical Reports," see links for 1980 and 2000 at: www.justice.gov/usao/resources/annual-statistical-reports (accessed April 28, 2016).

9. See appendix A for full details on my methods and appendix B for detailed profiles of these three districts.

10. Foucault 1982, 786.

11. Reicher 2004.

12. For Michel Foucault (1982), understanding power requires grounded empirical investigation that takes "the forms of resistance against different forms of power as a starting point. To use another metaphor, it consists of using this resistance as a chemical catalyst so as to bring to light power relations, locate their position, and find out their point of application and the methods used. Rather than analyzing power from the point of view of its internal rationality, it consists of analyzing power relations through the antagonism of strategies" (780).

13. The most comprehensive and insightful analysis of the effects of the guidelines on the distribution of legal power is Stith and Cabranes' *Fear of Judging: Sentencing Guidelines in the Federal Courts* (1998).

14. U.S. Sentencing Commission 2007; Rosenmerkel, Durose, and Farole 2009.

15. Garland 2001, 5; Lynch 2012.

16. All of these statistics are from the U.S. Department of Justice, Office of the U.S. Attorneys, "Annual Statistical Reports," available online for the years 1955 to 2014 at: www.justice.gov/usao/resources/annual-statistical-reports (accessed May 10, 2016).

17. McDonald and Carlson 1993; U.S. Sentencing Commission 2014 (totaling all three categories of sentenced drug defendants).

18. The Sentencing Commission's own analyses indicated that racial disparities were not limited to who was charged. In its 2004 report on the first fifteen years of the guidelines, the commission reported that black drug defendants had 20 percent higher odds and Latinos had 40 percent higher odds of receiving prison sentences than otherwise similar white drug defendants. Those sentences were also likely to be longer, even after controlling for differences in case facts. Specifically, both black and Latino drug defendants received prison sentences that were about 10 percent greater than otherwise similar white drug defendants. When the built-in sentencing differentials by drug substance were factored in, the gap between sentences imposed on black and white defendants ballooned in the guidelines era, largely due to the crack statute. The commission reported that black drug defendants' sentences were about 60 percent longer than white drug defendants' sentences (92.1 months compared to 57.9 months). See U.S. Sentencing Commission 2004.

19. U.S. Department of Health and Human Services, Substance Abuse and Mental Health Services Administration (2009) data indicated that of adults reporting that they had ever tried crack, 72 percent were non-Hispanic whites and only 13 percent were black. Of those who had used crack in the prior year, 63 percent were white and 25 percent were black.

20. U.S. Sentencing Commission 2014. Latinos made up 31 percent of convicted drug trafficking defendants in 1992, which steadily rose to 48 percent by 2013, where it stayed in 2014. For the three drug offense categories combined, Latinos made up 50 percent of all sentenced defendants.

21. U.S. Sentencing Commission 1991, 1.

22. See, for example, Johnson, Ulmer, and Kramer 2008; Kautt 2002; Lynch and Omori 2014; Ulmer 2005; Wu and Spohn 2010. Ilene Nagel and Stephen Schulhofer conducted the seminal studies at the dawn of the guidelines era to reveal how the new rules were being circumvented. See Nagel and Schulhofer 1992; Schulhofer and Nagel 1997.

23. Welch and Thompson 1980.

24. See Michelle Alexander 2010. Politicians of all stripes joined the crack mandatory minimum frenzy. The 1986 law was foremost made possible by the liberal Massachusetts congressman Tip O'Neill, with the full support of the Black Congressional Caucus. David Sklansky (1995) points out that the crack treatment is contrary to the stated goal of using mandatory minimums to

punish "kingpins," since the higher-ups deal in crack's precursor, powder cocaine. Consequently, writes Sklansky, "Defendants caught trafficking in crack thus are almost always the street-level retailers of the cocaine trade, not the wholesalers" (288). New York's Rockefeller drug laws, which preceded the federal developments, were revolutionary for their harshness but did not distinguish so closely by illicit substance. These laws imposed long mandatory minimums on convicted traffickers of two or more ounces of illicit substances.

25. U.S. Sentencing Commission 2004.

26. Lynch 2011a; Beckett, Nyrop, and Pfingst 2006.

27. Lynch 2011b; Simon 2007.

28. John Pfaff (2011, 19) finds that increased felony filings at the state level accounted for the largest share of growth in prison admissions during the rise of "mass incarceration."

29. *United States v. Booker*, 543 U.S. 220 (2005); *Kimbrough v. United States*, 128 S.Ct. 558 (2007); *Gall v. United States*, 552 U.S. 38 (2007). *Booker* got around the problem that defendants have a right to have a jury determine any facts that necessarily increase their punishment by rendering the guidelines advisory. That way, judges could use non-conviction-related "relevant conduct" to punish as long as they did not have to do so under the guidelines.

30. The mandatory minimums serve as a floor for judges' discretion in cases where they apply. See Fischman and Schanzenbach 2012.

31. For instance, the bipartisan Smarter Sentencing Act was reintroduced for the third time in 2015 but never made it to a vote. Although it had several components, its greatest impact would have reduced the length and applicability of mandatory minimums. The most recent version of this legislation is even more modest in its reforms.

32. Holder 2013. Primarily, assistant U.S. attorneys were directed not to specify drug weights that would trigger long mandatory minimums in their charging documents when the defendant met certain criteria. He also urged prosecutors in this memo and in a follow-up memo not to use threats of sentencing enhancements to obtain guilty pleas.

33. See Rachel Barkow (2015) for a history of federal executive clemency and an argument for more robust use of this presidential power.

34. See, for example, the August 13, 2013, *New York Times* editorial characterizing Holder's announcement of the revised charging policy as a "transformational moment," part of a sea change in criminal justice policy in the United States (The Editorial Board, "Smarter Sentencing," *New York Times*, August 13, 2013).

35. Stith and Cabranes 1998, 2.

36. The National Association of Assistant United States Attorneys, which represents a subset of more conservative, antireform assistant U.S. attorneys, has been especially proactive in fighting against any changes that would lessen sentences or weaken prosecutorial tools. See the organization's positions at: http://www.naausa.org/site/index.php/resources/white-papers/90-jul-2015-dangerous-myths-of-drug-sentencing-reform/file (accessed June 16, 2016). For a critique of this organization's positions, see Families Against Mandatory Minimums 2015.

37. For a study that directly documents this phenomenon, see Lerman and Weaver 2014.

Chapter 1

1. Ronald Reagan, "Radio Address to the Nation on Federal Drug Policy," October 2, 1982; full text available at: www.presidency.ucsb.edu/ws/?pid=43085.
2. Anslinger worked in Germany, Venezuela, England, France, and Belgium for a variety of organizations before returning to the United States to work on the domestic prohibition effort, which was his post at the time of his appointment to the Federal Bureau of Narcotics in 1930. For a sympathetic biography of Anslinger see McWilliams 1989; for a more critical analysis see Kinder 1981.
3. Provine 2007, 81.
4. This is not for lack of trying. A number of legislative proposals that aimed especially to regulate opium importation and use and cocaine use failed in the early twentieth century. See Musto 1999. The Harrison Act was given additional enforcement teeth in 1919 when it was amended to explicitly deny medical professionals' ability to prescribe substances "simply to maintain an addict" (Provine 2007, 80). The full text of the Harrison Narcotics Tax Act of 1914 is available at: www.druglibrary.org/schaffer/history/e1910/harrisonact.htm. This act in many ways mimicked the legislative efforts happening in various states at around the same time, which prohibited distribution of narcotic and addictive substances except by pharmacists or doctors (Musto 1999).
5. Musto 1999.
6. Ibid.
7. Full text available at: www.druglibrary.org/schaffer/hemp/taxact/mjtaxact.htm.
8. On Anslinger's early red baiting and xenophobic tactics as means to gain political support for this and subsequent legislative proposals, see Kinder 1981.
9. There were mandatory minimums on the federal books for other criminal acts; these were the first for drug crimes. See Murakawa 2014.
10. Anslinger 1951, 747–48. Anslinger published articles not only in law reviews, as here, but also in numerous popular media venues, including *Reader's Digest* and *Time* magazine (Provine 2007).
11. Musto 1999.
12. Narcotics Control Act of 1956, Public Law 728 (HR 11619), 84th Congress, 2nd Session.
13. Vehicle Seizure Act of 1939, Ch. 618, 53 Stat. 1291 (1939).
14. Anslinger 1951, 746.
15. Informers Act of 1930, Ch. 829, 46 Stat. 850 (1930).
16. See, for example, Provine 2007; Musto 1999; Cohen 2006.
17. This began with the opium scare of the late 1800s in a backlash against Chinese immigrants, who had come to the western United States in large numbers to work as laborers. Regulation efforts centered on containing Chinese addicts within immigrant enclaves. As the broader population began to experiment with opium, the Chinese were framed as malevolent corruptors who used

opium to "seduce and enslave" innocent white women and children (Provine 2007, 71). For a popular, sensationalistic account of how such women were sucked in and enslaved by Chinese men peddling opium in New York, see Riis 1890, 94–97. African Americans were said to become irredeemable if they used cocaine, becoming driven to rape white women and to commit murder. Medical experts at the time suggested that the only viable intervention for the black cocaine addict was imprisonment, which itself was only "palliative, for he returns inevitably to the drug habit when released" (Dr. Edward Huntington Williams, "Negro Cocaine 'Fiends' New Southern Menace," *New York Times*, February 8, 1914; available at: www.druglibrary.org/schaffer/history/negro_cocaine_fiends.htm [accessed April 27, 2016]). Political and popular rhetoric asserted that white children in particular were targeted by black and Latino marijuana dealers for corruption, which spurred legislative efforts to regulate and criminalize the drug.

18. Anslinger's racism is discussed in Provine 2007, 83–89. Anslinger also pointed the finger at the Japanese, Chinese Communists, Italians, and other foreigners over the course of his career, depending upon his audience. See Kinder 1981.

19. Musto 1999; Provine 2007.

20. "Sourcebook of Criminal Justice Statistics Online," www.albany.edu/sourcebook/pdf/t5372010.pdf (accessed April 27, 2016).

21. U.S. Department of Justice 1954, "Title 2, Criminal Division, Narcotics Law Violations," 86, available at: www.justice.gov/archive/usao/usam/1953/title2criminaldivision.pdf (accessed on April 27, 2016).

22. Although Richman (2000) argues that the borders between state and federal criminal jurisdiction have been porous for most of the twentieth century.

23. Anslinger 1959a, 1959b.

24. This period of the federal government's domestic drug policy has been less comprehensively examined than either the preceding or subsequent periods. David Musto and Pamela Korsmeyer's *The Quest for Drug Control* (2002) is perhaps the most detailed and complete portrait of this period.

25. Ibid., 9.

26. Ibid.

27. Aronowitz 1967.

28. Public Law 89-793 (November 8, 1966).

29. The provisions and full explanation of this act were published in a National Institute of Mental Health pamphlet, a scan of which is available at: http://digital.tcl.sc.edu/cdm/ref/collection/gdp2/id/491 (accessed April 27, 2016).

30. Friedman, Horvat, and Levinson 1982. Title III of the act provided for treatment for addicts who sought it voluntarily, even though they had no pending charges or convictions in federal court.

31. Ibid.

32. Commission on Law Enforcement and Administration of Justice 1967, 1.

33. Ibid., 11.

34. Public Law 91-513, October 27, 1970, 84 Stat., available at: http://www.gpo.gov/fdsys/pkg/STATUTE-84/pdf/STATUTE-84-Pg1236.pdf (accessed April 27, 2016).

35. Despite this dramatic restructuring of drug laws, mandatory minimums for drug violations were not fully relegated to history. By 1975, Senator Edward

Kennedy had proposed legislation introducing a variety of new mandatory minimums, including for heroin trafficking offenses. See Murakawa 2014.

36. Nixon's original proposed version of this legislation and the version passed by Congress differed significantly on this issue: Nixon did not support wholesale rescission of mandatory minimums—only for first-timers charged with possession. See Peterson 1984.

37. Beale 1996.

38. *Perez v. United States* 402 U.S. 146 (1971). According to Chippendale (1994, 461), *Perez* set off a "federalization explosion" whereby Congress passed thousands of criminal laws that duplicated state laws.

39. Perhaps the most longstanding and pointed disagreements have to do with the DEA's steadfast commitment to keeping marijuana as a schedule 1 drug—in the same category as heroin, LSD, and Ecstasy—deemed to "have no currently accepted medical use in the United States, a lack of accepted safety for use under medical supervision, and a high potential for abuse." See U.S. Department of Justice, Office of Diversion Control, "Definition of Controlled Substance Schedules," www.deadiversion.usdoj.gov/schedules/#define (accessed April 27, 2016).

40. Comprehensive Drug Abuse Prevention and Control Act of 1970, Section 411, Title II, codified as 21 U.S.C. § 851. The 1984 U.S. Attorneys Manual made the discretionary nature of this provision explicit: "The language of section 411 indicates that the filing of a 'previous convictions' information is discretionary with the U.S. Attorney. Thus, for valid reasons in a given case, a U.S. Attorney may decide to forego the filing of such an information" (U.S. Department of Justice 1984, Title 9-100.320).

41. As Anslinger testified before Congress; his testimony was quoted on November 24, 1953 in newspapers across the country, for example, in the *Detroit Free Press*, November 24, 1953, 2.

42. Peterson 1984, 252.

43. See ibid., 255, quoting Congressman Sisks and Senator Dodd in the House and Senate debates.

44. Codified as 21 U.S.C. § 849(e).

45. Musto and Korsmeyer 2002. This law enforcement configuration migrated in many ways from the organized crime venue and has become a critical component of the contemporary war on drugs.

46. Nixon (1973).

47. See Brown (1985) for an interesting ethnographic examination of the ambiguities of this dual policy in action.

48. The following account of drug policy from the Nixon administration to the end of the Carter administration draws on Musto and Korsmeyer 2002.

49. Andreas and Youngers 1989.

50. Musto and Korsmeyer 2002.

51. There was also a bit of a drug scandal within the White House involving the top drug policy adviser, Peter Bourne, which led to his resignation and embarrassed the White House.

52. Lassiter 2015.

53. McGirr 2002.

Chapter 2

1. Contemporaneous critiques can be found in American Friends Service Committee 1971; Clark 1970; Frankel 1973; Mitford 1973.
2. Among many others, Francis Allen (1981) and David Garland (2002) offer comprehensive post-hoc analyses of the fall of rehabilitation.
3. For comprehensive and authoritative accounts of the making of the SRA and subsequent development of the Sentencing Guidelines, see Stith and Koh 1993; Stith and Cabranes 1998, chapters 1 and 2; Baron-Evans and Stith 2012.
4. Stith and Koh 1993.
5. See for example S.1437 § 100 (1978).
6. Stith and Koh 1993. In addition to the sentencing reform provision, the Crime Control Act reestablished the federal death penalty, increased punishments for marijuana offenses, and added a "career criminal" statute, among other features.
7. Murakawa 2014.
8. Stith and Koh 1993. For a rich treatment of the broader rise of the politics of law and order, see Beckett 1996. For an analysis of a longer political trajectory and comparative analysis of America's punitiveness in this period see Gottschalk 2006. For an examination of the effects of such politicization, including its transmission into the logics of schools, workplaces, and family life, see Simon 2007.
9. Public Law 98-473, October 12, 1984, at 98 Stat. 1976 (for full Crime Control Act). Sentencing Reform Act is Chapter 2 at 98 Stat. 1987, and establishment of Sentencing Commission is at 98 Stat. 2017.
10. U.S. Sentencing Commission 1987b, 1.1.
11. Public Law 98-473, October 12, 1984, at 98 Stat. 2018.
12. 18 U.S.C. § 3553(a)(2)(A)-(D).
13. See 28 U.S.C. § 994(h). "The Commission shall assure that the guidelines specify a sentence to a term of imprisonment at or near the maximum term authorized" for certain categories of defendants, including those convicted of drug violations, as specified in 28 U.S.C. §994(h)(1)(b).
14. 18 U.S.C. § 3624(b).
15. James B. Jacobs (1982) delineates how new determinate schemes across the country defined good time credits.
16. 18 U.S.C. § 3624(e).
17. Stith and Cabranes 1998.
18. Baron-Evans and Stith 2012.
19. Public Law 99-570, October 27, 1986.
20. Over time, methamphetamine came to be treated the same as crack; it is now the punitive "anchor." At the guidelines' inception the ratio of methamphetamine to crack was 50:1. Because the 1987 drug quantity table does not list methamphetamine, one must look to the drug equivalency table. There, methamphetamine has a 1:2 ratio to powder cocaine, which can then be compared crack in the quantity table. See U.S. Sentencing Commission 1987a, 242.

21. For a first offense, possession of at least five grams triggered the five years; for defendants with prior crack possession convictions, that threshold fell to three grams for one prior, then one gram for two or more priors (Public Law 100-690, 102 Stat. 4181, 1988). This section was repealed by the Fair Sentencing Act of 2010.
22. Full wording at 21 U.S.C. § 841(b)(1)(B). The prior can be for mere possession, so long as it was punishable by more than a year in prison. Because it actually increases both mandatory minimums and statutory maximums, it has implications for cases in which a mandatory minimum does not apply but where the career offender guideline does apply.
23. Public Law 100-690, § 6452(a)(2), 102 Stat. 4371 (1988).
24. As I noted in chapter 1, 21 U.S.C. § 851 was authorized by a provision of the Comprehensive Drug Abuse Prevention and Control Act of 1970 to temper automatic criminal history–related enhancements associated with the Anslinger-era mandatories. It requires prosecutors to file an information that they are seeking such enhancements and provide evidence of the prior but gives them discretion to not file. See Russell 2010 and Gleeson 2013.
25. Baron-Evans and Stith 2012. The USSC detailed its logic on this in the first *Guidelines Manual*, stating that two offense levels of the drug Sentencing Guidelines (for the five- and ten-year mandatory minimums) were dictated by the 1986 Anti-Drug Abuse Act, and that the others "are proportional to the levels established by statute," which was "essential to provide a logical sentencing structure for drug offenses." See U.S. Sentencing Commission 1987a, 2.46.
26. This is not unique to drug cases in the federal context. For instance, the child pornography guidelines are driven by quantity of images and the fraud guidelines are driven by dollar amounts defrauded or intended to be defrauded.
27. This was done to "discourage unnecessary litigation" over facts that would move a defendant up or down a level. See U.S. Sentencing Commission 1987a, 1.11.
28. If a mandatory minimum applies, it serves as the bottom below which a judge cannot sentence unless a prosecutor asks for a departure.
29. Not to mention extensive circuit court and Supreme Court case law interpreting the guidelines.
30. As of the 2015 *Guidelines Manual*, the two chapter 3 reductions are for "mitigating role" and "acceptance of responsibility." In contrast, there are five victim-related enhancements, one general aggravating role, three additional specific aggravating role enhancements, and four other specific offense characteristics that upwardly adjust the offense level in chapter 3. Chapter 3 of the *Guidelines Manual* also provides the rules for calculating offense level for multiple counts of conviction.
31. Ibid. The general relevant conduct guideline is at § 1B1.3.
32. The "mule" label is viewed by some as offensive. The USSC uses it to designate someone tasked with transporting drugs on his or her person, whereas a courier is someone tasked with moving drugs by a car or other vehicle. These are also sometimes referred to as mechanized mules. See Lerman (forthcoming).
33. A specific drug conspiracy statute was first authorized in the Comprehensive Drug Abuse Prevention and Control Act of 1970 (codified in 21 U.S.C. § 846), which means upon conviction, the drug offense penalties apply.

34. In the original version of the drug equivalency table, the standardized weight unit was "heroin weight." See U.S. Sentencing Commission 1987a, 2.42–2.44.
35. It also looked to existing models for guidance. It essentially mimicked several state models, such as Minnesota's, to include a criminal history axis, and it mimicked the federal parole scheme that was previously used to help determine release eligibility.
36. 28 U.S.C. § 994(d) (1)-(11).
37. For detailed discussion of how this happened in the early days of the commission, see Lynch and Bertenthal 2016.
38. U.S. Sentencing Commission 1987a, 4.9.
39. The 1984 act did repeal the "special dangerous drug offender" provision.
40. 28 U.S.C. § 994(n). This was one of the many delineated "duties of the Commission" in the SRA.
41. See U.S. Sentencing Commission 2015, 417–418 (on 5C1.2) for current language.
42. Froyd 1999. Congress directed the USSC to devise the specific contours of the safety valve.
43. Ronald Reagan, "Radio Address to the Nation on Federal Drug Policy," October 2, 1982, available at University of California, Santa Barbara, American Presidency Project: www.presidency.ucsb.edu/ws/?pid=43085 (accessed April 29, 2016).
44. Ibid.
45. Terence Dunworth and Charles D. Weisselberg (1992) report on increases, by year, of funding for the DEA and U.S. attorneys. Russell-Einhorn (2003) describes the emergence of such collaborations to target violence, gangs, and drug crime. He points out that there were less formal, shorter-term collaborations prior to the 1980s, but that this period institutionalized such collaborations as ongoing law enforcement strategies.
46. U.S. Department of Justice, Offices of the United States Attorneys n.d., statistical reports for 1980 and 1990.
47. Ibid., statistical reports for 2000 and 2010.
48. Although U.S. attorneys' offices also handle civil matters, and the civil caseload is actually larger than the criminal caseload, the bulk of their time is spent on criminal matters. According to the United States Attorneys' Office annual statistical report for 2000, "About 76 percent of attorney personnel were devoted to criminal prosecutions and 24 percent to civil litigation. Ninety-three percent of all attorney work hours spent in United States District Courts were devoted to criminal prosecutions and seven percent to civil litigation." See U.S. Department of Justice, Offices of the United States Attorneys n.d., annual statistical report for 2000, 2.
49. New York State's Rockefeller drug laws led the way in the 1970s; see also King and Mauer (2002) for an analysis of state-by-state drug law policies and practices.
50. Ibid.; Lynch 2012.
51. Even though federal prosecutors have held primary prosecutorial responsibility for cases crossing state or national borders for a long time, and they function as the primary law enforcement jurisdiction for serious offenses on Indian reservations and for crimes committed on federal land, the trend toward adopting scores of prototypical "state" cases was a new development.
52. U.S. Department of Justice 1985, Title 9, Ch. 101.400, pages, 18–19.

53. Ibid., 19.
54. Ibid.
55. Ibid.
56. The drug conspiracy statute is codified as 21 U.S.C. § 846; it was first enacted in 1970 and was amended in 1988.
57. U.S. Department of Justice 1985, Title 9, Ch. 101.600, subsection M.
58. Lee 1994, 5.
59. Ibid.
60. Ibid., 5. The remaining reasons were "4. Help to dismantle entire criminal organizations" and "7. Permit more than one trial to be held on the same conspiracy."
61. Stith 2008. The Office of the Attorney General has nominal authority over district-level U.S. attorneys and their AUSAs, but day-to-day prosecutorial policies and practices have typically been autonomously developed within districts.
62. Thornburgh Bluesheet (1989), "Plea Policy for Federal Prosecutors: Plea Bargaining Under the Sentencing Reform Act (March 13, 1989)," available at: www.ussc.gov/sites/default/files/pdf/training/annual-national-training-seminar/2014/DOJ_memo.pdf, 16.
63. Ibid., 17.
64. Ibid., 18.
65. Ashcroft 2003, 3.
66. As a point of contrast, while the likelihood of receiving a prison sentence increased significantly for federal white-collar crimes after the implementation of the Sentencing Guidelines, average sentence length was cut in half, from about thirty months to fifteen months (U.S. Sentencing Commission 2004).
67. The Bureau of Justice's State Court Processing Statistics data from 2006 indicate that about 36 percent of drug felony convictions in the seventy-five largest U.S. counties resulted in a prison sentence, and the mean sentence length was thirty-four months. See Cohen and Kyckelhahn 2010. At its peak, the annual share of state prisoners sentenced for drug felonies was 22 percent; it is now around 17 percent.
68. Berman 2010, 429. Proactive law enforcement strategy was also shaped by the constraints on judges. They aimed to develop and bring cases that hit the sentence benchmarks that were determined by drug weight. This was a new phenomenon directly attributable to the new sentencing structure, and has been referred to as "sentencing entrapment" or "sentencing factor manipulation." For more details see Thomas 1996.
69. As I noted in the introduction, this changed in 2005 as mandated by the *United States v. Booker* ruling.
70. U.S. Sentencing Commission 2011.
71. These statistics are derived from the consolidated database of USSC outcome data for this period, available to researchers as "Defendants Sentenced Under the Sentencing Reform Act."
72. All these statistics are derived from the consolidated database of USSC outcome data for this period. The differential in sentence length is in part the product of differences in typical case facts, including in drug substances and quantities involved and in defendants' prior criminal records, but the between-district differences in punitiveness exist above and beyond case-relevant factors. See Lynch and Omori (2014) for general procedure and dataset.

73. U.S. Department of Justice 1985, Title 9, Ch. 101, pt. 400, 19.
74. U.S. Sentencing Commission 2012b.
75. Over the same time period, Northeastern District's drug trafficking sentences were on average 81 percent of the guidelines' minimum, and Southwestern District's drug sentences averaged 73 percent of the guidelines' minimum. The national average for sentenced drug cases was 85 percent of the guidelines' minimum.
76. Data were missing from USSC data files for mandatory minimum applications in 1992.
77. In the federal system, petty offenses include both infractions and misdemeanors that can result in no more than six months of incarceration. Record keeping for petty offense convictions in federal court is sparse, whereas more precise data are readily available for class A misdemeanors and felonies. See Warner (2004).
78. Fast-track programs were first instituted locally and autonomously by several U.S. attorneys in border districts to deal with immigration cases. In 2003, the PROTECT Act authorized U.S. attorneys' offices to develop fast-track programs that conformed to a set of rules, and the USSC was directed to develop a specific departure guideline for participants in these "early disposition" programs. While the vast majority of the subsequently approved programs have been for immigration offenses, only crimes of violence are categorically excluded. For this history see Gorman 2009.

Chapter 3

1. That's not the worst of it. If the prosecutor had been so inclined, he could also have filed an 851 enhancement on the prior drug conviction, which would increase the statutory maximum from twenty to thirty years, thereby moving the "career offender" guideline to 188 to 235 months.
2. Delineated in U.S. Sentencing Commission 2015, § 4B1.1.
3. U.S. Sentencing Commission n.d.
4. So-called "state adoption" cases constitute a distinct subset of the federal drug caseload nationally, and a large subset in Northeastern District. These cases typically begin with local arrests and prosecutions, which are then dropped when an assistant U.S. attorney in the jurisdiction decides to indict in federal court.
5. Analysis of the 1992-to-2012 USSC data indicates that the same pattern does not hold for non-drug defendants. Except for one outlier year, 2009, the annual share of non-drug career offenders was 5 percent or less each year in those two decades.
6. Sometimes they are targeted in buy-busts by local law enforcement who work closely with the federal prosecutors in the drugs-guns-gangs unit. In these cases, the suspects are well-known to local police, and know their exposure. On "buy-busts" and other drug law enforcement strategies see Buerger 1992.
7. Interview NE061701.
8. Both oral statements by prosecutors and written case documents, particularly prosecutors' sentencing memos, use this language to describe this typology of defendant.
9. Thomas Hendley is a pseudonym.

10. This is not to say that those targeted are not committing the crimes for which they are charged but that such a strategy invites very insular judgment about who is worthy of targeting for proxy arrests and prosecutions that is untestable in any meaningful way. Such an approach not only challenges legal ideals but is susceptible to bias and error about the overarching assessment of "trouble."

11. See 21 U.S.C. § 860 for the full text of this enhancement statute.

12. For an account of local black leaders' role in pushing for tough drug laws in New York in the 1960s, see Fortner 2015.

13. The guidelines allow for either side to seek departures from the Sentencing Guidelines when the criminal history score does not adequately reflect prior criminal history (U.S. Sentencing Commission 2015). In this case, Hendley sought an upward departure based on section 4A1.3 of the Sentencing Guidelines, which "specifically encourages upward departures based on 'reliable information' that a defendant previously engaged in 'prior similar adult criminal conduct not resulting in a conviction'" (quoting from Hendley's sentencing memo in this case).

14. This sort of intervention reduces the structurally based criminogenic factors in defendants' lives to their own dispositional failings, which is at odds with much macro-criminological research and theory. In addition, as the noted criminologist Doris Layton MacKenzie (2000) has pointed out about this program, it has been hard to evaluate its effectiveness since the bulk of the evaluations have been done by the very proprietors of the program. This goes against standard protocol for evaluation research, especially when there are financial benefits attached to the program's success.

15. It had been a distinct municipality before being annexed into the larger city.

16. This kind of plea deal where the actual sentence terms are agreed upon by both sides is known colloquially as a "C plea." Pursuant to Federal Rule 11(c)(1)(C), if the judge accepts the guilty plea, he or she is bound to sentence the defendant to the terms agreed upon in the plea deal. A judge may reject the guilty plea if he or she does not want to impose the terms. In contrast, many plea agreements are a deal over the parties' recommendations to the judge, leaving the judge with discretion over the term of imprisonment.

17. In the direct quotes from court hearings, documents, and interviews, I use brackets to smooth and clarify language but strive to remain true to the verbatim excerpts.

18. See for example, the volume edited by Erickson et al. (1997), which includes contributions on the effectiveness of public health and harm reduction models.

19. Gary Alan Fine (2012, 36) would describe this as the "idioculture" of the organization—the "system of knowledge, beliefs, behaviors, and customs" that help define strategies for action.

20. Quote from Mr. Hendley's written response to the motion to terminate supervision.

21. This was a quote from the judge or her clerk, scribbled on the motion itself indicating denial, which was included in the official case court record on this motion.

22. Quote is from the hearing itself, inserted verbatim in the case docket.

23. In this context, this meant of all the young men whom he, as part of the task force, had prosecuted.

24. These types of cases, even though brought by several different AUSAs in the office, were regularly referred to as "Hendley cases" or "Hendley specials."
25. In many cases, informants are the only source of evidence for establishing drug weight for past deals that otherwise lack hard evidence. They are also used to fortify other evidence. So, for instance, in the case of recorded conversations that were carried out using code to disguise the topic, informants may "translate" the coded language into plain language. Or they may corroborate weight as captured in videos or photos.
26. U.S. Sentencing Commission (2011). The USSC's mandatory minimum report to Congress indicates that drug defendants in "manager" roles and higher were the most likely to receive substantial assistance departures and those at the lowest rungs, the least likely.
27. The threshold amounts are specified in the indictment to trigger specific mandatory minimums.
28. Because the defendants were born outside the country, verification of true identity is difficult. In the case of one defendant, the original complaint was issued under one alias, which remained his name up until his retained lawyer appeared for him on the day of formal indictment, twelve days into the case. The second name, also an alias, was used in his indictment and remained on the record all the way to the day he pleaded guilty, nine months later. At that hearing he informed the judge of what he characterized as his true name, under which the guilty plea was recorded and sentence was pronounced.
29. Nothing in his formal record indicates that this is the case here, but it is not unusual for some early busts to be quietly made, and those arrested put to work as informants within the larger conspiracy. The result is that their cases may take a slightly different path than the others, including in some cases, the conspirators never being charged.
30. Quote from fifth joint status report filed by the prosecution in this case.
31. As noted in chapter 2, the degree to which satisfying the fifth prong of the safety valve requires providing information about others varies by district; several defense attorneys characterized Northeastern District as one where prosecutors expected cooperation-level information.
32. Even though the guidelines are now advisory, judges are still required to use the correct guidelines' calculation as a starting point at sentencing.
33. Interview NE060601.
34. U.S. Sentencing Commission 2011.
35. But they can be considered for departures for adequacy. See U.S. Sentencing Commission 2015, § 4A1.2(h): "Sentences resulting from foreign convictions are not counted, but may be considered under § 4A1.3 (Adequacy of Criminal History Category)."
36. In the ten-defendant conspiracy that intersected with this case, sentences for the majority of defendants were well below typical Hendley case sentences, including several who simply received time served.
37. Interview NE040801.
38. This district had relatively low caseloads relative to the number of prosecutors and judges, so it was an ongoing challenge to defend their budget requests and fight cuts from their respective executive offices in Washington, D.C.
39. Interview NE061001.

40. Interview NE060703.
41. Interview NE061801. Some lawyers said they had never seen one of these low-level cases where the defendant was not black, several others mentioned occasional Hispanic defendants brought in on these low-level cases. None had ever seen a white defendant come in through the Hendley-type strategy. Nor did I ever observe any hand-to-hand drug sale cases where the defendant was not black.
42. During my original observation period in this site, in summer 2013, these cases made up the majority of the drug caseload in the Urban division of Northeastern District. Upon my return in 2014, they still predominated the drug caseload, although the overall numbers of drug prosecutions declined that year.
43. This is known colloquially as a trial penalty. Jeffrey T. Ulmer, James Eisenstein, and Brian D. Johnson (2010) calculated a penalty 15 percent above and beyond guidelines factors for federal defendants who were convicted at trial from 2000 to 2002.

Chapter 4

1. Interview S0400301.
2. As reported in his attorney's submitted sentencing memo.
3. "Flipped" means getting them to become cooperators.
4. Interview S072601.
5. For an analysis of federal drug conspiracy and the low bar for proving conspiracy, see Heller 1996.
6. Interview S070301.
7. From the judge's "Notice Contemplating Upward Variance."
8. This was not simply a case of gender bias. Judge Jenkins gave the woman's husband the same lenient sentence when he was sentenced later. He had an identical plea agreement to that of his wife.
9. Mr. Samuels's son was even more analogous to Aaron Crenshaw in terms of his sentencing situation. He pleaded guilty to sales of 4 grams of heroin, and as a career offender, his guidelines were 151 to 188 months. But Judge Jenkins went to near the top of those guidelines, sentencing him to 180 months— 15 years. Father and son remain incarcerated in the same prison as of this writing.
10. It is very difficult to capture how many defendants officially cooperate in this district because, unlike in most other districts, the mechanism for giving the sentencing break comes after sentencing, generally one to two years later, rather than at sentencing. This is done pursuant to Rule 35(b) of Title VII, Federal Rules of Criminal Procedure. This in itself is an interesting local cultural norm, but there are no aggregated statistics kept on the awarding of sentence reductions through the Rule 35 mechanism. Estimates given to me by longtime federal defenders were that 60 to 70 percent of all drug defendants in Middle division of this district cooperated for a sentencing break, and about 85 percent in South division.
11. Interview S070301.

12. In the North division of Southeast District, there was more demographic variety among drug defendants charged federally, in part because there was also a subset of international "mule" cases that came through the airport in the division.
13. South division of this district has consistently prosecuted guns and drugs together at double the rate of Middle division. There was a spike in gun enhancements among sentenced drug defendants in Middle division for several years following this initiative's implementation, but that trend retreated by 2001.
14. The state system also had some mandatory minimums, but they were much less severe than in the federal system.
15. Interview S04050102.
16. In the twenty-year period that began with this initiative, 83 percent of sentenced drug defendants and 93 percent of defendants sentenced for having a gun in furtherance of a drug or violent crime were African American in the division where this program started.
17. Interview S072202.
18. Interview S071501. My interview and observational data indicate that in other divisions and districts, if a defendant pleads guilty straight up, without entering into a plea agreement, the sentencing judge will routinely award "acceptance of responsibility" by virtue of the plea alone. A sentence at the low end of the guidelines, which here is considered a gift, is actually higher than the national norm, which is just 85 percent of that low end. And although 851 enhancements are typically used to compel a guilty plea, perhaps forcing a higher sentence than would be without that possibility, I did not see them used outside of this district to force cooperation.
19. Interview S071602.
20. Ibid.
21. Interview S07090102.
22. Interview S070301.
23. This can be a gray area, since lying, or even not being fully forthcoming, constitutes breaking the agreement. If the prosecutor wants a cooperating defendant to inform on loved ones and the defendant is not forthcoming, the agreement may be voided and the relevant conduct is in.
24. Interview S071501.
25. The "statement of facts" is usually drafted by the case prosecutor, sometimes in consultation with the defense, and lays out the facts of the case as agreed upon for the guilty plea. This document is the basis for probation's calculation of the offense level portion of the guidelines in most districts. Occasionally there are some disagreements between this document and the probation officer's assessment, but it is less common to have a wholesale proactive inquiry around things like drug weight in order to jack up the guidelines, as occurs in Southeast District.
26. Interview S071701.
27. A second 924(c) triggers a twenty-five-year mandatory minimum that must be served consecutive to any other sentence, so fifteen years was the mandatory minimum because he qualified as an "armed career offender" due to his record, and twenty-five additional years were for the 924(c) gun charge.

28. Interview S070901.
29. Interview S071502.
30. The pseudo-economic logic of plea bargaining is that not agreeing to plead guilty has to have some costs associated with it. In the federal system, this is formalized by the conferral, or withholding, of the "acceptance of responsibility" reduction in the guideline calculation. But it is also more informally imposed here, as well as in most American systems, by less generous sentencing upon conviction. For an empirical examination of the trial penalty in the federal system, see Ulmer, Eisenstein, and Johnson 2010.
31. Charles's testimony at Devon's trial and entries in the case docket indicate multiple efforts in this regard, including being removed from Bureau of Prisons to the custody of DEA agents to undergo a polygraph more than a year after being sent to prison.
32. His sentence was later reduced to 188 months as part of the crack retroactivity resentencing policy that was authorized by the U.S. Sentencing Commission in 2008 and was approved by Congress, following a guideline change that reduced crack guidelines two levels across the board. In effect, his offense level was decreased by two levels under the new formula and he was given the bottom of the guidelines at that new level. For more on this crack retroactivity policy, see Yellen 2008.

Chapter 5

1. Only 5 percent of drug trafficking defendants in this district received substantial assistance departures in both 2011 and 2012, as compared to about 18 to 23 percent in the mid-1990s.
2. A "mechanized mule" is typically at the lowest level of a drug trafficking operation who drives a vehicle that is transporting drugs. Mechanized mules may be fully aware of what they are doing, they may turn a blind eye so are willfully ignorant of the crime they are committing, or they may be completely duped and have no knowledge that they are moving drugs. They also may be transporting the drugs under some duress, in that traffickers have made covert or overt threats to gain their compliance.
3. Border-crossing cards are specialized visitor visas issued by the U.S. Department of State to Mexican residents under the provisions of the Immigration and Nationality Act § 101(a)(15)B, which allow holders to legally pass into the United States on a temporary basis for tourism, business, or both. To obtain the card Mexican citizens must prove that they are tied to Mexico and are compelled by circumstance to return there.
4. Stacy A. Wetmore, Jeffrey S. Neuschatz, and Scott D. Gronlund (2014) demonstrate how powerful informant testimony is relative to other forms of evidence.
5. He was the only person in the district that year who was convicted and sentenced for this crime, making it unusual in this respect as well.
6. The original driver was charged as the third defendant in this case. He entered into a plea agreement in which he admitted to importing more than five hundred grams of methamphetamine and testified at Abraham's trial.

The docket indicates he was sentenced the day before Abraham and his uncle were sentenced. Mysteriously, though, unlike almost all sentencing dispositions, no formal judgment was ever issued that indicated what his sentence was, and there is no record that he ever was turned over to the custody of the Bureau of Prisons.

7. 8 U.S.C. § 1325 is the misdemeanor illegal entry offense, and 8 U.S.C. § 1326 is the felony reentry offense.

8. Although some do backpack for a living, crossing back and forth for cash.

9. For a full argument and illustration of the melding of backpacking and immigration cases in this border district, see Lynch 2015.

10. For an account of the treacheries and challenges on the "migrant trail," see Martinez 2013.

11. There is also a smattering of identity fraud cases, where defendants used fraudulent documents at ports of entry. The other mass-processing route is Operation Streamline, which is limited to those accused of illegally entering or reentering the United States. In Southwestern District, between 70 and 120 arrestees per day are referred to this option. They begin and end their cases in a single day, including meeting an attorney, hearing charges against them, pleading guilty, waiving all rights, and being sentenced to a maximum of 180 days' incarceration. These mass-processing schemes mainly take place in the border division of this district, which processes the vast majority of criminal cases in the district.

12. In the urban division, several hours north of the border, the misdemeanor option is not available for backpackers. The standard deal there is a felony trafficking conviction with a sentence of thirteen months and a day.

13. I observed a handful of illegal reentry sentencing hearings where this sixteen-level enhancement was applied, which moved the imprisonment term up from just months to years. As of this writing, debate is under way to reform or eliminate this guideline enhancement.

14. Every day, U.S. Border Patrol officers here compile a list of 70 to 120 illegal reentry arrestees who are recommended for adjudication through Operation Streamline, which is the highest-speed fast-track criminal processing program in the nation.

15. 21 U.S.C. § 844.

16. I never saw a judge try to sentence above the stipulated range in this district. In other districts, judges were more likely to reject the terms of binding pleas because they wanted to sentence above rather than below the agreed-upon sentence.

17. For a systematic study of courier pay by substance, risk, and other characteristics of job, see Bjerk and Mason 2014.

18. For the history and state of the law concerning search powers at the border, see Nadkarni 2013.

19. On a few occasions, "pity 5Ks" or "pity free talks" were awarded to very sympathetic or pathetic defendants by prosecutors, even if they provided no usable information. In Southwestern, the lowest-level defendants were especially unlikely to have information to give and were often too scared to talk even if they did have some information.

20. In Erik Erikson's (1956) model of human development, "psychosocial moratorium" is a stage of development in late adolescence when people are trying to work out their identities by exploring different possibilities. It is analogized to a period of identity crisis.

21. Mr. Hopkins was first offered a noncooperation agreement that stipulated a sentence of between seventy-seven and ninety-six months. Once he agreed to cooperate, the agreement was amended to be open-ended as to sentence, depending upon the value of the cooperation.

22. His three codefendants eventually also pleaded guilty and were sentenced by the same judge. The two who were Mr. Hopkins's prior compatriots received sixty months each, and the driver received thirty-seven months.

23. This is exactly how the economists David Bjerk and Caleb Mason (2014) approached their analysis of border-crossing drug couriers.

24. Interview SW100402.

25. Interview SW101801.

26. Interview SW100401.

27. Interview SW102301

28. They would still be able to obtain discovery if they did not waive the preliminary hearing, but they would have to file a motion and schedule a hearing to get the judge to order that the evidence be turned over.

29. Although this was in part to ensure that defendants were properly informed of the immigration consequences, it also served as an adjudicatory logic that pervaded cases here, subsuming the kind of penal logics that animated sentencing hearings in both Northeastern and Southeast Districts.

Chapter 6

1. Stuntz 2011, 80.

2. Stith and Cabranes 1998, 3.

3. Fine 2012, 36.

4. Fiske 2009; Ross and Nisbett 1991.

5. For the classics, on conformity: Asch 1956; on obedience: Milgram 1965; on helping and altruism: Latané and Darley 1969.

6. On the Stanford Prison Study, see Haney, Banks, and Zimbardo 1973; Haney and Zimbardo 2009.

7. Sources for these statistics: Bureau of Justice Statistics 1989; U.S. Sentencing Commission 2014.

8. Dunworth and Weisselberg 1992.

9. Ulmer, Eisenstein, and Johnson 2010.

10. Human Rights Watch 2013.

11. Ibid.

12. For a full discussion of the ethics of incentive-based plea bargaining, see Grant 2014. For an empirical test of the economic model of plea bargaining, see Bushway and Redlich 2012.

13. Ulmer 2012.

14. Most states authorize active involvement of judges, although a few do not. See Batra 2015.

15. Emmelman 1997; see also Kohler-Hausmann (2013) on this as an adjudication strategy in misdemeanor court. Brian D. Johnson (2014) shows that in the federal system, conversely, drug cases have among the lowest rates of declination by prosecutors when compared to other offenses and that "young, black males" were less likely to have their cases dropped in this system.

16. Emmelman 1996, 1997, 2003.

17. The Sixth Amendment of the Constitution requires a "speedy trial," but in practice most defendants waive that right to provide their attorneys time to investigate and prepare the case. As Emmelman (1996) and others have observed, delay is also a good strategic move in obtaining favorable plea offers, especially for out-of-custody defendants.

18. See Court Statistics Project (website), "Two-Tiered Systems Have Three General Jurisdiction Judges per 100K Population," available at: www.court-statistics.org/Other-Pages/Examining-the-Work-of-State-Courts/20124_EWSC.aspx (accessed May 9, 2016).

19. United States Courts (website), "Table 6.2—U.S. District Courts—Combined Civil and Criminal Judicial Facts and Figures (September 30, 2010)," available at: www.uscourts.gov/uscourts/Statistics/JudicialFactsAndFigures/2010/Table602.pdf (accessed May 9, 2016).

20. Rule 11(c)(1) of the Federal Rules of Criminal Procedure.

21. My analysis is based on U.S. Sentencing Commission (USSC) data from 1992 to 2012, obtained from ICPSR. For a full discussion of the data compiled for the larger study, see Lynch and Omori 2014.

22. Interview RU06240102.

23. On the adoption of a "real offense" approach, see Schmitt, Reedt, and Blackwell 2013; Reitz 1993. The system is a "modified" real-offense one in that it incorporates aspects of the offense even if not elements of the conviction, but it made many traditional mitigating factors, such as the defendant's psychological state or other concerns, irrelevant to sentencing that had been central to sentencing pre-guidelines. Relevant conduct is subject to a lower standard of proof—preponderance of the evidence. Furthermore, it is not subject to the hearsay rule, so all kinds of unsworn statements can be used against the defendant as the basis for relevant conduct.

24. See U.S. Sentencing Commission 2013a.

25. Pursuant to Rule 11(c)(1)(c) of the Federal Rules of Criminal Procedure, these pleas, known colloquially as c-pleas, are binding as to terms, and a judge can merely accept or reject it on its terms. If the judge rejects it, the guilty plea can be withdrawn.

26. Interview NE060702.

27. Interview S071504.

28. Interview SW100302.

29. Interview NE061802.

30. Interview NE061201.

31. Interview S070301.

32. Interview S07090102.

33. Interview S072203.

34. 18 U.S.C. § 924(c). The 924(c) enhancement also applies in statutorily defined violent offenses. The penalties are even steeper if the gun was brandished or

discharged in the commission of a qualifying offense, or if the gun has certain characteristics such as being a short-barreled rifle or shotgun (ten-year
mandatory minimum on the first count), a machine gun, or equipped with a
silencer (thirty-year mandatory minimum on the first count).

35. The general consensus was that if the defendant was eligible, these were
going to be applied, and the negotiation worked off of that calculation.
Again, Southwestern was an outlier on this, as we saw with the career
offender backpacker.

36. Interview NE060703.

37. As described earlier, the 851 enhancement means that prosecutors can file
an information alleging an eligible prior drug conviction predicate that will
double mandatory minimums; two priors bring a life sentence without the
possibility of parole in drug cases where the base mandatory minimum is ten
years, should a prosecutor seek it.

38. Interview NE061001.

39. Interview S070301.

40. Interview SW100302.

41. Interview S071602.

42. Interview NE060601.

43. Interview S071602.

44. Interview NE060601.

45. Interview SW102301.

46. Interview SW100302.

47. The number of cases drops during the summer, when the extreme heat makes
it very dangerous to cross the border.

48. Interview NE061201.

49. Interview S070301.

50. Interview NE060301.

51. Interview SW101701.

Chapter 7

1. The charging power does not even have to be realized to be effective. As I
heard from attorneys, and as Miller and Eisenstein (2005) documented in their
qualitative study of a multi-jurisdictional initiative in a single federal district, the threat of federal indictment is routinely used against those arrested
on state charges to get them to plea to terms dictated by local prosecutors
and to compel cooperation. These uses of the hammer of federal law do not
show up at all in court records, except sometimes as the unnamed sources
of relevant conduct used against federal defendants. See also Phillips (2012),
whose detailed ethnography of a huge drug conspiracy sting operation in Los
Angeles illustrates how suspects and arrestees get sorted into federal or state
courts (or avoid prosecution altogether in a few cases).

2. An unpublished 2015 survey of federal defenders indicates that prosecutors
in 60 percent of the federal districts continue to use the 851 enhancement as
a coercive bargaining tool (Amy Baron-Evans, Sentencing Research Counsel,
Federal Defenders, communication with the author), even though Attorney
General Eric Holder directed U.S. attorneys not to do so in two separate direc-

tives (2013, 2014). Just as with any top-down directive, the frontline actors can and will find ways that formally comply but that circumvent the intent if it is counter to their purposes (Lynch and Omori 2014).

3. See U.S. Sentencing Commission 1987a chapter 1.
4. Stith and Cabranes 1998.
5. Gertner 2007, 534.
6. Interview S04050102. On the strategies used to circumvent the guidelines in the early years, see also Schulhofer and Nagel 1997. For a qualitative comparison, see Ulmer 2005. For a more recent quantitative analysis, see Johnson, Ulmer, and Kramer 2008.
7. Public Law 108-21, 117 Stat. 650, S. 151.
8. The amendment was drafted by a freshman congressman, Tom Feeney (R-Fla.) and is colloquially known as the Feeney Amendment. It specifically limited departures from the Sentencing Guidelines in a subset of sex and violence crimes. It did not constrain upward departures—the amendment was unidirectional in its concern regarding outside-of-guidelines sentences.
9. Stephanos Bibas (2004) predicted that under the Feeney Amendment, "prosecutorial leverage to plea bargain will be at an all-time high, resulting in fewer trials, more bargains, and higher sentences. Judges used to check prosecutorial harshness, but now they are increasingly powerless unless prosecutors deign to grant leniency" (295).
10. Interview NE06100102. The words "bad," "awful," and "horrible" were used to characterize this period by a number of the defense attorneys who had practiced at the time. None characterized it in a positive light.
11. Interview NE061201.
12. In some ways, the Feeney Amendment's success as a weapon against judicial leniency was its own undoing. Members of the federal judiciary—including some of the most conservative, law-and-order, and highest-ranked among them—while not unanimously opposed to the amendment, were infuriated by this direct attack on the very limited judicial discretion that remained in the guidelines era. Supreme Court Chief Justice William Rehnquist included a lengthy critique of the law in his 2003 year-end report (U.S. Supreme Court 2004). Taking particular issue with the new reporting requirements, he suggested that they "could appear to be an unwarranted and ill-considered effort to intimidate individual judges in the performance of their judicial duties" He also reiterated the collective concern expressed by the judiciary that members of their branch had not been consulted for their input on the proposal. A year later, Rehnquist joined the majority in *United States v. Booker*, which rendered the guidelines "effectively advisory."
13. 5K1.1 departures were applied in about 27 percent of all federally sentenced drug cases between 1992 and 2012. As demonstrated by the U.S. Sentencing Commission's (2011) analysis, the very way prosecutors grant these has been a huge source of disparity in terms of relative culpability of the drug defendant and of racial identity of the recipients.
14. For a related argument about the paradoxical power to grant mercy see Douglas Hay (1975), "Property, Authority, and the Criminal Law," in which Hay examines judicial power to reprieve those sentenced to death under the so-called "Bloody Code" in late eighteenth-century England.

15. Foucault 1982, 781.
16. Interview S040302.
17. As historian Khalil Gibran Muhammad (2011) has shown, the construction of black criminality was fundamental to the making of modern America, and continues to be reified through our criminal justice practices as well as our sociological explanations of those practices.
18. Large literatures on both dehumanization and social identity theory speak directly to this. On dehumanization: Haque and Waytz 2012; on social identity theory: Reicher 2004.
19. Nelson 2015. The group was founded in 1993. That version of the reform bill, the Smarter Sentencing Act of 2015 did not survive the legislative process. The legislation would have reduced the terms on mandatory minimum drug sentences, including eliminating the life sentence on the double 851 (the minimum would become twenty-five years).
20. National Association of Assistant United States Attorneys, "The Dangerous Myths of Drug Sentencing 'Reform,'" July 2015, available at: www.naausa. org/2013/images/docs/Dangerous-Myths-of-Drug-Sentencing-Reform.pdf (accessed May 9, 2016).
21. Ibid., 9.
22. Ibid., 12.
23. NAAUSA 2015, 11. The NAAUSA document does not speak for all federal prosecutors, and a number of former U.S. attorneys have been active on the other side of the reform debate as well, urging Congress to ease the punitive drug laws. For a more reformist view, see Lu (2007), a former federal prosecutor who has been involved in efforts to increase awareness of racial disparities in prosecutions, in part through spearheading the development of principles and guidelines for prosecutors.
24. Cotton 2016. Senators Cotton, Sessions, Hatch, and Perdue published a set of editorials in opposition to a current reform bill, the Sentencing Reform and Corrections Bill. Hatch is mainly concerned with adding the "mens rea" requirement favored by Koch Industries, among other corporate actors.
25. See Aviram (2015) and Gottschalk (2014) for recent book-length examinations of the prospects for and challenges to meaningful criminal justice reform more generally.
26. See Wilkins, Newton, and Steer (1991). William W. Wilkins, Jr., was the founding chairman of the U.S. Sentencing Commission. The race- and class-based concern about "unwarranted disparities" animated the original commission's guidelines-building project, but their solution became raising the floor. For a pointed critique of the Sentencing Commission for its lack of concern for disadvantaged defendants, see Tonry 1996.
27. U.S. Sentencing Commission 2013b. Statutory maximums are specified in 21 U.S.C. § 241.
28. For an extended study of snitching and its problems of unreliability (among others), see Natapoff 2009.
29. Tonry 1996.
30. Beckett, Nyrop, and Pfingst 2006; Lynch et al. 2013.
31. Drug priors can potentially bite four times, even in a single defendant's sentence: as criminal history points, as predicate convictions under the career

offender guidelines, as predicates under the armed career criminal statute, and as a predicate for an 851 enhancement. No other category of prior conviction can do that much to a sentence.
32. Davis 2007.
33. Simon 2001, 129.

Epilogue

1. As Harold J. Krent (2013) explains, there is a presumption against retroactively applying new laws to those whose cases have been finalized. This was made even more difficult by provisions of the 1996 Anti-Terrorism and Effective Death Penalty Act. Nonetheless, some of the crack policy changes have been made retroactive, subject to judicial approval on a case-by-case basis. Crack retroactivity applied to the U.S. Sentencing Commission's 2007 crack guidelines' two-level reduction, and again in 2011 after the passage of the Fair Sentencing Act in 2010. The rules governing the retroactive application of the guidelines and statutory changes are complex. In June 2015, the U.S. Sentencing Commission published "Primer: Retroactivity," available at: www.ussc.gov/sites/default/files/pdf/training/primers/2015_Primer_Retroactivity.pdf (accessed May 3, 2016), to provide guidance on the rules.
2. This was the plea agreement reached. He admitted to lying to his colleagues about sleeping with an eighteen-year-old female cooperator who was facing drug charges herself. The cooperator insisted she feared reprisals from the agent if she did not go along, but he was not charged with any crimes directly related to that. The agent was sentenced to probation.
3. He had filed an additional habeas corpus petition from prison. His first denial was of his direct appeal, which was handled by his trial attorney and challenged the way the judge "remedied" the prejudice caused when evidence of his heroin possession was illegally introduced by the prosecutor. After that, Harrison himself filed several successive habeas corpus petitions from prison. They alleged ineffective assistance of counsel because of how his attorney had managed the prejudicial evidence, and because the attorney had failed to challenge the life sentence as unconstitutionally severe and disproportionate.
4. See Department of Justice, "Announcing New Clemency Initiative, Deputy Attorney General James M. Cole Details Broad New Criteria for Applicants," available at: www.justice.gov/opa/pr/announcing-new-clemency-initiative-deputy-attorney-general-james-m-cole-details-broad-new (accessed May 3, 2016). As of August 9, 2016, President Obama had granted clemency to 562 people, and all but a small handful had been sentenced for drug crimes. Updated statistics are available at U.S. Department of Justice, "Pardons Granted by President Barack Obama," available at: www.justice.gov/pardon/obama-pardons (accessed August 9, 2016).
5. In 2013 Gleeson was as pointed as could be in his "statement of reasons" for imposing a 132-month sentence on a drug defendant, Lulzim Kupa, who had pleaded under the threat of the double 851. "If DOJ cannot exercise its power to invoke recidivist enhancements in drug trafficking cases less destructively and less brutally, it doesn't deserve to have the power at all." See Gleeson 2013, 60.

6. Judge Gleeson left the federal bench in March 2016 to return to private practice, but POP continues on.
7. Mr. Young contacted me after I published an editorial about the 851 enhancement in the *New York Times*. I subsequently read the public case file, including the transcript of his sentencing hearing. He urged me to use his true name, and I agreed to do so since I am only using public documents in discussing his story. A story about Mr. Young was recently published: Taylor Dolven and Daniela Porat, "How Christopher Young's 14-Year Plea Deal for Drug Crimes Turned into Life in Prison," *Vice News*, October 4, 2015, https://news.vice.com/article/how-christopher-youngs-14-year-plea-deal-for-drug-crimes-turned-into-life-in-prison (accessed May 3, 2016).
8. Chris Young was not the only one from this case to be convicted at trial. He was defendant number twenty-seven in a thirty-six-defendant conspiracy, indicating his relatively low rung in the conspiracy. Two others, defendants fourteen and twenty-two, also went to trial and were hit with the double 851. They were all convicted of at least one count and all three received life-without-parole sentences. The "kingpin" of the conspiracy received twenty-five years after pleading guilty.
9. This of course is legal formality. The judge had to impose these add-on sentences since they were mandated by the convictions, even though with a life sentence, there is no way to actually do five extra years in prison beyond the life sentence, much less five years of supervised release.

Appendix A

1. I have analyzed data from that district elsewhere, but do not include it here because it does not sufficiently add to my overall goals with this book.
2. Lynch and Omori 2014.
3. Church 1985; Nardulli, Eisenstein, and Flemming 1988.
4. On the limits of using the federal sentencing statistical databases, especially in the post-*Booker* period: Hofer 2007, 2009.
5. For instance, in districts that handle a large number of a given case type, established "going rates" are likely to be both resistant to change and less variable within the category (Nardulli, Eisenstein, and Flemming 1988), whereas in districts with small and infrequently adjudicated caseloads of given offense types, sentencing will likely be more individualized to start and perhaps more responsive to formal policy changes.
6. For full transcripts of the regional hearings and mandatory minimums hearings, see U.S. Sentencing Commission website, "Agendas and Witness Statement," available at: www.ussc.gov/Legislative_and_Public_Affairs/Public_Hearings_and_Meetings/hearings.cfm (accessed April 28, 2016).
7. More than a third of drug trafficking defendants from 1992 to 2009 were awarded substantial assistance departures at sentencing. See Lynch and Omori 2014.
8. As noted in chapter 1, the so-called "100:1" disparity between powder and crack cocaine quantity to trigger the same mandatory sentence has been reduced to 18:1, and mandatory minimums for simple possession of crack have been eliminated.

9. Koppel 2010.
10. Nachmanoff and Baron-Evans 2009.
11. Hofer 2006, 444.
12. Ibid.
13. To provide just one example of how this can play out, one of the districts in this study has among the lowest rates of 5K1.1 departures in the nation, but a large number of defendants get sentence breaks for cooperation through a different mechanism, called a Rule 35(b) motion, which does not show up in USSC outcome data, since the adjustment to sentence length occurs well after formal sentencing.
14. Nagel and Schulhofer 1992; Schulhofer and Nagel 1989, 1997.
15. My agreement with these offices and my social science research ethics require an assurance of confidentiality, including not identifying districts in any published work related to this project.
16. U.S. Sentencing Commission 2014.
17. I spent several years trying to gain close access outside of the public courtroom and also attempted to gain access through U.S. attorneys' offices in several districts and the federal probation office in one district. I even published an article in the *Federal Sentencing Reporter,* inviting court actors to partner with me in an effort to more fully understand the effects of *Booker.* See Lynch 2011c.
18. For an extended discussion, see, for example, Shermer and Johnson 2010.
19. For an exception in one state court context, see Emmelman 1996, 1997, 2003.
20. Alexander 2010; Engen 2009.

Appendix B

1. To derive this estimate I used district probation office codes where the presentence report was prepared, as coded in the USSC sentencing data, to determine the division in which cases were adjudicated.
2. South division is technically two divisions, but the judges are shared and almost all cases are heard in the larger division.
3. Ninety-four percent of Middle division's sentenced crack defendants were African American.
4. This percentage would be considerably higher if it included the vast number of drug possession convictions in the last several years. As I cover in more detail in chapter 5, nearly every person convicted of misdemeanor possession in this district is an unauthorized immigrant who has carried a backpack filled with marijuana across the border. These cases began to be pled out as misdemeanor possession cases rather than felony distribution cases as the courts along the border became overwhelmed by them.

═══ References ═══

Alexander, Michelle. 2010. *The New Jim Crow: Mass Incarceration in the Age of Colorblindness*. New York: New Press.

Allen, Francis. 1981. *The Decline of the Rehabilitative Ideal: Penal Policy and Social Purpose*. New Haven, Conn.: Yale University Press.

American Friends Service Committee. 1971. *Struggle for Justice: A Report on Crime and Punishment in America*. New York: Hill & Wang.

Andreas, Peter, and Coletta Youngers. 1989. "US Drug Policy and the Andean Cocaine Industry." *World Policy Journal* 6(3): 529–62.

Anslinger, Harry J. 1951. "The Federal Narcotic Laws." *Food, Drug, and Cosmetic Law Journal* 6(10): 743–48.

———. 1959a. "The Treatment of Drug Addiction." *Food, Drug, and Cosmetic Law Journal* 14(4): 240–47.

———. 1959b. "The Implementation of Treaty Obligations in Regulating the Traffic in Narcotic Drugs." *American University Law Review* 8(2): 112–16.

Aronowitz, Dennis S. 1967. "Civil Commitment of Narcotic Addicts." *Columbia Law Review* 67(3): 405–29.

Asch, Solomon E. 1956. "Studies of Independence and Conformity: I. A Minority of One Against a Unanimous Majority." *Psychological Monographs: General and Applied* 70(9): 1–70.

Ashcroft, John. 2003. "Memo Regarding Policy on Charging of Criminal Defendants." September 22. Available at: www.justice.gov/archive/opa/pr/2003/September/03_ag_516.htm (accessed May 10, 2016).

Aviram, Hadar. 2015. *Cheap on Crime: Recession-Era Politics and the Transformation of American Punishment*. Berkeley: University of California Press.

Barkow, Rachel E. 2008. "Institutional Design and the Policing of Prosecutors: Lessons from Administrative Law." *Stanford Law Review* 61(4): 869–921.

———. 2015. "Clemency and Presidential Administration of Criminal Law." *New York University Law Review* 90(3): 802–69.

Baron-Evans, Amy, and Kate Stith. 2012. "*Booker* Rules." *University of Pennsylvania Law Review* 160(6): 1631–743.

Batra, Rishi Raj. 2015. "Judicial Participation in Plea Bargaining: A Dispute Resolution Perspective." *Ohio State Law Journal* 76(3): 565–97.

Beale, Sara Sun. 1996. "Federalizing Crime: Assessing the Impact on the Federal Courts." *Annals of the American Academy of Political and Social Science* 543(1): 39–51.

Beckett, Katherine. 1996. *Making Crime Pay: Law and Order in Contemporary American Politics*. New York: Oxford University Press.

Beckett, Katherine, Kris Nyrop, and Lori Pfingst. 2006. "Race, Drugs, and Policing: Understanding Disparities in Drug Delivery Arrests." *Criminology* 44(1): 105–38.

Berman, Douglas. 2010. "Encouraging (and Even Requiring) Prosecutors to be Second-Look Sentencers." Afternoon keynote address at symposium "Examining Modern Approaches to Prosecutorial Discretion," Temple University, James E. Beasley School of Law (October 17). *Temple Political and Civil Rights Law Review* 19(2): 429–41.

Bibas, Stephanos. 2004. "The Feeney Amendment and the Continuing Rise of Prosecutorial Power to Plea Bargain." *Journal of Criminal Law and Criminology* 94(2): 295–308.

Bjerk, David, and Caleb Mason. 2014. "The Market for Mules: Risk and Compensation of Cross-Border Drug Couriers." *International Review of Law and Economics* 39: 58–72.

Brown, Barry S. 1985. "Federal Drug Abuse Policy and Minority Group Issues— Reflections of a Participant-Observer." *International Journal of the Addictions* 20(1): 203–15.

Buerger, Michael E. 1992. "Defensive Strategies of the Street-Level Drug Trade." *Journal of Crime and Justice* 15(2): 31–51.

Bureau of Justice Statistics. 1989. *Compendium of Criminal Justice Statistics, 1984.* Washington: U.S. Department of Justice, August.

———. N.d. "Federal Justice Statistics." Available at: http://www.bjs.gov/index. cfm?ty=dcdetail&iid=262 (accessed June 22, 2016).

Bushway, Shawn D., and Allison D. Redlich. 2012. "Is Plea Bargaining in the 'Shadow of the Trial' a Mirage?" *Journal of Quantitative Criminology* 28(3): 437–54.

Chippendale, Stephen. 1994. "More Harm Than Good: Federalization of Criminal Law." *Minnesota Law Review* 79(2): 455–83.

Church, Thomas W. 1985. "Examining Local Legal Culture." *Law and Social Inquiry* 10(3): 449–510.

Clark, Ramsey. 1970. *Crime in America: Observations on Its Nature, Causes, Prevention and Control.* New York: Simon and Schuster.

Cohen, Michael M. 2006. "Jim Crow's Drug War: Race, Coca Cola, and the Southern Origins of Drug Prohibition." *Southern Cultures* 12: 55–79.

Cohen, Thomas H., and Tracey Kyckelhahn. 2010. *Felony Defendants in Large Urban Counties.* Washington: U.S. Department of Justice.

Commission on Law Enforcement and Administration of Justice. 1967. "Task Force Report: Narcotics and Drug Abuse." Washington: U.S. Government Printing Office.

Cotton, Tom. 2016. "The Current Sentencing Reform and Corrections Act Is Dangerous for America." February 9. Available at: https://medium.com/Sen Tom Cotton/the-current-sentencing-reform-and-corrections-act-is-dangerous-for-america-56b78a43da31#.e1hcw0tsm (accessed May 10, 2016).

Davis, Angela J. 2007. *Arbitrary Justice: The Power of the American Prosecutor.* New York: Oxford University Press.

Dunworth, Terence, and Charles D. Weisselberg. 1992. "Felony Cases and the Federal Courts: The Guidelines Experience." *Southern California Law Review* 66(1): 99–153.

Emmelman, Debra S. 1996. "Trial by Plea Bargain: Case Settlement as a Process of Recursive Decisionmaking." *Law and Society Review* 30(2): 335–60.

———. 1997. "Gauging the Strength of Evidence Prior to Plea Bargaining: The Interpretive Procedures of Court-Appointed Attorneys." *Law and Social Inquiry* 22(4): 927–55.

———. 2003. *Justice for the Poor: A Study of Criminal Defense Work.* Burlington, Vt.: Ashgate Publishing.

Engen, Rodney. 2009. "Implications of Determinate and Presumptive Sentencing—Making Research Relevant." *Criminology and Public Policy* 8(2): 323–36.

Erickson, Patricia G., Diane M. Riley, Yuet W. Cheung, and Pat A. O'Hare, eds. 1997. *Harm Reduction: A New Direction for Drug Policies and Programs.* Toronto: University of Toronto Press.

Erikson, Erik H. 1956. "The Problem of Ego Identity." *Journal of the American Psychoanalytic Association* 4(1): 56–121.

Families Against Mandatory Minimums. 2015. "The Dangerous Myths of NAAUSA." *Federal Sentencing Reporter* 28(1): 24–38.

Fine, Gary Alan. 2012. *Tiny Publics: A Theory of Group Action and Culture.* New York: Russell Sage Foundation.

Fischman, Joshua B., and Max M. Schanzenbach. 2012. "Racial Disparities Under the Federal Sentencing Guidelines: The Role of Judicial Discretion and Mandatory Minimums." *Journal of Empirical Legal Studies* 9(4): 729–64.

Fiske, Susan T. 2009. *Social Beings: Core Motives in Social Psychology.* 2nd ed. New York: John Wiley.

Fortner, Michael Javen. 2015. *Black Silent Majority: Rockefeller Drug Laws and the Politics of Punishment.* Cambridge, Mass.: Harvard University Press.

Foucault, Michel. 1982. "The Subject and Power." *Critical Inquiry* 8(4): 777–95.

Frankel, Marvin E. 1973. *Criminal Sentences: Law Without Order.* New York: Hill & Wang.

Frase, Richard S. 1999. "Sentencing Guidelines in Minnesota, Other States, and the Federal Courts: A Twenty-Year Retrospective." *Federal Sentencing Reporter* 12(2): 69–82.

Friedman, Steven B., George L. Horvat, and Robert B. Levinson. 1982. "The Narcotic Addict Rehabilitation Act: Its Impact on Federal Prisons." *Contemporary Drug Problems* 11(1): 101–11.

Froyd, Jane L. 1999. "Safety Valve Failure: Low-Level Drug Offenders and the Federal Sentencing Guidelines." *Northwestern University Law Review* 94(4): 1471–507.

Garland, David. 2001. "Introduction: The Meaning of Mass Imprisonment." *Punishment and Society* 3(1): 5–7.

———. 2002. *The Culture of Control: Crime and Social Order in Contemporary Society.* Chicago: University of Chicago Press.

Gertner, Nancy 2007. "From Omnipotence to Impotence: American Judges and Sentencing." *Ohio State Journal of Criminal Law* 4(2): 523–39.

Gleeson, John. 2013. "Statement of Reasons in *USA v. Lulzim Kupa.*" U.S. District Court, Eastern District of New York. October 9. Available at: https://img.nyed.uscourts.gov/files/opinions/11cr345SOR.pdf (accessed June 21, 2016).

Gorman, Thomas E. 2009. "A History of Fast-Track Sentencing." *Federal Sentencing Reporter* 21(5): 311–17.

Gottschalk, Marie. 2006. *The Prison and the Gallows: The Politics of Mass Incarceration in America.* New York: Cambridge University Press.

———. 2014. *Caught: The Prison State and the Lockdown of American Politics.* Princeton, N.J.: Princeton University Press.

Grant, Ruth. 2014. *Strings Attached: Untangling the Ethics of Incentives.* Princeton, N.J.: Princeton University Press.

Haney, Craig, Curtis Banks, and Philip Zimbardo. 1973. "Interpersonal Dynamics in a Simulated Prison." *International Journal of Criminology and Penology* 1: 69–97.

Haney, Craig, and Philip Zimbardo. 2009. "Persistent Dispositionalism in Interactionist Clothing: Fundamental Attribution Error in Explaining Prison Abuse." *Personality and Social Psychology Bulletin* 35(6): 807–14.

Haque, Omar Sultan, and Adam Waytz. 2012. "Dehumanization in Medicine: Causes, Solutions, and Functions." *Perspectives on Psychological Science* 7(2): 176–86.

Hay, Douglas. 1975. "Property, Authority, and Criminal Law." In *Albion's Fatal Tree: Crime and Society in Eighteenth-Century England,* by Douglas Hay et al. New York: Pantheon Books.

Heller, Kevin Jon. 1996. "Whatever Happened to Proof Beyond a Reasonable Doubt? Of Drug Conspiracies, Overt Acts, and *United States v. Shabani.*" *Stanford Law Review* 49(1): 111–42.

Hofer, Paul J. 2006. "Immediate and Long-Term Effects of *United States v. Booker:* More Discretion, More Disparity, or Better Reasoned Sentences?" *Arizona State Law Journal* 38(2): 425–68.

———. 2007. "*United States v. Booker* as a Natural Experiment: Using Empirical Research to Inform the Federal Sentencing Policy Debate." *Criminology and Public Policy* 6(3): 433–60.

———. 2009. "How Well Do Sentencing Commission Statistics Help in Understanding the Post-*Booker* System?" *Federal Sentencing Reporter* 22(2): 89–95.

Holder, Eric. 2013. "Memorandum to the United States Attorneys and Assistant Attorney General." August 12. Available at: www.justice.gov/sites/default/files/oip/legacy/2014/07/23/ag-memo-department-policypon-charging-mandatory-minimum-sentences-recidivist-enhancements-in-certain-drug cases.pdf (accessed May 10, 2016).

———. 2014. "Guidance Regarding §851 Enhancements in Plea Negotiations." September 24. Available at: https://www.fd.org/docs/select-topics/sentencing-resources/memorandum-to-all-federal-prosecutors-from-eric-h-holder-jr-attorney-general-on-851-enhancements-in-plea-negotiations.pdf?sfvrsn=6 (accessed June 21, 2016).

Human Rights Watch. 2013. *An Offer You Can't Refuse: How Federal Prosecutors Force Drug Defendants to Plead Guilty.* December. Available at: www.hrw.org/report/2013/12/05/offer-you-cant-refuse/how-us-federal-prosecutors-force-drug-defendants-plead (accessed May 10, 2016).

Jacobs, James B. 1982. "Sentencing by Prison Personnel: Good Time." *UCLA Law Review* 30(2): 217–70.

Johnson, Brian D. 2014. "The Missing Link: Examining Prosecutorial Decision-Making Across Federal District Courts." Final Technical Report, prepared for National Institute of Justice. Washington: National Criminal Justice Reference

Service. Available at: www.ncjrs.gov/pdffiles1/nij/grants/245351.pdf (accessed May 10, 2016).

Johnson, Brian D., Jeffery T. Ulmer, and John H. Kramer. 2008. "The Social Context of Guidelines Circumvention: The Case of Federal District Courts." *Criminology* 46: 737–83.

Kautt, Paula. 2002. "Location, Location, Location: Interdistrict and Intercircuit Variation in Sentencing Outcomes for Federal Drug-Trafficking Offenses." *Justice Quarterly* 19(4): 633–71.

Kinder, Douglas Clark. 1981. "Bureaucratic Cold Warrior: Harry J. Anslinger and Illicit Narcotics Traffic." *Pacific Historical Review* 50(2): 169–91.

King, Ryan, and Marc Mauer. 2002. *Distorted Priorities: Drug Offenders in State Prisons.* New York: The Sentencing Project.

Kohler-Hausmann, Issa. 2013. "Misdemeanor Justice: Control Without Conviction." *American Journal of Sociology* 119(2): 351–93.

Koppel, Nathan. 2010. "Holder Memo Promises Greater Sentencing Discretion." *Wall Street Journal Law Blog*, May 28. Available at: http://blogs.wsj.com/law/2010/05/28/holder-memo-promises-greater-sentencing-flexibility/ (accessed May 10, 2016).

Krent, Harold J. 2013. "Retroactivity and Crack Sentencing Reform." *University of Michigan Journal of Law Reform* 47(1): 53–86.

Lassiter, Matthew. 2015. "Impossible Criminals: The Suburban Imperatives of America's War on Drugs." *Journal of American History* 102(1): 126–40.

Latané, Bibb, and John M. Darley. 1969. "Bystander 'Apathy.' " *American Scientist* 57(2): 244–68.

Lee, Gregory D. 1994. "Drug Conspiracy Cases." *FBI Bulletin* 63(10): 1–5.

Lerman, Amy E., and Vesla M. Weaver. 2014. *Arresting Citizenship: The Democratic Consequences of American Crime Control.* Chicago: University of Chicago Press.

Lerman, Kevin. Forthcoming. "Couriers, Not Kingpins: Toward a More Just Federal Sentencing Regime for Defendants Who Deliver Drugs." *UC Irvine Law Review.*

Lu, Lynn D. 2007. "Prosecutorial Discretion and Racial Disparities in Federal Sentencing: Some Views of Former U.S. Attorneys." *Federal Sentencing Reporter* 19(3): 192–201.

Lynch, Mona. 2011a. "Crack Pipes and Policing: A Case Study of Institutional Racism and Remedial Action in Cleveland." *Law and Policy* 33(2): 179–214.

———. 2011b. "Mass Incarceration, Legal Change, and Locale: Understanding and Remediating American Penal Overindulgence." *Criminology and Public Policy* 10(3): 671–98.

———. 2011c. "Expanding the Empirical Picture of Federal Sentencing: An Invitation." *Federal Sentencing Reporter* 23(5): 313–17.

———. 2012. "Theorizing the Role of the 'War on Drugs' in US Punishment." *Theoretical Criminology* 16(2): 175–99.

———. 2015. "Backpacking the Border: The Intersection of Drug and Immigration Prosecutions in a High Volume US Court." *British Journal of Criminology.* Prepublished September 28, 2015. DOI: 10.1093/bjc/azv105.

Lynch, Mona, and Alyse Bertenthal. 2016. "The Calculus of the Record: Criminal History in the Making of US Federal Sentencing Guidelines." *Theoretical Criminology* 20(2): 145–64.

Lynch, Mona, and Marisa Omori. 2014. "Legal Change and Sentencing Norms in the Wake of *Booker*: The Impact of Time and Place on Drug Trafficking Cases in Federal Court." *Law & Society Review* 48(2): 411–45.

Lynch, Mona, Marisa Omori, Aaron Roussell, and Matthew Valasik. 2013. "Policing the 'Progressive' City: The Racialized Geography of Drug Law Enforcement." *Theoretical Criminology* 17(3): 335–57.

MacKenzie, Doris Layton. 2000. "Evidence-Based Corrections: Identifying What Works." *Crime & Delinquency* 46(4): 457–71.

Martinez, Oscar. 2013. *The Beast: Riding the Rails and Dodging Narcos on the Migrant Trail.* New York: Verso.

McDonald, Douglas C., and Kenneth E. Carlson. 1993. *Sentencing in the Federal Courts: Does Race Matter?* Washington: U.S. Department of Justice, December.

McGirr, Lisa. 2002. *Suburban Warriors: The Origins of the New American Right.* Princeton, N.J.: Princeton University Press.

McWilliams, John C. 1989. "Unsung Partner Against Crime: Harry J. Anslinger and the Federal Bureau of Narcotics, 1930–1962." *Pennsylvania Magazine of History and Biography* 113(2): 207–36.

Milgram, Stanley. 1965. "Some Conditions of Obedience and Disobedience to Authority." *Human Relations* 18: 57–76.

Miller, Lisa, and James Eisenstein. 2005. "The Federal/State Criminal Prosecution Nexus: A Case Study in Cooperation and Discretion." *Law and Social Inquiry* 30(2): 239–68.

Mitford, Jessica. 1973. *Kind and Usual Punishment: The Prison Business.* New York: Random House.

Muhammad, Khalil Gibran. 2011. *The Condemnation of Blackness: Race, Crime, and the Making of Modern Urban America.* Cambridge, Mass: Harvard University Press.

Murakawa, Naomi. 2014. *The First Civil Right: How Liberals Built Prison America.* New York: Oxford University Press.

Musto, David. 1999. *The American Disease: Origins of Narcotic Control.* New York: Oxford University Press.

Musto, David, and Pamela Korsmeyer. 2002. *The Quest for Drug Control: Politics and Federal Policy in a Period of Increasing Substance Abuse, 1963–1981.* New Haven, Conn.: Yale University Press.

Nachmanoff, Michael, and Amy Baron-Evans. 2009. "*Booker* Five Years Out: Mandatory Minimum Sentences and Department of Justice Charging Policies Continue to Distort the Federal Sentencing Process." *Federal Sentencing Reporter* 22(2): 96–99.

Nadkarni, Sid. 2013. "Let's Have a Look, Shall We: A Model for Evaluating Suspicionless Border Searches of Portable Electronic Devices" *UCLA Law Review* 61(1): 146–94.

Nagel, Ilene H., and Stephen J. Schulhofer. 1992. "A Tale of Three Cities: An Empirical Study of Charging and Bargaining Practices Under the Federal Sentencing Guidelines." *Southern California Law Review* 66(1): 501–66.

Nardulli, Peter F., James Eisenstein, and Roy B. Flemming. 1988. *The Tenor of Justice: Criminal Courts and the Guilty Plea Process.* Urbana: University of Illinois Press.

Natapoff, Alexandra. 2009. *Snitching: Criminal Informants and the Erosion of American Justice.* New York: NYU Press.

Nelson, Steven. 2015. "Prosecutors Rally Against Sentencing Reform, Say Build More Prisons." *U.S. News and World Report*, July 17.

Nixon, President Richard M. 1973. "State of the Union Message to the Congress on Law Enforcement and Drug Abuse Prevention." March 14. Available at: www.presidency.ucsb.edu/ws/?pid=4140 (accessed May 10, 2016).

Peterson, Ruth D. 1984. "Discriminatory Decision Making at the Legislative Level: An Analysis of the Comprehensive Drug Abuse Prevention and Control Act of 1970." *Law and Human Behavior* 9(3): 243–69.

Pfaff, John F. 2011. "The Myths and Realities of Correctional Severity: Evidence from the National Corrections Reporting Program on Sentencing Practices." *American Law and Economics Review* 132(2): 491–531.

Phillips, Susan A. 2012. *Operation Fly Trap: LA Gangs, Drugs, and the Law.* Chicago: University of Chicago Press.

Provine, Doris Marie. 2007. *Unequal Under Law: Race in the War on Drugs.* Chicago: University of Chicago Press.

Reicher, Stephen. 2004. "The Context of Social Identity: Domination, Resistance, and Change." *Political Psychology* 25(6): 921–45.

Reitz, Kevin. 1993. "Sentencing Facts: Travesties of Real-Offense Sentencing." *Stanford Law Review* 45(3): 523–73.

Richman, Daniel C. 2000. "The Changing Boundaries Between Federal and Local Law Enforcement." *Criminal Justice* 2: 81–111.

Riis, Jacob A. 1890. *How the Other Half Lives.* New York: Charles Scribner's Sons.

Rosenmerkel, Sean, Matthew Durose, and Donald Farole. 2009. *Felony Sentences in State Courts, 2006.* Bureau of Justice Statistics. Washington: U.S. Department of Justice.

Ross, Lee, and Richard Nisbett. 1991. *The Person and the Situation: Perspectives of Social Psychology.* New York: McGraw-Hill.

Russell, Sarah French. 2010. "Rethinking Recidivist Enhancements: The Role of Prior Drug Convictions in Federal Sentencing." *UC Davis Law Review* 43(4): 1135–233.

Russell-Einhorn, Malcolm L. 2003. *Fighting Urban Crime: The Evolution of Federal-Local Collaboration.* National Institute of Justice Research in Brief. Washington: U.S. Department of Justice.

Schmitt, Glenn R., Louis Reedt, and Kevin Blackwell. 2013. "Why Judges Matter at Sentencing: A Reply to Starr and Rehavi." *Yale Law Journal Online* 123: 251.

Schulhofer, Stephen J., and Ilene H. Nagel. 1989. "Negotiated Pleas Under the Federal Sentencing Guidelines: The First Fifteen Months." *American Criminal Law Review* 27(2): 231–88.

———. 1997. "Plea Negotiations Under the Federal Sentencing Guidelines: Guideline Circumvention and Its Dynamics in the Post-*Mistretta* Period." *Northwestern University Law Review* 91(4): 1284–316.

Shermer, Lauren O'Neill, and Brian D. Johnson 2010. "Criminal Prosecutions: Examining Prosecutorial Discretion and Charging Decisions in U.S. Federal District Courts." *Justice Quarterly* 27(3): 394–430.

Sieber, Joan E., and Martin B. Tolich. 2012. *Planning Ethically Responsible Research: A Guide for Students and Internal Review Boards.* Thousand Oaks, Calif.: Sage Publications.

Simon, Jonathan. 2001. "Entitlement to Cruelty: Neo-Liberalism and the Punitive Mentality in the United States." In *Crime Risk and Justice,* edited by Kevin Stenson and Robert R. Sullivan. Cullompton, UK: Willan.

———. 2007. *Governing Through Crime: How the War on Crime Transformed American Democracy and Created a Culture of Fear.* New York: Oxford University Press.

Sklansky, David. 1995. "Cocaine, Race, and Equal Protection." *Stanford Law Review* 47(6): 1283–322.

Stith, Kate. 2008. "The Arc of the Pendulum: Judges, Prosecutors, and the Exercise of Discretion." *Yale Law Journal* 117(7): 1420–97.

Stith, Kate, and Jose Cabranes. 1998. *Fear of Judging: Sentencing Guidelines in the Federal Courts.* Chicago: University of Chicago Press.

Stith, Kate, and Steven Y. Koh. 1993. "The Politics of Sentencing Reform: The Legislative History of the Federal Sentencing Guidelines." *Wake Forest Law Review* 28(2): 223–90.

Stuntz, William J. 2011. *The Collapse of American Criminal Justice.* Cambridge, Mass.: Harvard University Press/Belknap.

Thomas, Mark. 1996. "Sentencing Entrapment: How Far Should the Federal Courts Go." *Idaho Law Review* 33(1): 147–83.

Tonry, Michael. 1996. *Malign Neglect: Race, Crime, and Punishment in America.* New York: Oxford University Press.

Ulmer, Jeffery T. 2005. "The Localized Uses of Federal Sentencing Guidelines in Four U.S. District Courts: Evidence of Processual Order." *Symbolic Interaction* 28(2): 255–79.

———. 2012. "Recent Developments and New Directions in Sentencing Research." *Justice Quarterly* 29(1): 1–40.

Ulmer, Jeffery T., James Eisenstein, and Brian D. Johnson. 2010. "Trial Penalties in Federal Sentencing: Extra-Guidelines Factors and District Variation." *Justice Quarterly* 27(4): 560–92.

University at Albany, Hindelang Criminal Justice Research Center. N.d. "Sourcebook of Criminal Justice Statistics." Available at: http://www.albany.edu/sourcebook/ (accessed June 22, 2016).

U.S. Courts. N.d. "Federal Judicial Caseload Statistics." Available at: http://www.uscourts.gov/statistics-reports/analysis-reports/federal-judicial-caseload-statistics (accessed June 24, 2016).

U.S. Department of Health and Human Services, Substance Abuse and Mental Health Services Administration. 2009. "Results from the 2009 National Survey on Drug Use and Health: Volume 1, Summary of National Findings." Available at: http://archive.samhsa.gov/data/NSDUH/2k9NSDUH/2k9Results.htm (accessed May 10, 2016).

U.S. Department of Justice. 1954. *1953 United States Attorneys Manual.* Washington: Department of Justice.

———. 1985. *1984 United States Attorneys Manual.* Washington: Department of Justice.

U.S. Sentencing Commission. 1987a. *Guidelines Manual.* Washington: U.S. Sentencing Commission.

———. 1987b. *Sentencing Guidelines and Policy Statements.* May 1. Washington: U.S. Sentencing Commission.

———. 1991. *Annual Report, 1990.* Washington: U.S. Sentencing Commission.

———. 2004. *Fifteen Years of Guidelines Sentencing: An Assessment of How Well the Federal Criminal Justice System Is Achieving the Goals of Sentencing Reform.* Washington: U.S. Sentencing Commission, November.

———. 2006. *Final Report on the Impact of* United States v. Booker *on Federal Sentencing.* Washington: U.S. Sentencing Commission.

———. 2007. *Sourcebook, 2006.* Washington: U.S. Sentencing Commission.

———. 2009. *An Overview of the United States Sentencing Commission.* Washington: U.S. Sentencing Commission.

———. 2011. "Report to Congress: Mandatory Minimum Penalties in the Federal Criminal Justice System." Washington: U.S. Sentencing Commission.

———. 2012a. "U.S. Sentencing Commission Preliminary Quarterly Data Report." Washington: U.S. Sentencing Commission.

———. 2012b. "Report on the Continuing Impact of *United States v. Booker* on Federal Sentencing." Washington: U.S. Sentencing Commission.

———. 2013a. "Use of Guidelines and Specific Offense Characteristics, Offender Based, Fiscal Year 2012." Washington: U.S. Sentencing Commission. Available at: www.ussc.gov/Data_and_Statistics/Federal_Sentencing_Statistics/Guideline_Application_Frequencies/2012/Use_of_Guidelines_and_Specific_Offense_Characteristics_Guideline_Calculation_Based.pdf (accessed May 9, 2013).

———. 2013b. *Drug Primer.* Washington: U.S. Sentencing Commission.

———. 2014. *Sourcebook, 2013.* Washington: U.S. Sentencing Commission.

———. 2015. *Guidelines Manual.* Washington: U.S. Sentencing Commission.

———. N.d. "Quick Facts: Career Offenders." Available at: www.ussc.gov/sites/default/files/pdf/research-and-publications/quick-facts/Quick_Facts_Career_Offender_FY14.pdf (accessed May 10, 2016).

U.S. Supreme Court. 2004. "2003 Year-End Report on the Federal Judiciary." January 1. Available at: www.supremecourt.gov/publicinfo/year-end/2003year-endreport.aspx (accessed May 10, 2016).

Warner, Mary C. 2004. "The Trials and Tribulations of Petty Offenses in the Federal Courts." *New York University Law Review* 79(6): 2417–48.

Welch, Susan, and Kay Thompson. 1980. "The Impact of Federal Incentives on State Policy Innovation." *American Journal of Political Science* 24(4): 715–29.

Wetmore, Stacy A., Jeffrey S. Neuschatz, and Scott D. Gronlund. 2014. "On the Power of Secondary Confession Evidence." *Psychology, Crime & Law* 20(4): 339–57.

Wilkins, Jr., William W., Phyllis J. Newton, and John R. Steer. 1991. "The Sentencing Reform Act of 1984: A Bold Approach to the Unwarranted Sentencing Disparity Problem." *Criminal Law Forum* 2(2): 355–80.

Wu, Jawjeung, and Cassia Spohn 2010. "Interdistrict Disparity in Sentencing in Three U.S. District Courts." *Crime and Delinquency* 56(2): 290–322.

Yellen, David. 2008. "The Sentencing Commission Takes On Crack, Again." *Federal Sentencing Reporter* 20(4): 20–22.

Zimring, Frank, and Gordon Hawkins 1993. *The Scale of Imprisonment.* Chicago: University of Chicago Press.

═ Index ═

Boldface numbers refer to figures and tables.